The Dumbest Things
Ever Said or Done

Bob Fenster

**Andrews McMeel
Publishing**

Kansas City • Sydney • London

This book is dedicated to
everyone who ever thought:
Gee, that was a dumb thing to do.
But not dumb enough.
If I really knuckle down,
I can do something even dumber.

And then they do.

Andrews McMeel Publishing, LLC
an Andrews McMeel Universal company
1130 Walnut Street, Kansas City, Missouri 64106

www.andrewsmcmeel.com

14 15 16 17 18 RR2 10 9 8 7 6 5 4 3 2 1

ISBN: 978-1-4494-5712-9

Book design by Lisa Martin • Illustrations by Matt Taylor

Contents

 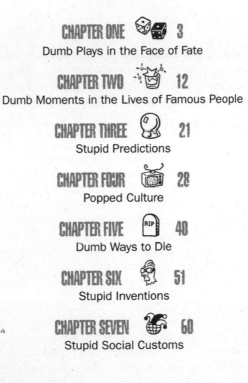

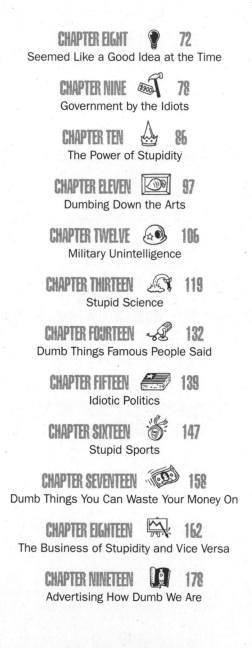

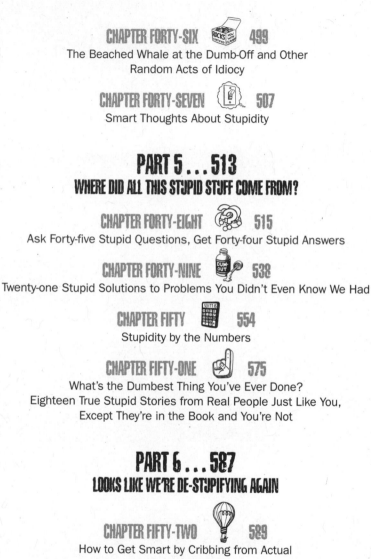

Acknowledgments

My biggest thanks to:

New York City for bringing me up with an early appreciation for absurdity.

My good friend Marilyn Green, a living library of curiosities, for sharing some of the gems in this book from her own collection.

My three sons—Robert Charles Conaway Bothwell, Nicholas Hammett Bothwell Fenster, and Edward Nash Bothwell Fenster—who all started laughing at an early age.

Introduction

Don't kiss a rattlesnake on the mouth.

There's one life lesson you might safely assume we don't need to be taught.

Put on the parachute *before* you jump out of the plane. Stop wasting the taxpayers' money on research to find out why convicts want to escape from prison.

We should be able to get across these low bridges of human effort without too much trouble.

Strangely enough, we seem to be a race of rattlesnake kissers.

In 1990, a guy showed up at an Arizona hospital with an unusual problem: He'd been bitten on the tongue while kissing a rattlesnake on the mouth.

But you figure, okay, lesson learned. No one is going to pull that dumb stunt again.

Wrong.

Ten years later, a man in Florida kisses a rattlesnake on the mouth—and gets away with it. So he does it again. And the second time, the snake points out to him why most people don't kiss rattlers.

Why did these men do such a stupid thing? Because they belong to the only species that keeps track of how dumb it is.

Anytime you think you've seen someone do the dumbest thing you can imagine, keep your eyes open for what's coming next.

Or just start reading this book.

It will make you wonder: If we are all as smart as we think we are, then how can everyone else be as dumb as we think they are?

Being human, we play defense. I may have made some dumb mistakes in my life, but I'm not as stupid as *those* guys.

This book is all about those guys.

PART 1
The Stupid Chronicles

CHAPTER ONE

Dumb Plays in the Face of Fate

Fate overwhelms intelligent strategies at every turn. Still, there are times when you can grab fate and ride the surge to triumph.

Or not. Consider:

In 1990 the University of Arizona poison control center treated a man who was bitten on the tongue while kissing a rattlesnake.

A Venezuelan farmer kept his family's hard-earned fortune, some $1,600, in a straw basket. He lost everything in 1971 when his pet goat ate the basket and everything in it.

The farmer retaliated by eating the goat. No goat ever tasted $1,600 good.

Drug-addicted comic Lenny Bruce was clowning around in a hotel room, rehearsing a routine about the difficulties a Jewish Superman would face, when he flew out the fifth-story window, broke his arm, and injured his back.

If you're a gambler, you know how rare it is to go on a prolonged winning streak. A sailor hit an incredible streak of good luck one night in 1950 at a Vegas craps table. He made twenty-seven straight passes with the dice, throwing twenty-seven winners in a row.

He could have won up to $268 million on that streak (betting the house limit with each roll). Granted, not many people would have bet that hard. But he should have won smaller but still vast amounts by any reasonable betting system.

Instead, the sailor bet so lamely that he walked away from that once-in-a-million-lifetimes streak with $750.

It's equally tough to pick winners at the racetrack. Then stupidity steps in and adds insult to insult: Every year an estimated $1 million is lost, in addition to all the other losses, by people who mistakenly throw away winning tickets.

A Japanese politician, running behind in the polls, didn't need a campaign manager, media adviser, or focus group to devise this original strategy: He faked an assassination attempt in order to gain the sympathy vote.

To make the attack look convincing, the politico stabbed himself in the leg. He severed an artery and bled to death before he could make his final campaign speech.

Sometimes fate grabs you by the collar and shouts, "Here's your golden opportunity. Make the most of it!" And we respond, "Now how can I really mess up this one?"

In 1920 the Republican Party offered Hiram Johnson a chance to run as vice president to Senator Knox of Pennsylvania. But Johnson didn't want to be vice president. He wanted to be president. He wouldn't take second position on the ticket, even though insiders told him that Knox wasn't likely to survive a full term because of a bad heart.

Fate even offered Hiram Johnson a second chance for glory. Once more, he was asked to take the vice president's slot, this time under the man who upset Knox for the nomination, Warren Harding. Again Johnson declined, saying he would take the presidency or nothing.

Both Knox and Harding, who was elected president, died within a few years. If Johnson had run as vice president with either man, he would have become president, the position he craved so much.

Instead, Calvin Coolidge, who knew how to answer when fate knocked, took Hiram Johnson's place in the White House and history.

In 1999 two Milwaukee teenagers were playing a game of fast draw with family pistols. Before starting the game, they checked the clips to make sure there were no bullets inside. They didn't check the chambers.

They drew. They shot. One boy was killed, shot through the head. The other boy took a bullet through the neck that severed his spinal column and left him paralyzed. He was then charged with murder.

A New York City boy died in 1989 while elevator surf-ing—riding on the top of an elevator car as it zips up and down a high-rise.

That was a dumb way to die, and it should have put an end to such a dangerous sport. Instead, other boys plunged with eyes wide open into the realm of foolish defiance of fate when they continued to elevator surf.

That year, ten more boys were crushed at the top of the elevator shaft or fell to their death off fast-plunging cars.

Boxer Gene Tunney won a controversial heavyweight champi-onship decision in 1927. When Jack Dempsey sent him to the canvas in the seventh round, the referee saved Tunney from a knockout by giving him an extra-slow count.

Three men died from heart attacks while listening to radio reports of that strange seventh round.

The capper came from a Tunney fan who was wildly cheering for his fighter while watching round-by-round recaps posted on a news board in Los Angeles.

Was the fan dumb for cheering a fight he couldn't see? No, for not putting down the ice pick before he started jumping up and down.

The fan was rushed to the hospital after stabbing himself with the ice pick in the middle of a cheer.

Athletes can be as self-destructive as fans. Consider the baseball player who in 1889 played with shotgun shells in his pockets. While he was batting, a wild pitch plunked him in the leg and his pants exploded.

Or the hockey goalie who put a pack of matches in his uniform pocket before taking the ice in 1930. A slap shot struck the goalie's pocket, ignited the matches, and set his uniform on fire.

Billiard champion Louis Fox was playing a big money match in upstate New York in 1865 when a fly landed on his cue ball. Unable to shoo the fly away, Fox miscued, lost the game, fled the hall in shame, jumped into the river, and drowned.

In 1975 an English couple were watching their favorite TV sit-com when the man was seized by a fit of laughter that lasted for half an hour. He laughed himself right into a fatal heart attack.

Have you ever seen English sitcoms? They're not that funny.

After the funeral, his wife wrote to the show's producers, thanking them for making her husband's last moments such happy ones.

In 1982 an Arizona man drove into the desert to take some target practice. He turned his shotgun on one of the legally protected giant saguaros and pumped twice.

The blasts cut the cactus in half. It fell on the man and crushed him to death.

Bungee jumping is not a new way to defy the fates. Young boys from the South Pacific island of Vanuatu maintain a tradition of building fifty-foot towers of sticks. To prove their manhood, they climb to the top and jump off, headfirst.

The boys knot vines to their ankles. They guesstimate the vines to be slightly shorter than the distance from the top of the tower to the ground, minus their height.

Sometimes they're right.

Teenage boys in Brazil prove their courage by surfing on the top of speeding electric trains. The boys who don't squat low enough under the trestles are decapitated. Others lose their balance and grab for the wires. If they don't fall to their death, they get electrocuted.

An Arizona man out hunting in 1971 shot himself in the leg. Nothing dumb about that. Happens often enough. But to call for help, the injured man fired off his rifle—and shot himself in the other leg.

A farmer in Uruguay tried to perform self-dentistry in 1977 by shooting a painful toothache with his pistol. He managed to extract the offending tooth, but also blew out his jaw.

In 1976 a New Orleans woman sued the government to nullify the Louisiana Purchase. The court denied her suit, ruling that she was too late, since the statute of limitations had expired 167 years ago.

What's the injury rate among football players? One hundred percent. Among professional boxers, 87 percent will suffer brain damage. Careers in both professional sports are short, risky, and financially rewarding only for a small percentage of those who jump in headfirst.

Doesn't slow down the volunteer rate in either sport.

A man in Clermont, France, blew up his house with his washing machine. He told police that he was trying to remove a grease stain from a shirt by pouring a cup of gasoline in the washer. When the machine changed cycles, a spark ignited the gasoline and blew out the first floor of his home, knocking him unconscious.

"I feel a bit stupid," the man admitted later.

To offer thanks for his fiancée's healthy recovery from a life-threatening illness, a Brazilian man walked penance halfway across the country, carrying a large cross on his back.

While he was gone on this spiritual trek, his fiancée married another man.

The owner of a vegetarian health spa in Mexico insisted in his will that he be buried only in the no-smoking section of the cemetery.

Back in 1973 the Denver Broncos were nothing like the Super Bowl champs they would become more than two decades later. After a particularly bad loss, one Denver fan wrote the following suicide note: "I have been a Broncos fan since the Broncos were first organized and I can't take their fumbling anymore."

Then the fan shot himself in the head. Whatever the Broncos had was catching, because he fumbled the shot and lived.

In 1999 after the United States had been shocked by a series of shootings in which high-school students had brought guns to school to kill fellow students and teachers, a woman high-school teacher in Ohio suggested the following as a topic for a writing assignment: "If you had to assassinate one famous person who is alive right now, who would it be and how would you do it?"

In 1929 a man complaining of stomach problems required surgery. The doctors removed from his stomach buttons, nails, thimbles, salt-shaker tops, safety pins, carpet tacks, coat-rack hooks, beads, pins, and a nail file.

When the Boston Strangler was terrorizing that city in the 1960s, a Brockton woman collapsed and died of fright when a strange man knocked on her front door one day. Turned out he was an encyclopedia salesman.

A South African man shot his friend in the face while both men were taking target practice, shooting beer cans off each other's heads.

The shooter lost the contest, while the winner was seriously wounded.

CHAPTER TWO

Dumb Moments in the Lives of Famous People

It's not that the famous are dumber than you or I. Well, maybe it is.

But when they hit those low poses, the rest of us are out there watching with a certain amount of glee. Most of *our* embarrassing moments we can keep to ourselves.

☆

In the seventeenth century, England's King Charles II collected the powdered remains from mummies of Egyptian kings. In an attempt to become as great as they were, Charles rubbed the powder all over himself.

He eventually achieved his goal, although not in the way he expected. He died just as they had.

☆

Israel's Queen Jezebel carefully put on her full makeup before committing suicide by throwing herself out a tower window. She didn't want to leave an ugly corpse.

Apparently, it didn't occur to the queen what would happen to her carefully made-up face when she hit the ground.

Movie star Warren Beatty had this bright moment of self-realization: "I'm old, I'm young. I'm intelligent, I'm stupid. My tide goes in and out."

☆

But Beatty wasn't able to match this gem of revelation from England's Princess Diana: "Brain the size of a pea, I've got."

☆

Russia's Ivan the Terrible ordered an elephant killed because it did not bow down to him.

☆

Queen Christina of Sweden had a miniature cannon built and shot tiny cannonballs at the fleas in her house.

☆

King James I of England liked to gamble at cards. He had two court attendants whose duties consisted of royal card facilitation. One of the lackeys held the cards for the king, while the other told him which cards to play.

So what exactly did the king like about playing cards?

☆

New York businessman Abe Hirschfeld made a fortune operating parking lots. He then bought the *New York Post*, but was forced to sell the paper after sixteen days when his staff published an entire issue trashing the boss.

Hirschfeld went on to start another newspaper (at a time when papers all over the country were folding). It folded within five months. He then ran for political office and lost three times, twice as a Democrat, once as a Republican.

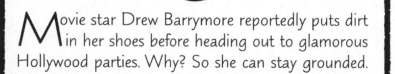

Movie star Drew Barrymore reportedly puts dirt in her shoes before heading out to glamorous Hollywood parties. Why? So she can stay grounded.

Mao Tse-tung of China was a chain smoker (though not, one assumes, during the rigors of the Great March).

Mao defended his habit by declaring that smoking was "a form of deep-breathing exercises." He also didn't brush his green teeth or take baths.

☆

Yukio Mishima, one of Japan's greatest writers, led his militant followers to take control of a Japanese army base in 1970. He made an impassioned speech to the soldiers there, demanding a return to the noble ways of the ancient samurai.

When his pleas were scorned, Mishima committed ritual suicide, and a follower cut off his head in the samurai way.

Mishima was not alone among creative fortunates who negated the talent that made them great in the first place. Other writers and artists had difficulty remembering that you can't continue to produce great work if you're dead, and that suicide is a long-term solution to a short-term problem.

1. The master painter Vincent van Gogh shot himself to death at thirty-seven.
2. American poet Hart Crane became an alcoholic and committed suicide at thirty-two.
3. Edgar Allan Poe, one of the most original writers in American history, drank himself to death with the help of drugs.
4. The magical Welsh poet Dylan Thomas, loved and beloved around the world, drank himself to death at thirty-nine.
5. Poet Sylvia Plath committed suicide. So did the poets Thomas Chatterton, Anne Sexton, Randall Jarrell, and Robert Lowell.
6. The Russian writer Maksim Gorky shot himself in the chest but survived the botched suicide attempt.
7. Debt-ridden writer Joseph Conrad shot himself in the heart, but survived.
8. Concert pianist Arthur Rubinstein hung himself with his own belt. It broke. He survived.

☆

King Ludwig II of Bavaria spent a fortune building the fairy tale medieval castle of Neuschwanstein in non-medieval 1860.

The fortune he spent on the castle wasn't his. It belonged to the state treasury, which was one reason Ludwig was declared insane and sent to an asylum.

One of the other reasons: Ludwig invited his horse to dinner.

A king must work harder than ordinary men to achieve insanity.

☆

Movie star Humphrey Bogart, one of the smartest tough guys in film, flunked out of prep school after failing geometry, English, French, and Bible studies.

> Future playwright Eugene O'Neill was kicked out of Princeton University for throwing a beer bottle through the window of the college president, who later became president of the United States—Woodrow Wilson.

Peanuts cartoonist Charles Schulz had his cartoons rejected by his high-school yearbook, then was turned down for a cartoonist's job at the Walt Disney studio.

☆

Silent movie star Charlie Chaplin, who ingratiated himself with people around the world as the persecuted little tramp, played the persecutor in his not-so-private life.

He seduced actress Lita Grey when she was sixteen and he thirty-five, after grooming her to become a starlet. When she became pregnant, he offered to pay for an abortion or give her money to marry another man. Only when threatened with statutory rape and a paternity suit did he consent to marry Lita.

During their marriage, Chaplin threatened to kill her, tried to convince her to commit suicide, and still fathered two children with her. They divorced after two years.

☆

Jazz Age writer F. Scott Fitzgerald was declared the spokesman for his rebellious generation. His first novel, *This Side of Paradise*, was a success, but his subsequent books, including the now-famous *The Great Gatsby*, were financial flops.

Yet Fitzgerald and his wife, Zelda, continued to live and spend wildly, although they no longer had the resources for it.

Fitzgerald could have found financial salvation when he was contracted to write for a movie studio. But he was so difficult for Hollywood producers to work with that the studio fired him.

He died young and in debt, while the flamboyant Zelda died in an asylum after a nervous breakdown. A classic case of great promise, squandered thoughtlessly.

☆

American poet Ezra Pound was such an intellectual master that it took other intellectuals to appreciate his mastery. Yet the acclaimed poet took sides against his own country during World War II, calling Hitler "a saint" and accusing the Jews of being evil, rather than the victims of a vast evil.

Tried for treason, Pound spent twelve years in a hospital for the criminally insane. Near the end of his life he admitted, "Everything that I touch, I spoil. I have blundered always."

This is an accurate description of the kind of monumental stupidity that only a vastly intelligent person can achieve.

☆

Convicted killer Sirhan Sirhan offered this unique plea for parole from prison: "If Robert Kennedy were alive today, he would not countenance singling me out for this kind of treatment."

Sirhan was turned down for parole and remained in prison, where he had been sentenced for assassinating Robert Kennedy.

☆

Philip III, king of Spain in the 1600s, died from a fever he contracted from sitting for too long in front of the fire.

Since he knew he was overheating, why didn't the king move away from the fire? It wasn't his royal job. The palace's fire-tending attendant, whose job it was to pull back the king's chair, was off duty.

☆

When the English poet Alexander Pope read his translation of *The Iliad*, Charles Montagu, the earl of Halifax, objected to several passages and strongly suggested that Pope rewrite them.

The poet tried to negotiate a reasonable course between the demands of poetry and those of the aristocracy: He returned to Lord Halifax a few months later, thanked him for his perceptive suggestions, and read him the corrected lines.

The earl heartily approved the changes. What the earl didn't know was that Pope had made no changes.

Writers have since used the Pope approach to rewriting on countless newspaper and magazine editors down through the years.

Newspaper magnate Joseph Pulitzer once tried to build a billboard for his *New York World* that could be seen on Mars. He abandoned the plan when he couldn't decide what language the Martians could read.

Oscar Levant, the witty radio and TV star who was also an accomplished pianist, drank forty to sixty cups of coffee a day, then complained endlessly about his insomnia.

Pulitzer Prize–winning poet John Berryman, an alcoholic, tried to kill himself by jumping off a bridge into the Mississippi River. He missed the water and landed on the riverbank.

In the eighteenth century the earl of Bridgewater chose his favorite dogs to join him at table for dinner. The dogs, wearing custom-made leather boots, were draped in linen and served by butlers.

If the dogs exhibited poor table manners, the earl banished them from the table.

Queen Elizabeth had needs beyond those of the average royalty. She employed one maid, whose sole job was to tend to the queen's gloves.

Elizabeth had more than two thousand pairs of gloves, which meant a typical pair could go six years without being twice tugged upon the queenly hands.

☆

France's King Louis XV spent the equivalent of $15,000 a year on coffee.

While we're brooding over java, it was the English custom in the 1600s not to put sugar or cream into coffee, but mustard. No one stepped forward to claim his share of fame for that move.

CHAPTER THREE

Stupid Predictions

Stupidity self-promotes. Half the perceived intelligence in the world comes from people who learned to keep their big mouths shut.

Consider the following people who didn't:

Charles Duell, commissioner of the U.S. Office of Patents, in 1899: "Everything that can be invented has been invented."

Oxford professor Erasmus Wilson: "When the Paris Exhibition [of 1878] closes, electric light will close with it and no more will be heard of it."

The *Literary Digest* in 1899: "[The automobile] will never, of course, come into as common use as the bicycle."

Professional well drillers when Edwin Drake tried to convince them to help him drill for oil in 1859: "Drill for oil? You mean drill into the ground to try and find oil? You're crazy."

A Western Union executive rejecting a new technology in 1876: "This 'telephone' has too many shortcomings to be seriously considered as a means of communication. The device is inherently of no value to us."

An editorial in a Boston newspaper in 1865: "Well-informed people know it is impossible to transmit the voice over wires and that were it possible to do so, the thing would be of no practical value."

French physiology professor Pierre Pachet in 1872: "[Louis Pasteur's] theory of germs is a ridiculous fiction."

Lord Kelvin, president of England's Royal Society in 1895: "Heavier-than-air flying machines are impossible."

An American newspaper editor suggesting in 1889 that the great British writer should find another trade: "I'm sorry, Mr. Kipling, but you just don't know how to use the English language."

Sir John Eric Ericksen, British surgeon to Queen Victoria in 1873: "The abdomen, the chest, and the brain will forever be shut from the intrusion of the wise and humane surgeon."

Marshal Ferdinand Foch, professor of military strategy at France's École Superieure de Guerre, in the days before World War I: "Airplanes are interesting toys, but of no military value."

H. M. Warner, head of Warner Bros. studio, rejecting a new movie technology in 1927: "Who the hell wants to hear actors talk?"

A business partner of radio pioneer David Sarnoff explaining in the 1920s why they should not go into the radio business, as Sarnoff suggested: "The wireless music box has no imaginable commercial value. Who would pay for a message sent to nobody in particular?"

Yale economist Irving Fischer, a week before the 1929 stock market crash that led to the Great Depression: "Stocks have reached what looks like a permanently high plateau."

Engineer Lee DeForest in 1926: "While theoretically and technically television may be feasible, commercially and financially I consider it an impossibility."

Newspaper columnist Dorothy Thompson upon visiting Germany in 1931: "When finally I walked into Adolf Hitler's salon in the Kaiserhof Hotel, I was convinced that I was meeting the future dictator of Germany. In something less than fifty seconds I was quite sure I was not."

The *Daily Express*, a British newspaper: "Britain will not be involved in a European war this year [1938], or next year either."

Movie studio boss Irving Thalberg explaining why he didn't want to make *Gone with the Wind*: "No Civil War picture has ever made a nickel."

Actor Gary Cooper on his decision to reject the lead role in *Gone with the Wind*: "I'm just glad it'll be Clark Gable who's falling on his face and not Gary Cooper."

Thomas Watson, IBM chairman, evaluating the business potential of a new contraption in 1943: "I think there is a world market for maybe five computers."

Popular Mechanics forecasting the relentless march of science in 1949: "Computers in the future may weigh no more than 1.5 tons."

An editor in charge of business books for Prentice Hall publishers in 1957: "I have traveled the length and breadth of this country and talked with the best people, and I can assure you that data processing is a fad that won't last out the year."

An IBM engineer in 1968 asked this plaintive question about the microchip: "But what is it good for?"

Ken Olson, founder of Digital Equipment Corporation, in 1977: "There is no reason anyone would want a computer in their home."

The *New York Daily News* in 1951 about the debut of a new Giant, the future Hall of Famer Willie Mays: "Just so-so in center field."

Tommy Holmes, minor league baseball manager: "That kid can't play baseball. He can't pull the ball."

Holmes was referring to Hank Aaron, who pulled the ball often enough and far enough to become baseball's all-time home run leader.

Composer Robert Schumann on fellow composer Frederic Chopin: "Nobody can call that music."

Since then we've heard that remark applied to jazz, rock 'n' roll, and rap. It never stops the musicians from making what nobody can call music.

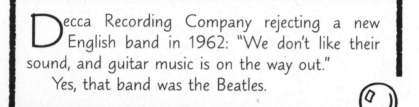

Decca Recording Company rejecting a new English band in 1962: "We don't like their sound, and guitar music is on the way out."
Yes, that band was the Beatles.

Business Week magazine in 1958: "Though import sales could hit 425,000 [cars] in 1959, they may never go that high again."

Within a few years, Japanese carmakers alone would be selling three times that number of cars in the United States.

Steve Jobs on attempts to get major electronics companies to manufacture the personal computer he designed with partner Steve Wozniak: "So we went to Atari and said, 'Hey, we've got this amazing thing, even built with some of your parts, and what do you think about funding us? Or we'll give it to you. We just want to do it. Pay our salary, we'll come work for you.' And they said,

'No.' So then we went to Hewlett-Packard, and they said, 'Hey, we don't need you. You haven't got through college yet.'"

Jobs and Wozniak went on to start Apple Computer.

$$\textcircled{?}$$

A Yale professor explaining the poor grade he gave business student Fred Smith in 1966 for his research paper proposing an overnight delivery system: "The concept is interesting and well-formed, but in order to earn better than a C the idea must be feasible."

After college, Smith founded Federal Express.

$$\textcircled{?}$$

The *Wall Street Journal* a year before Bill Clinton's reelection: "He will lose to any Republican nominee who doesn't drool onstage."

CHAPTER FOUR

Popped Culture

Pointing out the stupidities of pop culture seems almost too easy. Still, who can resist?

A movie-theater manager in Seoul, South Korea, found that *The Sound of Music* ran too long. He fixed the problem with some clever editing that hadn't occurred to the musical's director: He cut out the songs.

Paul McCartney woke up one morning humming the melody to what became one of the most popular songs in history, *Yesterday*. Would the song have been as popular if he had kept the original lyrics: "Scrambled eggs. I love your legs"?

There will always be stage mothers, but not many like the woman from Detroit who sent her two daughters (ages eight and ten) on a bus to Hollywood in 1938, telling them to report to central casting, then send for the rest of the family as soon as they became movie stars.

Los Angeles authorities put the girls on the next bus home.

When the TV sitcom *Laverne and Shirley* was syndicated to Thailand, local translators found it necessary to explain the behavior of American sitcom women with the following remark: "The two women depicted in the following episode are from an insane asylum."

Which explains most of what we see on TV.

The producers of the hit TV show *Miami Vice* spent more money to produce a typical episode than the Miami Police Department spent each year to run the Miami vice squad.

TV's *Sesame Street* became wildly successful by making education enjoyable for young children. But not everyone was happy with that accomplishment.

Professional educators complained that Muppet creator Jim Henson made education too much fun, so that kids found real school boring.

Advice to would-be movie stars: Don't slug the boss if you enjoy the perks of being rich and famous.

Silent-screen star John Gilbert punched out studio chief Louis B. Mayer, one of the most powerful men in Hollywood, over a wisecrack Mayer made when Gilbert was stood up at the altar by actress Greta Garbo.

Mayer swore revenge and got it when talking pictures took over the industry. The mogul convinced Hollywood and the world that Gilbert was through in motion pictures because he had an effeminate voice.

Gilbert drank himself to death within a few years. Mayer went on to become even more extraordinarily rich, powerful, and unsluggable.

Filmmaker Frank Capra's warm-hearted fantasy *It's a Wonderful Life*, one of two all-time favorite holiday movies, bombed at the box office when it was first released in 1946.

The movie was such a failure that years later Capra didn't even bother to renew the copyright. That slipup interested TV stations, which realized they could show the movie without being obligated to pay royalties.

This time around, audiences loved the movie, and *It's a Wonderful Life* became one of the most popular films of all time.

It's hard to break into showbiz, harder still if you try it without the benefit of brains.

In 1929 an aspiring actor named Charles Loeb mailed himself in a box from Chicago to a Hollywood film studio. That gambit got him past the studio gates, but more dead than alive. He recovered from his injuries, but he did not land a part because no one was going to hire anyone that wacko.

Remember that Cinerama epic, *Krakatowa, East of Java*? Only two problems with the title: The volcano is spelled "Krakatoa" and it's not east of Java, it's west. Close enough for Hollywood.

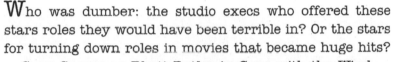

Who was dumber: the studio execs who offered these stars roles they would have been terrible in? Or the stars for turning down roles in movies that became huge hits?

Gary Cooper as Rhett Butler in *Gone with the Wind*.
Robert Redford as Michael Corleone in *The Godfather*.
Anthony Hopkins as Gandhi.
Marlon Brando as Lawrence of Arabia.

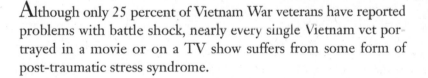

Although only 25 percent of Vietnam War veterans have reported problems with battle shock, nearly every single Vietnam vet portrayed in a movie or on a TV show suffers from some form of post-traumatic stress syndrome.

A kids' favorite around the world, the *Muppet Show* was banned in Turkey in 1979 because TV executives there thought Miss Piggy would offend Muslims, who don't eat pork.

In 1956 a TV producer for the U.S. Steel Hour made certain changes in the script for a drama about the true story of a black teenager who was kidnapped and murdered by racists in Mississippi.

The producer, not wanting to cross anyone, changed the black teenager to a Jew, moved the story from the South to New England, and eliminated the murder.

Orson Welles's 1938 radio play, a dramatization of H. G. Wells's *War of the Worlds*, was a ludicrously unbelievable account of a landing and an attack by extraterrestrial aliens.

During the broadcast, the announcers made clear several times that the show was a work of fiction.

Nevertheless, a million listeners thought that space aliens really had invaded the United States. People panicked in the streets.

Two people in Kansas City went to the hospital with alien-inspired heart attacks, while fifteen people in Newark, New Jersey, were treated for shock. One Pittsburgh woman tried to poison herself so the aliens wouldn't get her.

When the crossword puzzle was invented in 1913, it became a worldwide craze, particularly in the United States and England. One of the major side effects of the craze: a tremendous boost in the sale of dictionaries.

Yet dictionaries, being instruments of snobs at the time, refused for seventeen years to recognize that *crossword* was a word.

A Los Angeles radio station informed a woman who called into one of their phone-in shows that the station had a policy that only calls from people under the age of fifty got on the air.

A Florida news anchor interrupted her morning broadcast in 1974 to announce, "In keeping with Channel 40's policy of bringing you the latest in blood and guts, and in living color, you are going to see another first—attempted suicide."

She then pulled out a gun and shot herself on air.

British movie director Tony Kaye brought a monk, a rabbi, and a priest into the New Line studio to help him negotiate to have his name taken off his first film, *American History X*.

"I want to put the fear of God into every production company in this industry," Kaye explained.

Rock singer Carl Perkins's most popular song was *Blue Suede Shoes*. Late in his career, he put on blue suede shoes for all of his concerts.

He wore the showy shoes with dread because after the performance fans would mob the stage to step on his blue suede shoes, exactly as the song urged them not to do.

"You can't believe how much of a problem that becomes," Perkins reported. "My feet get horribly sore. . . . I've seen my fans get older, which means they put on weight, so every year it seems my feet get crushed more."

To promote a bad romantic movie, *The Love Letter*, DreamWorks studio mailed anonymous mash notes to film critics around the country. The letter told the critic that the besotted admirer had been watching and worshipping him or her from afar, and had fallen madly in love with him or her.

The letters were typed by hand and mailed in plain envelopes from the cities in which the critics lived, so that the reporters wouldn't suspect that the letters came from a PR agent in Hollywood. This in an industry whose stars are regularly stalked, and sometimes murdered, by adoring fans.

An Indian movie producer decided to set a record by producing a feature film in twenty-four hours. He hired fifteen directors, fourteen to shoot the film and one to shoot the making of the film. The producer had no script, but gave the actors the idea of what he wanted and then let the cameras roll.

This effort came as no surprise in India, where record setting is such a passion that a man set a record by slicing a cucumber into 120,000 pieces, while another ate a brick in thirty minutes and thirty-three pounds of salt in five days.

How far can *Star Wars* mania go? Anyone can stand in line for three days to see a movie. But a twenty-eight-year-old father of three from Tucson, Arizona, showed real commitment: He legally changed his name to Obi-Wan Kenobi, the Jedi knight played by Alec Guinness in the original movie and Ewan McGregor in the prequel.

In 1949 Harry Cohn, head of Columbia Pictures, dumped a young actress because she had no star quality. Actually, he probably dumped many young actresses. This one turned out to be Marilyn Monroe.

The movies made comic Charlie Chaplin such a huge star that he became one of the founders of United Artists studio and assumed control of his own art. Therefore, we might be surprised that the great clown missed the significance of movies entirely.

"The cinema is little more than a fad," Chaplin explained in 1918. "What audiences really want to see is flesh and blood on the stage."

Here are some other farsighted know-nothings who looked greatness squarely in the face and missed it completely:

1. Rock-band manager Eric Easton helped put together the Rolling Stones in 1963. He told the band there was one thing holding them back. "The singer will have to go," Easton explained, referring to the gawky Mick Jagger.

2. "That the character Snow White is a failure in every way is undisputable," critic V. F. Calverton wrote about the 1938 debut of Walt Disney's first full-length animated film. "Another Snow White will sound the Disney death-knell."

3. "Displays no trace of imagination, good taste or ingenuity," film critic Russell Maloney wrote in the *New Yorker*

in 1939. "I say it's a stinkeroo." Maloney was referring to *The Wizard of Oz*.

4. "Hollywood often uses its best players, writers and directors for its epic phonies," Manny Farber observed in the *New Republic* in 1942. "Warner's is *Casablanca*."

5. "This is third-rate Hitchcock," Dwight Macdonald declared in Esquire in 1960. He meant *Psycho*.

6. "As difficult to sit through as a Black Mass sung in Latin," Michael Sragow complained in the *Los Angeles Herald Examiner* in 1979, referring to one of the most exciting thrillers of all time, *Alien*.

7. "Murphy's aggressive one-upsmanship through most of the film kills your interest in him as a performer," Pauline Kael commented in the *New Yorker* about Eddie Murphy in *Beverly Hills Cop*, the film that made him one of the most popular movie stars in the world.

8. "Spielberg . . . may indeed have made the most monumental molehill in movie history," John Simon predicted in 1982, condemning one of Spielberg's huge hits, *Close Encounters of the Third Kind*.

9. "The biggest disappointment of 1965. . . . The film bumbles along to boredom," Andrew Sarris wrote in the *Village Voice* about *Dr. Zhivago*.

10. "If sharks can yawn, that's presumably what this one is doing," Stanley Kauffmann said about *Jaws* in the *New Republic*. "It's certainly what I was doing all through this picture."

11. "The film is simply a bore. . . . So save your money," Christopher Hitchens advised *New Statesman* readers who might be tempted to see *Raiders of the Lost Ark*.

12. "A standard-issue baby-faced actor," David Denby

declared, dismissing the star of *Risky Business*, Tom Cruise, in *New York* magazine in 1983.

13. "Not only can he not act, he cannot even look and sound halfway intelligent," was how John Simon blasted the star of *The Deep*, Nick Nolte, in 1977.

14. "How a society as dynamic as our own throws up such a monstrosity is beyond the scope of this review," Henry Hart wrote about Elvis Presley in the movie *Love Me Tender*.

15. "At no time are we watching a young man who demonstrates a natural or exciting flair for dancing," Gary Arnold commented in the *Washington Post* about John Travolta in the disco movie that made his career, *Saturday Night Fever*.

16. "And then there is Diane Keaton's scandalous performance," John Simon wrote in *New York* magazine in 1977. "It is not so much an actress playing a role as a soul in torment crying out for urgent therapy—in bad taste to watch and an indecency to display."

    Simon was referring to Keaton's star turn in *Annie Hall*, the role for which she won an Oscar.

One movie star saw clearly through the fog that seemed to dim the bulbs of so many others. "People don't credit me with much of a brain," Sylvester Stallone said. "So why should I disillusion them?"

Tex Antoine, New York's popular TV weatherman, lost his job after beginning a report with this remark: "It is well to remember the words of Confucius: 'If rape is inevitable, lie back and enjoy it.'"

The dumbest mistake many moviemakers commit is making them in the first place. The following films incorporated some swell oversights, proving that no matter how gigantic your budget and your ego, you can make the smallest error and it will last for years.

1. In *The Wrong Box*, a story set in Victorian England, you can see numerous TV antennas on the rooftops of London.

2. In *Carmen Jones*, as actress Dorothy Dandridge walks down the street, you can track the camera and sound crew walking with her by their reflections in a store window.

3. During the big car chase in *Bullitt*, Steve McQueen's car loses three hubcaps. Later when the chase ends with his car crashing into a wall, three more hubcaps fly off.

4. Alec Guinness won an Oscar for *The Bridge on the River Kwai*, but his name was misspelled as "Guiness" in the credits.

5. In *Goonies*, a kid remarks that his favorite adventure was fighting the octopus. Only they never fought the octopus because the big octopus fight ended up on the cutting-room floor.

6. In *Jailhouse Rock*, Elvis Presley must have been sent to prison for multiple crimes because in one scene he wears a shirt identifying him as prisoner No. 6240. In the next scene, he's prisoner No. 6239.

In 1963 the producers of a movie called *Four for Texas*, a comedy about the Old West starring Frank Sinatra and the Rat Pack, screen-tested actresses in the nude, then shot nude scenes with the actresses who won the roles.

The producers knew the censors would cut out all the nude scenes, which had nothing to do with the rest of the story, before the film was released.

The movie *Heaven's Gate* would have been a flop for one simple reason: It was a lousy movie. But it took some real effort to turn it into a megaflop.

A loser of gigantic proportions requires, most of all, a director losing his grip.

Michael Cimino, who directed the epic Western, demanded millions of dollars' worth of authenticity. He spent megabucks on a wagon train with eighty wagons, hundreds of horses, and 1,200 extras who had to be taught how to ride, drive wagons, and use bullwhips.

He built a gigantic skating rink, and paid for 250 extras to take lessons on the use of antique ice skates. He rented a yacht, a brass band, and an authentic nineteenth-century train, which had to be rerouted from Denver to Idaho because it was too large for twentieth-century train tunnels.

Throw all that—plus twenty retakes of simple scenes and 1.5 million feet of film—into a bad movie and you've got the kind of legendary blunder that makes Hollywood the envy of million-dollar idiots the world over.

CHAPTER FIVE

Dumb Ways to Die

As dull as we grow in our daily routines, we show vast ingenuity in finding new and stupid ways to get ourselves killed.

Life's partner in crime, death, has always been a fast worker. But some people go out of their way to find death before death finds them.

A South Korean wife hanged herself in humiliation in 1987. The source of her shame? She had forgotten to set her clock ahead when the country switched to daylight savings time, and her husband had to leave for the company picnic without his lunch.

A drunk security guard asked a fellow worker at a Moscow bank to stab his bulletproof vest to see if it would protect him against a knife attack. It didn't.

An Alabama man died from rattlesnake bites after playing snake catch with a friend.

A sixteen-year-old English boy deodorized himself to death because he was obsessed with smelling nice. The coroner said the boy suffered a heart attack because he had ten times the lethal dose of propane and butane in his blood, built up from spraying his body for months with extreme amounts of deodorant.

In 1841 England's greatest daredevil, Samuel Scott, performed stunt acrobatics while hanging by a rope with the noose around his neck from London's Waterloo Bridge.

One day the noose slipped. Scott strangled to death on the bridge while the audience cheered, assuming it was part of the act.

So many rock stars die young, you'd think it was a career move. They kill themselves in car crashes, plane crashes, drug crashes. They overdose on booze and overstuffed sandwiches.

Then there was Terry Kath, lead singer for Chicago, one of the hot bands of the '70s. Playing with a gun, Kath pointed it at his head. His famous last words to friends were, "Don't worry. It's not loaded. See?"

A seventy-three-year-old man died of exposure during the freezing winter of 1989 in Rochester, New York, when he became stuck in a trash can on his own front porch.

People who passed by thought he was just fooling around, so no one stopped to help.

In 1933 a Japanese schoolgirl killed herself by jumping into an active volcano. Her death started a fad, with more than three hundred other Japanese children killing themselves the same way.

Tourists flocked to the island to watch people jump into the volcano. Police finally stopped the fad by erecting fences around the crater and making it illegal to buy a one-way ticket to the island.

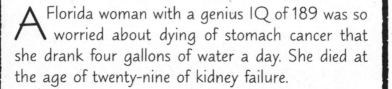

A Florida woman with a genius IQ of 189 was so worried about dying of stomach cancer that she drank four gallons of water a day. She died at the age of twenty-nine of kidney failure.

In 1857 a South African girl of the Gcealeka Xhosa tribe had a vision that if her people destroyed all their worldly possessions, the spirits would lead them to glorious victory over the white men who had stolen their country.

Her tribe followed the girl's vision, destroyed everything they owned, and 25,000 of them starved to death.

A veteran skydiver who was also a cameraman filmed the exploits of fellow skydivers with a camera strapped to his helmet. So it must have come as quite a surprise to the pro when he jumped out of a plane in April 1988, after having remembered to load and adjust his camera but forgetting to put on his parachute.

Actress Peg Entwistle, twenty-four, despairing of ever becoming a movie star, jumped to her death off the H in the famous Hollywood sign in 1932.

After her death, a friend opened a letter that had just arrived in the mail. The letter was from a movie producer, offering Entwistle a role in a picture. She would have played a girl who commits suicide.

Every golfer alive will relate to the impulse behind this stupid death in 1982 when a New Orleans golfer, playing badly on the 13th hole, threw his club away in disgust. The club hit his golf cart and broke in two. The shaft rebounded off the cart and stabbed the golfer in the neck, severing his jugular vein.

Army deserter Richard Paris went to Vegas on his honeymoon in 1967. He used fourteen sticks of dynamite to blow himself up, along with his bride and five other honeymooners.

Famed playwright Tennessee Williams suffocated to death at the age of seventy-one when he bent his head back to squirt in nose spray, the cap fell into his mouth, and he partially swallowed it.

Writers should watch what they swallow. Sherwood Anderson died at sixty-four when peritonitis set in after he swallowed a snack at a party but didn't remove the toothpick first.

Barnstorming pilot Lincoln Beachey decided his aerial stunts were growing too dangerous. Before he went looping, he strapped himself into the plane so he wouldn't fall out and kill himself.

Losing a wing during a dive, his plane crashed into San Francisco Bay. He drowned because he couldn't get free of the straps.

Henry Flagler, one of the founders of Standard Oil, died in 1913, attacked by his own door. The millionaire built himself a mansion in Florida, complete with fancy automatic doors. One of the closing doors caught him from behind and knocked him down the stairs. He died from the injuries.

Doesn't it make you mad when your team loses a close game it should have won? It made plenty of Peruvian soccer fans mad in 1964 when Argentina beat the national team on a disputed last-minute goal. Three hundred angry fans were killed in the ensuing riot.

That's small-time fatal stupidity compared to the riot that started 1,400 years ago over an unpopular call in a Constantinople chariot race. That riot claimed 30,000 lives. No record exists of whether the umpire was among them.

When Sherlock Holmes's creator, Arthur Conan Doyle, turned to lecturing about the spirit world, his speeches were so convincing that several New Yorkers who heard him speak at Carnegie Hall killed themselves so they could get to the spirit world sooner.

In 1929 firemen in Kent, England, put on a public demonstration of their skills, using nine young boys as pretend victims to be rescued from a burning house.

One of the firemen forgot the smoke bombs they had planned to use and actually set fire to the house. All the boys died in the blaze, while the crowd cheered, thinking the boys were actually dummies.

In Liverpool, England, an elderly man was following his 224-pound wife up the stairs one night in 1903. She lost her balance and fell backward, hit her head on the floor, and died instantly.

Her husband lay trapped under her body for three days. By the time friends found them, he had also died.

In 1983 a San Diego woman, arrested for shoplifting, swore she would hold her breath until she turned blue if the police didn't release her. They didn't, she did, and she died.

To commemorate the death of the Great Houdini, Joe Burrus, a latter-day escape artist, tried to better one of Houdini's stunts in 1990. He was chained and locked, then buried in a clear plastic coffin. Seven tons of concrete were poured on top of the coffin. But before Burrus could escape, the weight of the concrete crushed the coffin and he died on the same day as the master himself.

When silent-screen star Rudolph Valentino died at the age of thirty in 1926, a New York woman shot herself, an English actress poisoned herself, and two Japanese women committed suicide by volcano.

None of the women had ever met Valentino. They had all fallen for him in the movies.

When James Dean died young while speeding in his sports car, he sparked another round of fan suicide.

Two Parisians fought a duel with muskets in hot-air balloons in 1808. One man shot the other man's balloon, and his rival died from the plunge.

The *London Times* reported the accidental death of a boy who was rowing in the Mersey River with his friend in 1869. The boat capsized. The boy couldn't swim. Every time his friend tried to rescue him, the boy's dog bit him, trying to protect his master from attack. The master drowned.

An Australian man was shooting pool in his garage when he thought up a cute trick shot. He hoisted himself onto a ceiling crossbeam and hung by his feet while he cued up.

He fell, hit his head on the concrete, and died of brain damage, although he may have suffered the brain damage prior to the fall.

In 1901 Maud Willard threw herself over Niagara Falls in a barrel, but the fall didn't kill her as it has other daredevils.

What got Maud? She forced her dog into the barrel with her. The dog pressed its nose up against the barrel's single air vent, and Maud suffocated.

The Austrian Hans Steininger proudly held the sixteenth-century record for the world's longest beard. One day, while climbing up the stairs, he tripped on his beard and died from the fall.

Patients from a Cleveland mental institution were evacuated during a 1933 fire. Nine of the women patients went back inside to get out of the cold. They burned to death.

It's all fun and games during spring break at Daytona Beach, Florida, unless death plays along.

In 1989 an Illinois college student on spring break was playing the popular motel sport of balcony Frisbee. He leaned out too far for a catch and fell to his death. His is the only recorded fatality to mar the pacific sport of Frisbee.

Jessie Sharp was an expert kayaker, so good he thought he could kayak over Niagara Falls. Which he did in 1990, but only once.

In Mortar, Italy, a dog shot and killed its master. The man was out hunting when his dog fell into a ditch. When the hunter held out his rifle to help the dog up, it pawed the trigger.

In Sunderland, England, a twenty-seven-year-old man was rushed to the hospital after reporting difficulty breathing. The man had glued his nostrils shut after confusing a bottle of glue with nasal spray.

Coworkers in Stafford, England, wanted to do something special for their pal's fiftieth birthday, so they threw him a party, even hired an exotic dancer to pop out of a cake.

The man got the shock of his life when the naked dancer who popped out turned out to be his daughter. The shock proved too much for the birthday boy, who dropped dead from a heart attack.

Two brothers in Los Angeles decided to remove a bees' nest from a backyard shed by blowing it up with an illegal firecracker. They lit the fuse and ran back inside their house. The explosion blew in a window, cutting up one of the brothers badly enough to require stitches.

When the brothers headed toward their car, the wounded one was stung three times by the surviving bees. Neither of them knew that the stung brother was allergic to bee venom. They found out too late when he died of suffocation on the way to the hospital.

A Minneapolis man was charged with murder in the death of his cousin. The two young men were playing a game of Russian roulette and used a semiautomatic pistol.

A New Jersey man choked to death on a sequined pastie he had removed with his teeth from an exotic dancer's costume. "I didn't think he was going to eat it," the dancer told police. "He was really drunk."

Two Canadian friends died in a head-on collision, earning a tie in the game of chicken they were playing with their snowmobiles.

A Frenchman tried a complex suicide in 1998. Standing on a tall cliff, he tied a noose around his neck, securing the rope to a large rock. He then drank poison and set fire to himself. As he jumped off the cliff, he fired a pistol at his head.

The bullet missed him and cut through the rope so he didn't hang himself when he plunged into the sea. And not only did the cold water extinguish his burning clothes, but the shock of it made him vomit up the poison.

He was dragged out of the water by a fisherman and taken to a hospital, where he died of hypothermia.

A West Virginia fast-food worker died while trying to use short, tie-down straps to bungee jump off a seventy-foot railroad trestle.

The man taped several of the straps together, wrapped one end around his foot, and anchored the other end to the trestle. Then he jumped.

But as police explained, the length of the cord that he had assembled was greater than the distance between the trestle and the pavement below.

An Austrian circus dwarf was performing trampoline stunts at an outdoor show in Zambia when he took a bad bounce and landed in the yawning mouth of a hippopotamus. Half swallowed, the man suffocated before the hippo's jaws could be pried open.

CHAPTER SIX

Stupid Inventions

For every lightbulb we invent, a dozen guys are working on a dozen versions of self-contained, firefly-powered illumination devices.

Stupid inventions often demonstrate as much ingenuity and hard work as the inventions that change the world. Inventors of useless, ridiculous, and totally idiotic contraptions miss genius rank on a single fault. They could not answer the question: What in the world ever made you think we needed something like that?

Although they never took the world by storm or otherwise, patents were awarded to: a rocking chair–powered vacuum cleaner, a rocking chair–powered butter churn, a yegg-proof safe that exploded when it was opened, an army helmet with a gun on top that soldiers fired by blowing into a pneumatic tube, a cannon that shot live snakes at the enemy, and a submarine aircraft carrier.

Let's not forget these other perfectly brilliant but stupid inventions:

Railroad trains built with rails on top of every car.

The idea was when a fast train caught up to a slower train on the same track, it could pass by climbing up atop the slow train, rolling over the cars, and sliding down the other end.

Eyeglasses for chickens, so that other chickens wouldn't peck their eyes out.

Shoulder braces for hats. The braces enabled you to transfer the weight of the hat from your head to your shoulders, thus permitting "free circulation of air entirely around and over the head of the wearer," according to the patent application.

These metal hat supports would subsequently afford an "unobstructed exhibition of the ornamentation and trimming of the wearer's hair."

As would not wearing a hat.

In 1884 a Brit named Harry Fell was granted a government patent for making gold from wheat. His plan: Soak the wheat in water for ten hours, then dry the liquid, which turns into gold.

Fell may not have been a fool, only ahead of his time. Farmers subsequently perfected the technique of turning nonwheat into gold by getting the government to pay them not to farm.

A mechanical buggy whip that enabled a wagon driver to apply the whip to any horse in the team in only seven easy steps, none of which involved the manual snapping of the whip.

Breath-powered foot warmers. This apparatus was fashioned from tubes that ran inside your shirt, then bifurcated down each pant leg.

The top of the tube plugged into a funnel that strapped under your chin, into which you exhaled. The warmth of your exhalations floated down the tubes, keeping your feet toasty on cold days and strangers at a safe distance.

A dimple maker that worked on the principle of the rotary hand drill.

A mechanical baby patter to help put tots to sleep by patting them on the butt.

The patter was to be used in conjunction with the automatic baby-burping apparatus, which looked like one of those circus props used for launching acrobats.

A two-person topcoat for snuggling on cold days.

A movie theater in which the audience entered and exited through trap doors under each seat so they wouldn't step on one another's toes going out to the candy counter.

A cow decoy for hunters, which enabled two men to hide inside and wait for their unsuspecting prey—or a bull.

An automatic hair-cutting machine, whose use was to be followed by the automatic scalp-massaging machine, which required the user to stand on his head inside the apparatus.

A farm plow with a rifle welded onto the blade so that a man could farm and fire at the same time when the need arose.

A giant hot-air balloon powered by eagles. Or if you preferred, by vultures or condors.

A fishing lure in the shape and design of a naked woman, presumably used to lure sharks.

A rotary, gear-operated, automatic hat tipper designed to enable men to keep their hands free while tipping their hats politely with a nod of the head.

A combination cheese grater and mousetrap.

A smelly navigation system to help ships sail in fog without crashing into one another.

Each ship would be equipped with pumps that would propel nauseating odors to warn other ships of its presence.

Thick elastic shoes for jumping out of burning buildings. When you landed on your feet in the street below, the elastic would absorb the impact.

If you had to jump out of a particularly tall building, you simply added the accompanying parachute to your personal safety system. The chute fit neatly on top of your head and was held in place by a strap under your chin.

A jet-powered surfboard, intended, no doubt, for use in slow oceans.

Fake sideburns attached to sunglasses for the Elvis look.

A car burglar alarm that combined a detection circuit with a flamethrower.

A self-perfuming business suit.

A rifle that pitched baseballs, invented by a professor in 1897. It was intended to replace unreliable pitchers who couldn't get the ball over the plate often enough.

Strangely enough, the pitching rifle was actually tried in games. Even stranger, it wasn't pitchers who convinced the commissioner to ban the rifle from baseball. Batters didn't like it because without the motion of the pitcher's arm they couldn't pick up the pitch.

In 1953 a skier tired of waiting in long lift lines, invented self-propelled skis that powered skiers uphill. The device required skiers to fit belts under their skies and strap gas engines to their backs.

The power ski never took off because no one could figure out what the skier would do with the backpack engine at the top of the hill.

Dozens of inventors have created dozens of ways to help golfers find lost golf balls. The continued prevalence of lost golf balls will testify to the success of these attempts:
1. Coating golf balls with chemicals that would cause insects to swarm to the ball, thus identifying its location for the insect repellent–coated golfer.
2. Injecting odiferous chemicals into golf balls so golfers could sniff out their lost drives.
3. Inserting a tiny amount of radioactive chemicals inside the ball so it would click when the golfer approached with a Geiger counter.

If this device had ever been used, it would have replaced lost golf balls with lost golfers.

The Hun warriors of the fourth century invented the fearsome visage as a psychological weapon of war.

To strike fear into their enemies, the Huns would bind the heads of their infant boys so that by the time they grew old enough to fight they had deformed faces.

A tricycle with a printing press attached to the rear wheels that printed two different advertisements on the street as you rode along.

This device was designed in 1895 before the advent of the traffic jam.

A mechanical swimming bicycle upon which the pedaling swimmer lay supine, cranking with both hands and feet to turn a propeller that moved you through the water.

A flying machine in which the pilot rode inside a cage attached to a circular frame. The machine was carried through the air by a dozen eagles strapped into leather jackets hooked onto the frame.

A complete lifesaving system consisting of a flotational body suit that kept a shipwrecked swimmer vertical in the water for days.

The suit was outfitted with drinking water, food, torches, rockets, cigars, and reading material to help pass the time until rescuers arrived.

In 1891 a French engineer designed a daredevil ride specifically for the Eiffel Tower.

The ride consisted of a gigantic, bullet-shaped chamber big enough to seat fifteen people. The chamber would be hoisted to the top of the Eiffel Tower, then dropped to free fall into a champagne glass–shaped reservoir of water at the bottom of the tower.

The effect of the adventure, although it was never built, was described as a thrill. Something may have been lost in the translation from the French.

A machine for electroplating corpses was invented in 1891, so that you could coat your loved ones in a millimeter of copper and put them on display in their favorite easy chairs.

In 1886 two German brothers invented the photographic hat, consisting of a camera bolted inside a hat, to make cameras more portable.

A folding stool sewn inside the bustle of a nineteenth-century lady's skirts, which automatically unfolded into a seat when the lady sat down and folded back up for easy storage when she stood up.

A diet feedback tape that played antieating messages every time you opened your fridge.

A long-distance, pest-killing machine called the Coetherator. A farmer would take a picture of his field, put the photo in the machine, and fill it with insecticide. The machine would then kill the pests miles away from the field.

Bad food concoctions (most of them promoted by food marketing groups trying to increase sales of their product) aren't the same thing as bad food, although they can be.

But how would you know that any of the following foods were bad? You weren't actually going to try grape pesto pizza, peanut butter and Jell-O sandwiches, berries with green peppercorn sauce, pear-and-tomato pizza, tongue salad with cherries and hard-boiled eggs, spaghetti-squash waldorf salad, peanut-stuffed prune salad, onion wine, jalapeño pepper ice cream, cheeseburger-flavored popcorn, or fig ice cream?

Even geniuses aren't always so bright. When Thomas Edison invented the first phonograph in 1877, he wasn't thinking about the gigantic music industry he had just created. He thought the phonograph would be used as a device for people to record messages that would then be sent from one central telephone office to another, much the way people sent telegrams.

It took the public sixteen years to convince Edison that the phonograph had a future in the music business.

Many of the inventions mentioned above actually won patents. Historically, an idea didn't have to be doable to be patented. It only had to be unique, which was often its best feature.

These ideas and many others so impressed the man in charge of the U.S. Patent Office that he resigned, suggesting that the office be closed since there was nothing left to invent.

The year: 1875.

CHAPTER SEVEN

Stupid Social Customs

When we look back far enough, we find the beliefs held by people in earlier societies to be stupid, foolish, and blatantly false. Yet we confidently hold our own beliefs to be obviously true.

At least we won't be around in a few hundred years to hear them laughing at us. So let's laugh backward:

In Victorian England proper library etiquette demanded that books written by women not be shelved next to books written by men, unless the authors were married to each other.

In the twelfth century, Europeans believed that trees gave birth to birds.

For centuries, until Magellan's ships circumnavigated the globe, Europeans believed that no people could possibly live on the other side of the earth, even if it *was* round.

Forget about people falling off the bottom of the planet, this belief was religious, and was proved theologically.

If there were people on the other side of the earth, the intelligentsia reasoned, they wouldn't be able to see Jesus arrive at the Second Coming. Since God wanted everyone to witness that event at the same time, He wouldn't allow people to live out of sight of it.

For thousands of years comets were presumed to be condensations of people's sins. That's why they brought pestilence, famine, war, and the death of kings.

In medieval France priests and judges maintained that animals could be possessed by Satan. On the gallows in the French countryside, cows and pigs were hung by the neck until dead to release the devil within.

Because the meat of convicted stock was sinful, cow corpses were burned, not butchered. Thus, people starved while watching their farm animals slaughtered but not used for food.

We're much too civilized to condone such stupidity today. But in 1916, a circus elephant that killed three men was lynched using a railroad derrick and steel cables to hang her.

When high heels were invented in France in 1590, they were worn by men, who used them to assume a position of power over other men.

Men soon found that dominance was difficult to maintain when you were falling down after every other step.

So high heels were passed on to women, where they became a symbol of sexual subservience. Upper-class women wore heels to demonstrate that they were too rich to have to move.

During the French Revolution, women abandoned their heels as elitist. In a counterrevolutionary gesture, ballerinas started dancing on their toes to simulate high heels.

In the seventeenth and eighteenth centuries, rich men showed their class stature by shaving all the hair off their heads, then donning elaborate powdered wigs.

The wigs were often made from the hair of dead poor people, which was the cheapest way for wig makers to gather supplies.

Human sacrifice was once practiced by religions all over the world, as a ritual that brought their people a little closer to God, with the person being sacrificed a little closer than everyone else.

The early Babylonians sacrificed animals on their altars. Then priests would read God's will in the dead animal's liver. Why? The Babylonians thought the liver was the home of the soul.

The ancient goddess Cybele of Anatoli was popular with devout Romans in the second century B.C. The Romans worshipped her by bathing in the blood of sacrificed bulls.

The Catholics did it. So did the Protestants. They lashed heretics and witches by the thousands to stakes, set them aflame, and watched them burn. Isn't that a human sacrifice? It was to the poor people who were burned.

What exactly is a witch or a heretic? Anyone you burn at the stake in the name of God.

In the 1700s English judges would test accused witches by drowning them. If a woman was a real witch, the water would reject her, they reasoned. Therefore, all a woman had to do to prove her innocence was drown.

Thousands of innocent women died that way.

The branding of women as witches possessed by the devil continued over several hundred years in England, France, Germany, Spain, Italy, and the American colonies. Under the direction of men of God, these women were tortured until they confessed, at which point they were killed.

Anyone who tried to suggest that these women weren't witches and that the Church should stop torturing and killing women in the name of the Prince of Peace was tortured and killed in the name of the Prince of Peace.

In the eighteenth century the London hospital for the insane, called Bedlam, raised money by charging Londoners admission to see cages filled with chained prisoners, a human zoo.

The ancient Aztecs of Mexico honored people in religious ceremonies by sending them to the gods, which meant they first had to get rid of their bodies, as that was the only way to get there.

To prepare people for the sacred journey, Aztec priests would cut open the lucky travelers' chests and rip out their hearts. To dedicate a new temple, the Aztec king Ahuitzotl sacrificed 80,000 hearts to the gods.

Throughout the Middle Ages it was believed that certain kings had the power to heal the sick by touch. In 1684 a mass of the lame and the ill gathered to be touched by King Charles II of England.

The crowd grew so large and eager for kingly salvation that seven people were cured of their diseases by being trampled to death.

In Alexandria in the second century there was a law against women tricking men into marriage by applying makeup to deceive the men about their looks.

In our age men trick women into marriage by asking them.

If September is the ninth month of the year, why do we call it the seventh? We also get October, November, and December wrong.

The names of these months in Latin mean seven, eight, nine, and ten, respectively, but they are our ninth, tenth, eleventh, and twelfth months.

Well, we came close.

It worked out that way because March used to be the first month of the year. By that system, September was the seventh, October the eighth, and the other two followed in order.

But when the first month of the year was changed to January, the names of the last four months were not changed. Why? Because that's the way we are.

The Cracker Jack people have packed more than 16 billion toys in their boxes of candied popcorn since 1912. Aside from collectors, almost nobody still has any of them.

In seventeenth-century Europe, sneezing was considered a sign of good breeding. That's why members of the upper classes started sniffing snuff: to promote sneezing so they could demonstrate their superiority.

In France in the 1600s the remains of executed murderers were considered good-luck charms. Crowds would gather to pick apart the charred remains of people beheaded and burned, ignoring the obvious fact that these murderers had not been lucky for their victims or, ultimately, for themselves.

Today's hair extremes have nothing on eighteenth-century England, where fashionable women sported wigs up to four feet high. Hairdressers decorated these wigs with stuffed birds, fruit plates, and model ships.

To support such a structure of hair, the women had to sleep sitting up. To hold such elaborate hair sculptures together, the wigs were matted with lard. Since women often wore the wigs continuously for months, the lard attracted insects and mice.

🌐

A fad among Englishwomen in the late nineteenth century: nipple rings. The women believed the rings would enhance the size and shape of their breasts.

🌐

For most of recorded history, Europeans wrote without vowels. Reading was guesswork.

For example, the English word written *grnd* could mean grand, grind, or ground.

Vowel guesswork was haphazard and a silly method of writing for people trying to communicate. But the Europeans compounded their thickness by writing their sentences crammed together without spaces between the words.

🌐

In the Middle Ages Chinese peasants built homes in caves they dug out of soft clay. When a powerful earthquake hit northern China in 1556, the walls of a cave city were so weakened that 800,000 people were buried alive inside their cave homes.

The plague of the fourteenth century led to a confounding attempt at disease prevention in Germany and France: Flagellants marched from town to town, lashing one another with metal-tipped whips.

Their theory was that public atonement for sins would spare them from the Black Death. This method of plague control worked particularly well for the flagellants who died from excessive blood loss due to overenthusiastic whipping.

The Spanish Inquisition treated people like animals and vice versa. Believing that witches inhabited the bodies of cats, the Church ordered thousands of cats destroyed.

A popular pastime in sixteenth-century Paris was the public burning of bagfuls of cats to celebrate Midsummer Day.

In the seventeenth century pointed table knives were declared illegal in France. Why? Cardinal Richelieu was offended by the sight of uncouth diners picking their teeth with their knife points.

That's why, in our time, we use knives with rounded ends at table.

In the Middle Ages Spanish nobles found Spanish ladies difficult to kiss because the women always kept sharp toothpicks in their mouths all day and night.

In medieval times, when people ate out of a common dish, it was considered uncouth to gnaw on a bone and then throw it back in the pot for others to pick at. It was also considered low class to spit across the table or blow your nose on the tablecloth.

While knives and spoons were popular throughout the Western world, forks were generally unknown until the eleventh century. Instead, people took food from the common dish with their hands.

You could tell a nobleman from a peasant because the upper class washed their hands first and didn't take meat that displeased them from their mouths and put it back in the pot.

When a Byzantine noblewoman tried to introduce the use of the fork into Venetian society, she created a scandal. She was deemed overly refined. When she became ill, religious leaders declared that she was being punished by God for her sin of the fork.

In sixteenth-century Italy a proper gentleman did not wash his hands after relieving himself because the washing would remind decent people of the business he had just been about.

At the height of their civilization, Romans considered stuffed mice a dinner delicacy.

In some African cultures a woman's sex appeal was determined by the size and shape of the gap between her upper two front teeth. Some women, unlucky enough to be born gapless, would file down their teeth to achieve that gappy look.

No telling how long before Beverly Hills plastic surgeons pick up on that status symbol.

In Colonial America people thought they could cure stomachaches by placing big boots on their bellies.

Among the people of northern Spain, a village's babies were placed on the ground and a man, symbolizing the dangers infants face in life, leaped over them.

If he landed on the other side without landing on the babies, that symbolized their safe passage through the early years. If he didn't, it didn't.

Among the Berber tribes of North Africa, parents arranged marriages for daughters as young as ten. After a five-day wedding ceremony, the young couple was divorced so the daughter could marry someone else.

Among ancient Persians only the king had the right to use an umbrella to ward off sun or rain.

Two thousand years later, the royalty of Siam maintained

their rankings through umbrella status: The higher you stood among the elite, the larger your umbrella and the wider the decorative rings.

In thirteenth-century Germany knights would enter riddle contests that were as serious as jousts. Just as a loser in a tilt often lost his life although it was but a sporting contest, so a knight who could not answer a riddle was often put to death.

This practice may be seen as a primitive way of culling the weak-minded from the stock. But that hardly seemed necessary, as there were already a multitude of opportunities to be killed in the Dark Ages.

Norse followers of the god Odin would hang themselves so they could share the power of their god. One Norse saga recounts the efforts of a woman who hung her son so that Odin would help her brew better ale.

Superstitions about the sacrificial power of death by hanging remained into the nineteenth century, when executioners would sell remnants from hangings as good-luck charms.

English burglars believed that the severed hand of a hung man would enable them to open locks, while a bit of skin from a hanging victim would prevent a house from catching fire.

Among some African tribes, kissing was viewed as a threat of cannibalism because smooching reminded people of the way snakes would tongue victims before dining upon them.

Sailors of the Middle Ages believed that wearing rings in their ears would save them from drowning if their ship sunk.

In ancient Ireland before a king was crowned, he took a bath in the broth prepared from a boiled horse. Ever hear the Irish expression "A broth of a boy"?

When tobacco was introduced to Europe in the sixteenth century, all gentlemen (and some ladies) smoked the plant in pipes. Cigarettes were considered low class, only smoked by beggars who couldn't afford pipes.

Among the ancient Maori, it was believed that scratching the head could release the soul from the body. When you scratched your head, you immediately had to sniff your spirit back into your skull by putting your fingers up your nose.

CHAPTER EIGHT

Seemed Like a Good Idea at the Time

Let's start an empire. Say, this conquering stuff is fun; pass the wine. Oops, here come the barbarians.

Whether we're emperors or fools, play out a good idea long enough and you might run into that pitfall where smart moves go to stumble.

An antidrug group in New York distributed free pencils to school kids with the antidrug message, "Too Cool to Do Drugs."

It started out okay, but got worse and worse when the kids actually used the pencils. As the pencils were worn down and sharpened, the message changed to: "Cool to Do Drugs." Then: "Do Drugs."

When movie star Warren Beatty directed *Reds* in 1981, he wanted the extras on the set to understand the historical significance of the true story of an American writer who campaigned for workers' rights.

After the director explained the history of the workers' movement, the extras understood his lecture so well that they went on strike against Beatty for higher pay.

In 1985, to celebrate a year in which no one had drowned in city pools, two hundred New Orleans lifeguards threw a big party. During the party, one of the guests drowned.

Looking for relief, an Englishman picked up a tube of hemorrhoid cream. Oops, wrong tube. He got the superglue instead, and glued his buns together.

Inventor Charles Goodyear lived in poverty when he wasn't stuck in debtors' prison because none of his inventions worked. He was a man sparked by ideas that had great promise and no realization.

Failure, debt, doubt, the urge to tinker, and the need to stop tinkering and get an honest job—those were his constant, clashing companions.

Finally, Goodyear promised his wife that he'd stop conducting experiments in their kitchen and find a job that paid the bills.

Of course, he didn't. The man was an inventor. But he knew he was in trouble one day when he heard his wife coming up the stairs, home early. Instead of looking for a job, he'd been experimenting again with attempts to vulcanize rubber.

To avoid antagonizing his wife, he quickly swept his experiment into the kitchen stove. The stove was still hot, which is why Goodyear finally succeeded with one of his crazy experiments, discovering the process for creating heat-resistant rubber.

There's your dumb move turning into a good idea. But despite the importance of that invention, Goodyear died broke anyway.

Oddly, or perhaps not, Goodyear wasn't the only scientist who owed a discovery to a fearsome wife.

German inventor Christian Schönbein discovered smokeless gunpowder when he spilled one of his experiments in his wife's kitchen. Afraid that she would soon return and discover the accident, he mopped up the chemical spill with his wife's apron, then set the apron in front of the fire to dry.

The apron exploded because of cellulose nitration, and Schonbein had a new invention to market.

🔔

The founder of the Wrigley chewing-gum empire wasn't a chewing-gum man. William Wrigley, Jr., was trying to make a living in the baking-powder business. To increase sales, he gave away chewing gum to anyone who bought enough of his baking powder. Consumers didn't care for his baking powder, but they liked the gum.

Wrigley recognized a good idea when he stumbled across one and got out of the baking-powder business, with all its frustrations, and into the chewing-gum business.

Later the family spent a good part of its fortune to get into the baseball business by buying the Chicago Cubs, which was when the Wrigleys learned what frustration was really all about.

One man's lame move can make another man's career.

Actor Ronald Reagan got his start in Hollywood when he was hired to replace actor Ross Alexander, who killed himself at the age of twenty-nine.

Reagan later turned down the chance to play Rick in *Casablanca*. If Reagan had been smart enough to take the role, *Casablanca* would have become a forgotten film. And Bogie would have become president.

Sometimes being dumb pays off. A woman in San Francisco in the 1970s attempted suicide but failed. Put in a hospital room for observation, the woman climbed out of bed, opened the window, and jumped out.

She survived that suicide attempt too. Then she sued the hospital and won damages because they had not put her safely in a room out of which she couldn't have jumped.

A Little Rock, Arkansas, woman wanted to get her driver's license, like everyone else she knew.

Unlike everyone else, she failed the written test 103 times—even though you're allowed to study the booklet in the test room right up until you take the test. She finally passed the test on try 104.

Peter the Hermit, a French holy man, led a peasants' crusade at the turn of the eleventh century to seek salvation in Jerusalem. Peter may have been mad, but he gathered a huge following because salvation seemed preferable to the miserable, brutally abrupt life of being a French peasant in the Dark Ages.

The peasants, who took to ravaging villages along their journey to the sea, never made it to the Holy Land, where they would probably have been slaughtered by Saracens. Instead, they were slaughtered by the armies of France, who didn't like the idea of peasants marching, to their salvation or anywhere else.

When the minuet was introduced into French society in the 1600s, it was intended to demonstrate the grace of the upper class.

French dancing masters refined the minuet, which had begun as a folk dance, to the degree that books were written about proper performance. One book contained a lengthy chapter devoted to the correct manner in which the wrist was to be turned and sixty pages explored the details of the gentleman's bow.

Like Buddhist monks around the world, the Chogye order in South Korea practice meditation and nonviolence—except when they deal with one another.

Rival factions of peace-loving monks have been battling for control of the group for years, often erupting into fistfights. In 1999 the Buddhist battle escalated, as monks meditatively beat one another with metal pipes, stones, and bottles.

Ethereal dancer Isadora Duncan made Irish playwright George Bernard Shaw a proposition that sounded good on the face of it: that they have a baby together. "With my body and your brains," she said, "what a wonder it would be."

Shaw turned Isadora down, explaining, "But what if it had my body and your brains?"

💡

The ABC television network has made millions in advertising by broadcasting *Monday Night Football* over the decades. But the CBS network had first chance to run what has become one of the most popular sports shows of all time.

CBS turned the proposal down, the network president saying, "Preempt Doris Day? Are you out of your mind?"

💡

Russian scientist Elie Metchnikoff tried to kill himself with an overdose of morphine in 1873 but survived. Seven years later he tried to kill himself again with an injection of deadly bacteria. That didn't work either.

His subsequent research into bacteriology won Metchnikoff a Nobel Prize in 1908.

💡

William Sidis mastered Latin and Greek by the age of five. At the age of nine, he developed a new method of computing algorithms. He entered Harvard at eleven, graduating at sixteen.

Sidis then spent the rest of his life working as a dishwasher and clerk, amassing one of the world's largest collections of streetcar transfers.

CHAPTER NINE

Government by the Idiots

We get the government we deserve, which doesn't say much for us or them.

In 1975 the head of the Federal Energy Administration flew around the country speaking to business and civic groups about the need to conserve energy.

He spent $25,000 of the taxpayers' money on 19,000 gallons of fuel to spread the word not to waste so much money by using so much fuel.

The federally funded Law Enforcement Assistance Administration spent $27,000 to study why prison inmates want to escape prison.

The U.S. Consumer Products Commission bought 80,000 buttons for a campaign promoting safe toys. The buttons had to be destroyed because they were too sharp and were coated with lead paint.

When President Reagan's daughter Patti got married, there were more police officers and Secret Service agents at the ceremony (180) than there were guests (134).

In 1658 Virginia passed a law forcing all lawyers to leave the colony, thereby making Virginia as close to Eden as any American territory has come. The law was repealed in 1680. It's been downhill ever since.

Papal politics reached a new low in 897 when Pope Stephen VI brought Pope Formosus to ecumenical trial, not at all deterred by the fact that Formosus was already dead.

Pope Stephen had his predecessor's corpse seated in the courtroom in purple robes. Pope Formosus was tried and convicted.

Prior to the French Revolution, a man served fifty years in prison for whistling at Queen Marie Antoinette. Perhaps she shouldn't have been so surprised when she found the peasants revolting.

After the Clinton-Lewinsky scandal, officials of Madame Tussaud's wax museum in Sydney, Australia, had to seal shut the zipper on the pants of the Clinton dummy. Visitors kept opening it up as a gag.

In 1975 Congress retrofitted the elevators in the Capitol building to make them automatic. Then Congress continued to spend the taxpayers' money to pay the salaries of elevator operators to operate automatic elevators.

The federal government spent nearly $300,000 to build a community center in the woods between two Michigan towns. Money ran out before the roads to the facility could be finished, so no one from either town was able to use their center. It eventually collapsed of disrepair.

It doesn't take a huge federal bureaucracy to accomplish something really dumb. Even the local school board can manage the deed.

A thirteen-year-old Arizona boy was inspired to build a model rocket after seeing the movie *October Sky*, the true story of NASA rocket scientist Homer Hickam. The boy took his rocket, made out of a potato-chip canister and fueled with three match heads, to school.

School officials classified the rocket as a weapon and suspended the boy for the rest of the year, based on its zero-tolerance weapons policy.

Civilian employees at the Seattle Police Department received special training in proper sitting methodology, after two people in the department's fingerprint and photo unit slid off their chairs and fell to the floor.

A department supervisor circulated a memo on proper procedures titled "Chairs, How to Sit In." He advised, "Take hold of the arms and get control of the chair before sitting down."

"Some people know how to sit in a chair," a department safety officer explained, while others "need some instruction."

The post office printed a batch of international stamps in 1999 featuring a picture of the Grand Canyon and this message across each stamp: "Grand Canyon, Colorado."

The Grand Canyon is located in Arizona.

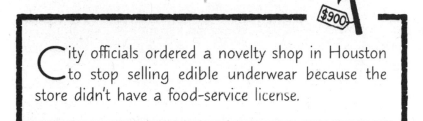

City officials ordered a novelty shop in Houston to stop selling edible underwear because the store didn't have a food-service license.

Long considered a pest by western ranchers, prairie dogs are prestigious pets in Japan, where the rodents sell for $30 apiece.

American ranchers would be happy to get rid of the critters, for profit or gratis. But the Colorado Division of Wildlife won't let ranchers export prairie dogs as pets because no species of wildlife may be sold, since they belong to the public. However, because they are considered pests, it's perfectly legal in Colorado to shoot, poison, or drown the prairie dogs.

How well are our government-run schools doing in educating the American people?

The Colonial Williamsburg Foundation put the system to the test with a survey of our historical knowledge.

The survey found that 79 percent of Americans knew that the slogan "Just do it" came from a Nike ad, but only 47 percent knew where "Life, liberty and the pursuit of happiness" came from.

Worse, 55 percent identified Obi-Wan Kenobi as the person who said, "May the force be with you" in *Star Wars*. Only 9 percent knew that George Washington was a general in the Revolutionary War.

The United States government spends billions on defense each year to kill all our enemies, anyone who was thinking of becoming our enemy, and most of the people who just look at us funny.

But the feds also spend countless millions on nondefense: developing new weapons that are never actually put into use. These projects get canceled before completion, but not before costing us millions in tax dollars.

Here are millions of dollars worth of nothing: the B-1A and XB-70 bombers, the ANP nuclear airplane, and the Roland SA, Navaho, Snark, Rascal AS, and Skybolt missiles.

Probably those millions went into deciding upon names for the nonweapons.

The Anglo-Saxons of England initiated an official justice system in the fourth century A.D. Prior to that time, justice was administered by the victor to the victim, following the system known as the Whim. Early Anglo-Saxon justice wasn't much of an improvement.

Under the English system, a man accused of a crime would be forced to close his hand around a poker that had been turned red in a fire. This wasn't the punishment; it was the trial. The man was declared innocent if his wounds healed after three days.

When Caligula was just another struggling assassin trying to move up the Roman ladder of success, a soothsayer told him he'd never make it all the way to emperor, that he had as much chance of getting the top job as he did of riding across the waters of the Bay of Baiae without a boat.

But Caligula was a hard-working assassin. After eliminating the competition, he became emperor of all of Rome, although it was not a position with much job security, even for someone of Caligula's talents.

Upon taking control, Caligula ordered scores of ships lashed together across the three miles of the bay, then covered the ships with wooden planks, piled dirt on top, and rode his horse across the Bay of Baiae.

Three years later he was assassinated by his guards, their way of protesting all the unpaid overtime they put in killing Caligula's enemies.

When the revolutionary tribunals couldn't convict counterrevolutionaries quickly enough following the French Revolution in 1793, the courts simply eliminated such time-consuming legal maneuvers as the defense.

Some 25,000 people were executed for crimes against the state, at which point the people who masterminded the executions were executed.

In 1981 a nine-year-old girl was executed in Iran for attacking government officials. By law, Iranian boys could not be put to death until they turned fifteen.

In an effort to cure the working class of their addiction to gin, the British government passed a law in 1832 officially favoring beer over gin. Workingmen throughout Britain responded to the legislation by drinking beer as a chaser to their gin.

In 1962 a Massachusetts man refused to pay the increased tax on his house. He burned it down instead. The government charged him for the tax increase anyway.

In 1971 a state representative in Rhode Island introduced legislation to charge couples a $2 tax each time they made love. Quickly calculating their own tax liabilities, politicians on both sides of the aisle voted the bill down.

In Yemen in 1968 a pet monkey was tried for arson, convicted, and executed by a police firing squad.

At the same time that the federal government was spending millions of dollars on programs to convince teenagers and others not to kill themselves by smoking cigarettes, Congress authorized a $328 million subsidy to support the nation's tobacco farmers, who were losing money because of the decline in cigarette sales.

The Department of Agriculture found a governmentally clever way to save money on its school lunch programs in the 1980s. The bureaucrats simply declared that they didn't have to buy actual vegetables for nutritionally needy kids because ketchup and relish were vegetables.

In the 1840s the French government passed a law saying that criminals could not be arrested between the hours of sunset and sunrise.

When Harold Ross, publisher of the *New Yorker*, had his fictional magazine character Eustace Tilley registered in the New York City phone book, city administrators sent Tilley a tax bill.

CHAPTER TEN

The Power of Stupidity

King Otto, a nineteenth-century ruler of Bavaria, set the benchmark for the royal class by making it his kingly routine to start each day by shooting a peasant.

Otto and other power-mad rulers may have a tough time convincing anyone of their qualifications for heavenly admittance. But does that mean the persecuted poor can waltz right through the gates as a belated reward for their noble poverty?

The history of power says that given a chance, the amateur despot class turns as cruel and heartless as the usual sadistic suspects.

More dogs have been kicked by the poor than by the rich. Give a poor man a taste of power, and he begins to act as cruelly stupid as the rich man.

For two hundred years in Russia a sect called the Brothers and Sisters of Red Death had a rule against marriage but not against sexual intercourse, as long as the act was followed by suffocating the participants with red pillows.

The sect finally disbanded in 1900 when one hundred members burned themselves to death in anticipation of the millennial end of the world.

In 1358, long before anyone conceived of a popular revolution against a corrupt aristocracy, French peasants suddenly had their fill of being used as pike fodder by the lords of the land.

Tired of being starved, beaten, raped, and killed, the poor actually got off their skinny butts and did something about it. They revolted.

Did they overthrow the aristocracy and start a noble society where everyone was treated as equals, with Christian kindness and respect for the rights of all?

Not in the fourteenth century, they didn't, although they had some trouble getting it right in the fifteenth, sixteenth, seventeenth, eighteenth, nineteenth, and twentieth centuries too.

Meanwhile, back in 1358 the French rebels abused and slaughtered the powerful in a fashion that would have made a king proud. They tied up aristocrats and forced them to watch as their wives and daughters were raped, tortured, and killed.

Within a month, turn-around day was over. The aristocrats brought in better-armed soldiers, and the revolting peasants were put in their place again, at the end of a pike or in the center of a noose.

But the powerless had proven their point: Given the chance, you couldn't tell them apart from the powerful.

The thirteenth century saw mankind make progress on at least one front: political repression. The most noted scientist of his age, Roger Bacon conceived of telescopes, microscopes, cars, steamships, airplanes, and underwater diving suits, even though there was no technology to support his theories in the 1200s and no labs in which to test them by experiment.

For Bacon's efforts to point the way out of the Dark Ages, the powers that ruled (the council of lords and the Church of the Lord) condemned him to prison.

Prison can wear down even a great visionary so that he sees the futility of his work in a world whose ignorance is insurmountable for the simple reason that the ignorant refuse to be surmounted.

"Would that I had not given myself so much trouble for the love of science," Bacon concluded miserably.

How many other people of illuminating intelligence have reached the same conclusion: that their ability to see what others will not is more of a curse than a blessing?

Is history replete with the silences of people who could have made a difference but chose not to under the pain of persecution?

♛

In the 1850s a Chinese visionary named Hung Hsiu-Ch'uan heard God say that he was the younger brother of Jesus.

To fulfill his vision, Hung organized the God Worship Society, which called for the Christ-like virtues of equality and morality.

Such beliefs can elevate people to moments of religious beneficence, or drive them to acts of vast stupidity. Equality and morality led Hung to declare a war against China's rulers that lasted fourteen years and cost 20 million lives—all in the name of the younger brother of the Prince of Peace.

When his rebellion finally failed, Hung committed suicide. So did 100,000 of his followers, making other religion-based suicides pale in comparison.

What do the following rulers have in common?

1. British prime minister David Lloyd George, who called Adolf Hitler a "great man."
2. Idi Amin, dictator of Uganda, who tried to exterminate the East Indians and Pakistanis in his country, whom he labeled "the Jews of Africa."
3. Nguyen Cao Ky, U.S.-supported premier of South Vietnam, who in the late '60s suggested that he could beat the Viet Cong if his country only had "four or five Hitlers."

No, not just their admiration for the world's most successful lunatic. But the obvious fact, which only rulers a little low on ammunition could miss, that Hitler would have happily exterminated all of them if he had succeeded with his master plan to conquer the world.

♙

Dón't get us started on the stupid atrocities of the French and Russian Revolutions, which were supposed to be the second and third wave of glorious rectification of the wrongs of the elite through the enlightened intelligence of the common man.

Those two bloody revolutions do make you wonder why the American Revolution was so relatively free of barbarism.

Actually, even the American Revolution had its share of stupid atrocities. But certainly nothing like the bloodbaths into which the revolutionaries managed to pour themselves in France and Russia.

In the American Revolution, neither side represented the poor. The colonists, led by Franklin, Jefferson, and Washington, were hardly peasants. America was a rich land waiting to be grabbed and they were grabbing.

Because many of the revolutionaries had been born in the new land, they didn't have centuries of hatred to avenge. Angry, would-be mobs lacked a convenient palace to torch. The British aristocracy that the American colonists revolted against were too far away to be dragged through the streets by their throats.

For their part, the British officers knew they were leading an army against people they weren't very much different from.

Still, there was the occasional dumb atrocity, such as the Wyoming Valley massacre in 1778, in which Tories encouraged their Indian allies to torture and slaughter Pennsylvania colonists who had been their neighbors for no particular military objective.

It's only by comparison to other revolutions that the American adventure looks clean.

♛

The worst acts of revolution belong to those suave sophisticates, the French. During the Reign of Terror in 1793–94, the victorious revolutionaries got so carried away with their self-righteous revenge that they slaughtered their countrymen by the thousands for crimes against the people, then for accusations about crimes against the people, then for the potential to engender accusations.

In Nantes the guillotine wasn't able to keep up with the volume of executions ordered by the tribunal. Condemned aristocrats, priests, government officials, and anyone else who ticked off the tribunal were crowded onto ships, which were then capsized in the river.

Any of the condemned who tried to escape drowning were pushed under the water with boat hooks.

The river became so littered with corpses that the contaminated water spread a fatal disease throughout the city. In their lust for vengeance, the revolutionaries accidentally killed themselves.

Then there's the Russian Revolution.

In 1917 after successfully overthrowing the czar, the Bolsheviks agreed to a stupid peace treaty with Germany, which convinced Germany that Russians were fools.

The Bolsheviks were eager to stop fighting the Germans so they could rush home from the front and kill several hundred thousand of their own people in a civil war that prevented the country from solving its farming, manufacturing, and financial problems.

After winning the civil war, the Bolsheviks were in no condition to deal with famine, which killed millions more, and which led the Germans a decade later to assume that the Russians were still fools and could be conquered during World War II.

The Russians may have been fools, but so were the Germans, who ignored the lessons of Russian winters and Napoleon's ill-fated attempt to conquer Russia, and the willingness of Russians to die fighting any enemy under the fatalistic theory that they were bound to die fighting one enemy or another, or each other, so what's the difference?

None of the stupid excesses of the power-mad Communists during these thirty years of slaughter—the civil wars, the famines, the collapse of Russian industry, or the German invasion—slowed Joseph Stalin as he murdered millions of his own people, which at least prevented them from dying of starvation or German bullets.

The American nation was founded on the concept of freedom and the inalienable rights of all people. Unless those people happened to be Africans.

Millions of people who were going about their own business lost their homes, their families, or their lives so that other people didn't have to pay for hired help.

The legacy of slavery still plagues America today in racism, crime, and poverty.

What would have happened if the Americans who promoted liberty had actually upheld their beliefs and never stolen the liberty of Africans? America would be a better place today, and so would Africa.

Back to more common forms of power madness: In 1976 the charismatic Rev. Jim Jones of the People's Temple explained to his devout followers that "if you love me as much as I love you, we must all die or be destroyed from the outside."

Over nine hundred people either committed suicide or were helped along the path of death by people more devout than they. Parents killed their own children in the name of God.

After the mass suicides, the religion was declared a cult.

Jack Anderson wielded power in Washington through his investigative newspaper column, but not as much power as he thought. After the shah of Iran was overthrown by revolutionaries, Anderson claimed that he had predicted in his column the shah's fall from power years earlier.

The only problem: When people checked Anderson's old columns, it turned out he had not made the prediction.

In the ninth century, Erigena was one of the few enlightened scholars. He argued quite reasonably that "reason and authority come alike from the one source of Divine Wisdom."

The Church didn't take kindly to such wild heresy and banned Erigena's writings. Four centuries later, they were still considered heresy, so Pope Honorious III had his work burned as "hereditary depravity."

An evangelist was fined $1,700 in Salisbury, England, for a stunt in which he went up in a motorized paraglider so he could preach from above the rooftops to sinners on the ground. "I thought that maybe if they heard this voice booming out from the sky, they would think it was God," he explained.

In the thirteenth century thousands of French children believed a shepherd boy who claimed to have seen a vision of Christ. The children followed their young leader on a crusade to liberate the Holy Land.

The children were put aboard ships owned by French merchants, promised a free journey to Jerusalem, then sold into slavery instead.

The Assyrians were the most cultured people of the ancient world: productive farmers, deft craftsmen who promoted the age of bronze tools, merchants and traders who traveled the known world.

All that changed during the thirteenth century B.C., when they became the terror of the Mideast, amassing huge armies and annihilating their enemies. Their specialty: blinding captives, thousands at a time, to prevent slave revolts.

The fact that blind men then made poor slaves with limited abilities was lost on the Assyrians, who are also now lost.

At the height of the Roman fascination with gladiators, contest preliminaries entertained the crowds with the slaughter of unarmed men hunted down by armed fighters. The victor's reward: His weapons were then taken from him, and he became the next victim.

Reform-minded religious leader Martin Luther preached the value of the common man before the eyes of God and attempted to attain relief for the poor from a corrupt religious power base.

Interpreting Martin Luther's message of enlightenment their own way, German peasants in 1524 revolted and slaughtered dozens of German aristocrats.

Martin Luther tried to explain to the rebellious peasants that "the duty of a Christian is to be patient, not to fight."

The peasants went about the German countryside patiently killing the rich, claiming to be doing God's will.

God had nothing to say about the matter when the German army caught up with them and slaughtered thousands of peasants until there were none left to revolt.

In the Dark Ages, when Christianity was battling to take control of heathen European tribes, witches and pagans were condemned and killed for partaking in hysterical rituals, during which they would become possessed by the devil and dance about in an uncontrollable passion for hours, sometimes stripping naked as the Evil Force had its way with them.

From the 1300s to as late as the 1800s in Europe and America, devout Christians would become possessed by the spirit of God and dance about in an uncontrollable passion for hours, sometimes stripping naked as the Lord had His way with them.

Among the Kwakiutl Indians, tribal power was determined by who destroyed more of his own possessions. Thus, the truly power mad not only burned all their tools, weapons, and household items, but burned down their own houses.

They were then left with the power of nothing.

The power happy don't always resort to violence. Sometimes they try to rule by law.

As the popularity of automobiles grew in the late 1800s, the Pennsylvania Farmers' Anti-Automobile Society drafted the following regulations: "In the event a horse refuses to pass a car on the road, the owner must take his car apart and conceal the parts in the bushes. Automobiles traveling on country roads at night must send up a rocket every mile, then wait ten minutes for the road to clear."

The Pennsylvania legislature did not put these rules into law, as you'll note by the rarity of people dismantling their cars in front of horses.

CHAPTER ELEVEN

Dumbing Down the Arts

Artists often have no more idea of what they're doing than the put-upon outsider who stares and wonders: Is that art? Am I supposed to like that? Or am I just too gaga to get it?

Who knows, who cares, of course.

A frustrated writer came up with a novel scheme to test the intelligence of book publishers. He retyped into manuscript form *The Painted Bird*, Jerzy Kosinski's award-winning novel, and submitted it, under his own name, to a dozen big publishers.

They all rejected the manuscript as not being worthy of publication, including the house that had actually published Kosinski's book.

Vincent van Gogh, now considered one of the greatest painters in history, was a failure in his own time. Art critics in the nineteenth century scorned his work; collectors ignored him.

Van Gogh sold exactly one painting during his life, although they now bring millions when collectors sell them to one another.

German composer Richard Wagner wore gloves whenever he conducted a work by Felix Mendelssohn. After the music was over, Wagner threw away the gloves.

Why? Mendelssohn was Jewish.

Turn-of-the-century entertainer Tony Minnock had one of the most bizarre talents ever seen on the stage: He could withstand pain.

His act consisted of having himself nailed to a cross, like Christ, while singing to the audience.

Theodore Geisel's first book was rejected by twenty-three New York publishers before one dared to print it. *And to Think that I Saw It on Mulberry Street* went on to sell millions of copies, as did the rest of Dr. Seuss's many books.

Dubliners, a collection of short stories by one of history's greatest writers, James Joyce, was rejected by twenty-two publishers before getting into print. The entire first edition was bought by a book hater, who burned every copy.

An eighteenth-century merchant, Timothy Dexter, wrote and published his autobiography. The book contained not a single mark of punctuation—except for the last page, which consisted of line after line of periods, commas, exclamation points, and question marks, with the instruction to readers that "they may peper and solt [the book] as they plese."

Spelling wasn't a big issue with Dexter either.

How many of these books would have become best-sellers if their authors had kept the less-than-inspired original titles?

Bar-B-Q (*The Postman Always Rings Twice*)
Ba! Ba! Black Sheep (*Gone with the Wind*)
The Old Leaven (*The Sun Also Rises*)
The Various Arms (*To Have and Have Not*)
Something Happened (*Of Mice and Men*)
A Jewish Patient Begins His Analysis (*Portnoy's Complaint*)
The Terror of the Monster (*Jaws*)

Artists often claim it's their work that matters, the song not the singer. Unfortunately, governments believe that noble lie too.

Auguste Rodin, France's great sculptor, was broke, starving, and freezing during the harsh winter of 1917. He asked the French government if he could live in the museum where his sculptures were housed.

Government officials turned down the artist's request, and he froze to death in an unheated garret. Rodin had donated many of those sculptures for free to his beloved country.

The French writer Guy de Maupassant liked sex more than writing. He was eventually admitted to a mental institution, where he would lick the floors and refuse to urinate. He died of syphilis at the age of forty-two.

English writer Thomas De Quincey (*Confessions of an English Opium Eater*) often set fire to his own hair while reading bedtime stories to his children. Somehow he lived to be seventy-four.

Before Ed Sullivan became famous as the wooden host of a Sunday TV show, he was a theater critic in the 1920s. In his first review, he suggested the playwright August Strindberg should rewrite the second act of his play *The Father*.

Sullivan missed one crucial fact: Strindberg had been dead for nearly a decade.

A critic for the *San Francisco Chronicle* wrote a scathing review of the San Francisco Ballet Company's performance, particularly damning the lead ballerina.

After the review was published, people who had attended the performance pointed out that the critic had not—or he would have known that the particular ballet he criticized was changed at the last minute and the particular ballerina he blasted never actually danced that night—good, bad, or otherwise.

The editor of the *Chicago Tribune* refused to admit that Henry Miller's risqué novel *Tropic of Cancer* had made the best-seller list. So he simply stopped printing the full list.

Instead, the *Tribune* printed a selective column called "Among the Best-Sellers."

Artist Cosimo Cavallaro created a work of installation art by renting a New York City hotel room for $100 a night and covering everything in it with melted cheese. Gruyère, mostly, with Swiss and other varieties thrown in as the muse directed.

While fans of melted-cheese art had this work take their breath away, its main function seemed to be providing writers with a string of cheese puns: "Cavallaro has created a muenster. The art was as gouda it could get."

Need a reason to read those little signs on the walls in museums? Here's one posted at the *Titanic* museum in Indian Orchard, Massachusetts: "These postcards were donated by Janet Ripin, on behalf of her great-uncle, George Rosenshine, who perished in the *Titanic* disaster and had been in a steamer trunk for many years."

Heinrich Heine, the nineteenth-century German poet, left everything he owned to his wife when he died, on one condition: She had to get remarried.

That way, Heine said, "There will be at least one man who will regret my death."

The great playwright George Bernard Shaw wrote some of the finest, most intelligent speeches in the English language. Unfortunately, he didn't know how to stop talking. When he was eighty-two, Shaw came out in favor of the Fascists, Mussolini and even Hitler.

When the artists and animators who made cartoons for Hollywood movie studios organized into a union in the 1930s, the labor bosses didn't know where to put them.

They initially made the animators part of the Brotherhood of Painters and Paperhangers.

In medieval times the Catholic Church banned women from the stage in order to protect their morals. But the Church still wanted operas sung and needed singers with high voices.

The Church and its medical advisers solved that problem by castrating young boys so their voices wouldn't change as they grew older. The castratos were then trained to sing the women's roles.

This practice continued into the nineteenth century.

Belgian musician Joseph Merlin built the first roller skates in 1760. To make a big impression upon the aristocracy, he wore the skates to a London gala.

Thinking the skates alone wouldn't be enough of a sensation, Merlin rolled into the ballroom playing his violin. Therefore, he had no hands free to stop himself, and he crashed into a mirror. He nearly died from his injuries.

In 1561 a book called *Missae ac Missalis Anatomia* was published, containing fifteen pages of errata. The whole book ran to only 172 pages of text, setting a world record that has yet to be beaten for abominable proofreading.

British censors crept in slow motion through John Ford's 1935 drama about the Irish Rebellion, *The Informer*, and cut out every reference to the IRA or the rebellion—129 cuts in all, making the film completely unintelligible when it was released in England.

Hadji Ali, an Egyptian stage performer, had a brief career in the 1930s as the "Amazing Regurgitator." He would swallow buttons, jewelry, coins, and goldfish, then selectively regurgitate them.

An Englishwoman impulsively kissed a painting in an art museum in 1977. It cost the museum $1,260 to remove her lipstick from the canvas.

"I only kissed it to cheer it up," the woman explained. "It looked so cold."

Are you more superstitious than actors? Almost impossible.

We all know that the preferred wish of good luck to an actor about to go onstage is "Break a leg," when the actual breaking of a leg would be rather bad luck.

Theater tradition also maintains that a cat adopted by a theater brings good luck, as do shoes that squeak when you make your entrance.

Bad luck stems from including a picture of an ostrich in a stage set, whistling in the theater, or repeating the last line of a play during rehearsal.

If you can avoid all that, your career may be set, although it would also help if you could act a little.

A Japanese artist constructed a portrait of the Mona Lisa entirely from toast in 1983.

In the 1600s in England anyone caught singing or playing music in a tavern was whipped and imprisoned.

These punishments weren't a critical judgment, but a belief among royalty that romantic ballads and songs of any kind were a subversive threat to their reign.

The brilliant cellist Yo-Yo Ma put his concert cello in the trunk of a taxi at a New York hotel, then left it behind in the cab when he arrived at the concert hall.

"I did something really stupid," Ma said. "I just forgot."

Ma's 266-year-old cello was valued at $2.5 million. Ma may have been incredibly absentminded, but he was also incredibly lucky. Police tracked down the taxi and found the cello in the trunk.

In the sixteenth century a musician invented the cat organ. Cats were placed in a resonant box, with their tails extending through holes in the bottom of the box. The musician then played the chorus by yanking their tails.

CHAPTER TWELVE

Military Unintelligence

They also serve who only sit and send us to our senseless doom.

The history of military idiocy is a long one because in no other field of endeavor are the entrance requirements so low and the effort so exhaustive.

Yes, sir, General, we'd be happy to go on that impossible mission and die. After all, we may be soldiers, but we're also idiots.

How many millions of stalwart young men have thought: Is this really how I should be throwing away my life?

Unfortunately, the thought comes as they charge across some crowded plain or up a barren hill into the face of certain death, at the precise instant that some order-issuing general on a hillside to the rear thinks: Oops.

Maybe that wasn't such a great idea.

Oh well, too late now. Better luck in the next war, chaps.

As a race, we applaud courage precisely because it flies in the face of all intelligence.

It took great courage for French knights to charge into the rain of English arrows from the longbows at Agincourt. But what idiots.

A little less courage and a little more brain power might have led the French to alternate strategies. They might have circled the outnumbered English to neutralize their longbows, instead of charging en masse down a narrow vale directly into the flight of massed points, thereby presenting the enemy with their single chance for triumph.

The Duke of Wellington once said, "There's nothing on earth so stupid as a gallant officer."

Yet could Wellington's army, or any army, have won a single battle without such gallant stupidity? War depends on men willing to shut down their brains, which counsel survival, and charge onto the enemy pikes. Remarkably, such men are never in short supply.

The Charge of the Light Brigade in 1854: How gallant, how stupid, how British.

In the Crimean War, an idiot captain ordered the six hundred men in the British Light Brigade, armed only with swords, to attack an entrenched Russian force consisting of six battalions of riflemen, six divisions of cavalry, and thirty cannon.

The Light Brigade lost four hundred of its six hundred men in twenty-five minutes. But they were not defeated until Russian soldiers on the surrounding hills fired into the battle, killing as many of their own men as the enemy.

During the Revolutionary War, George Washington led the Continental Army to their first victory by surprising the British troops at the Battle of Trenton in New Jersey.

Washington shouldn't have been able to surprise anyone. A Loyalist spy trying to report Washington's plans wasn't allowed in to see the British commander because the colonel wouldn't be interrupted while playing cards.

When the desperate spy finally sent in a note explaining that the enemy was advancing for a sneak attack, the British colonel put the note in his pocket unread and continued to play cards. It was his deal.

The note was later found on the dead colonel's body after Washington's victory.

In 1628 the Swedish navy built its largest and most dangerous warship, with sixty-four guns mounted on two decks. The ship proved dangerous to its own crew because of its inept design, and sank in Stockholm Harbor as it was launched for its maiden voyage.

> The French army invented a blast-resistant boot allowing soldiers to walk over mine fields. One problem: The boot was so heavy and hard to walk in that the soldiers would be shot down by snipers long before they were not blown up by mines.

The Roman emperor Valens wisely sent for reinforcements so they could wipe out invading Goths.

Valens must have been affronted by his own sensible strategy because before the reinforcements could arrive, he led his outnumbered troops in a charge against the enemy.

The Goths must have been shocked to see Valens charge, since they had remained stationary, making no threat against the Romans, who could have waited at their leisure for reinforcements.

Instead, Valens managed to achieve the slaughter of two-thirds of his own army, including himself.

In Scotland William Wallace (the Braveheart portrayed in the movie by Mel Gibson) had his bravery greatly aided by English arrogance, that curious pride of stupidity.

In 1297 a superior English force, led by de Warrenne, planned to annihilate Wallace's ragged army, but first had to cross the river Forth. Warrenne chose for his crossing Stirling Bridge, even though the Scots could be seen waiting on the other side and the bridge was so narrow only two men could cross at a time.

A mile upstream lay an undefended ford, wide enough for thirty English soldiers to march across side by side.

The Scots waited patiently at Stirling until a third of the English army had crossed the narrow bridge, then slaughtered them. A small detachment of Scot spearmen were able to bottle up the bridge, preventing the rest of the superior English army from riding to the rescue.

Wallace was undoubtedly as brave as Mel Gibson portrayed him, but his bravery would have been of little historical note if de Warrenne had not been quite so insistently vainglorious.

Most bad leaders make mistakes of aggression, but inactivity can be as stupid as hyperactivity.

Union general George McClellan prolonged the Civil War by his hesitancy to engage the enemy, even though his forces were far superior in number to the Confederates.

In the battle over Munson's Hill, McClellan declined to attack after evaluating the hill as too heavily fortified with Rebel cannon.

After the Southern troops escaped under cover of darkness, Union soldiers discovered that the cannon that turned back McClellan from certain victory were logs painted black.

The general's indecision through a lengthy campaign grew so frustrating that President Lincoln wrote him this letter before relieving McClellan of his lack of command: "If you don't want to use the army, I should like to borrow it for a while. Yours respectfully, A. Lincoln."

"Military strategy consists in making one mistake less than the enemy," the military strategist Hans Delbruck said. That task is often made easier by the insistent stupidity of enemy leaders.

In the second Boer War, British commander Lt. Gen. Charles Warren lost the battle of Spion Kop because he spent twenty-six hours personally directing the forces committed to the vital mission of ferrying the general's personal baggage across the river.

By the time Warren successfully completed that campaign, Boer reinforcements had arrived and dug in. Warren committed his troops to the attack just in time to get them decimated. No reports on the casualties among Warren's luggage.

At the Battle of Loos in 1915, ten thousand inexperienced British troops were sent in a frontal charge against German positions.

The British commander lied to his own men, telling them they were being sent to pursue routed German defenders.

Instead, the British marched directly into entrenched German machine guns, which mowed down eight thousand of them. The British could not break through because their leaders had provided them with no tools to cut the barbed wire.

German casualties? None.

The Germans were so astounded by the slaughter that they did not fire upon the British survivors as they retreated.

This is not to imply that the Germans were necessarily smarter. After all, they lost World War I, which wasn't as inevitable as it now seems.

In fact, the German army was on the verge of capturing Paris when they took a detour into the French wine country. They proceeded to get so drunk that by the time they resumed the attack, French and American reinforcements were in place.

The Germans soon sobered up enough to surrender.

During World War I, Corporal Alvin York's company was nearly wiped out. A sharpshooter, York managed to gun down twenty-five German soldiers, one at a time, luring them from shelter with the mating calls he'd used hunting turkeys back home in the hills of Tennessee.

One German soldier after another grew curious about the strange sounds. "Every time one of them raised his head, I just touched him off," York said, explaining how he came to panic a German battalion into surrender and win himself a Medal of Honor.

On the other side of World War I, a single German soldier captured a French fort.

The infantryman on a reconnaissance patrol stumbled through a tunnel that led him into Fort Douaumont, where the French troops had posted no guards.

The surprised German soldier locked the enemy inside their barracks and opened the gates to his company.

In the Battle of Verdan, in which the fort was retaken, the French army lost 100,000 men.

At Crecy in 1346 the French army attacked a much smaller force of English troops, composed primarily of longbow men, who stopped the first wave of French infantry. Before these foot soldiers could find cover, French mounted knights attacked along the same route, blocking their retreat, which also blocked their advance.

Instead of clearing the way for the survivors of the first wave, the French knights attacked their own infantry, while the English longbows slaughtered both groups at their leisure.

In 1750 British general James Abercromby attacked the French at Ticonderoga in New York state, near the Canadian border. His army outnumbered the defenders five to one and could have defeated them with a flanking attack, or an artillery bombardment, or even a siege.

Instead, Abercromby managed to wrest defeat from certain victory by sending wave after wave of his unfortunate soldiers in direct attacks against the French middle, the only fortified position the French held.

When a detachment of British troops actually managed to reach the French fortifications, they could not assault the nine-foot-high breastworks because the British had forgotten to bring ladders along on the charge.

In the 1916 Battle of the Somme, British commander Lt. Gen. A. G. Hunter-Weston ordered a frontal assault on German forces, telling his officers that the German defense had been destroyed by an artillery bombardment—even though everyone could see plainly that the German fortifications were intact.

The British charged directly into the German machine guns, and twenty thousand of them were slain in the first thirty minutes of the futile attack.

During World War I, soldiers on the Allied side were supplied with grenades mounted on sticks. The idea was to reach back and hurl the grenade over the trench, using the stick to leverage the throw, like a lacrosse player throwing a ball downfield.

But the grenades were designed to explode on impact, and trenches weren't wide. Many Allied soldiers lost their lives when they reached back and banged the grenade end of the stick on the back side of the trench.

Everything stupid that can happen in battle happened to the American forces in the war against Spain, fought in Cuba in 1898. The only reason the Americans won the war was that the Spanish side was even dumber.

First, the American army didn't have enough men or supplies. Being forced into the war too soon by rabble-rousing politicians, the army didn't have enough time to train new recruits.

They chose an inexperienced general to lead the expedition to Cuba. He chose the wrong port from which to embark. The port didn't have room for enough ships and had only one railroad track, so supplies and men backed up for miles trying to load.

The general also chose the wrong place to land in Cuba, at a port where there was no way to off-load horses. Soldiers forced their horses overboard. Many horses, being even dumber than their riders, swam the wrong way, out to sea, and drowned.

The initial assault was so badly managed that a small force of Spanish soldiers could have ended the war right there by preventing the landing. But the Spanish commander didn't bother to send that small force of soldiers, so the Americans landed clumsily but unopposed, which was about the only way they could have landed.

The war's most famous battle, for San Juan Hill, was

only famous because it was so badly planned, led, and fought that vast American courage, and a vast number of American lives, were required to win it.

American soldiers suffered through repeated blunders by their officers, whereas with a modest amount of intelligent leadership and planning they might have won the battle much more easily.

A few scenes from the fight will suffice to explain how the Americans, who outnumbered the Spanish sixteen to one, almost managed to lose what seemingly could not be lost:

1. The American commanders didn't bother to gather reconnaissance, so they had no idea of how many Spanish soldiers were dug into the hill, or which were the best approaches to take to capture it.

   Instead, they used a hot-air balloon for their only reconnaissance during the battle. While the officer in the balloon could provide little actual information to the commanders on the ground, the balloon did serve one functional purpose— unfortunately, for the enemy.

   The balloon had to hover above the American troops so the observer inside could shout his observations to officers below. The Spanish defenders simply poured artillery and rifle fire into the jungle below wherever the balloon went.

2. The American attack was led by a National Guard unit composed of inexperienced soldiers armed with outdated rifles that fired old-fashioned black powder. The puffs of powder from their own rifles marked them as targets for the Spanish soldiers,

who returned more accurate fire with more modern weapons.

This American regiment proved so ineffective that they had to lie down in the grass to allow other units to pass them by and attack.

3. When the Americans reached Spain's first line of defense, barbed wire, they found that no one had brought wire cutters. Also, no one had provided for artillery support.

   Unable to break through the wire, American troops had to hide in the jungle vegetation. When a battery of Gatling guns arrived, the American soldiers cheered. This gave away their positions, and the Spanish fired at the sounds, killing many men they couldn't see.

4. When the Americans finally started to advance up the hill, their artillery opened fire too late, hitting more Americans than Spanish.

5. All of this could easily have been avoided, since the Americans' naval guns could have forced the Spanish to abandon the hill or surrender. Only one problem with the naval guns: The Americans never used them.

The Americans did finally win the battle, at great cost, because the Spanish general was an equal match for the American general in terms of incompetence. He sent no reinforcements to a hill that could have been held.

Is it any wonder that German officers, in Cuba as observers, were not impressed with the American army, and didn't think it would be much of a fighting factor in wars to come in Europe?

After having failed to take the city of Syracuse by siege in 413 B.C., the Athenian army prepared to escape by sea before they were trapped by Spartan reinforcements.

As the Athenian soldiers started to board their ships, they came under the influence of a lunar eclipse. The Athenians disembarked, considering the eclipse a bad omen for sailing.

They were right in their reading of the omen, in a way, because the Spartan reinforcements arrived in time to block the harbor and kill 47,000 Athenians. The 7,000 survivors spent the rest of their miserable lives watching lunar eclipses as quarry slaves and wondering exactly how bad sailing away could have been.

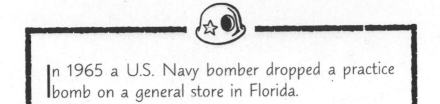

In 1965 a U.S. Navy bomber dropped a practice bomb on a general store in Florida.

After two women officers in the U.S. Army were refused the Combat Infantryman's Badge for their actions in battle in the 1990 invasion of Panama, an army spokesman couldn't deny that the women had done their share in the fight.

Although women soldiers weren't allowed to go into battle, the battle had come to them. Displaying true army logic, he explained the denial of their medals this way: "We have a combat exclusion policy for women, but that doesn't mean women are excluded from combat."

Former Nazi general Sepp Dietrich complained in 1965 that Nazi veterans weren't being well treated, identifying them as a "persecuted community."

The Vietnam War can be seen as folly on many levels. American soldiers who don't want to fight a war fighting for people who don't want them fighting it, kept there by American politicians who know the war can't be won the way it's being fought.

But we'll look at only one stupid aspect of the war because it is so modern in its foolishness: American soldiers were routinely sent to Vietnam for short tours of duty—one year at a time—in an effort by political leaders to prevent unrest among the GIs.

The stupid result: Just as American soldiers were learning to adapt to guerrilla war in the jungle, they were shipped home and new, jungle-ignorant troops were sent in.

In that way, the casualty rates among American soldiers were always kept higher than they had to be because experienced troops would have avoided many of the stupid deaths into which raw recruits stumbled.

CHAPTER THIRTEEN

Stupid Science

For many dark centuries the dumbest science was: There was no science.

Anyone suggesting scientific investigation was branded a heretic and burned at the stake.

Science-deprived generations had to stagger along making a mess of the world in unscientific ways, believing that the universe was created by one of a variety of unknowable gods, rather than by one of a variety of unknowable theories of physics.

Now that our new and improved world is guided by a dominating science, we are no longer prey to the stupidities of ignorance. We are, instead, prey to the stupidities of science.

In 1971 Japanese scientists designed an experiment to study landslides. They watered-down a hill with fire hoses to create the effect of a massive rainstorm.

The hill collapsed. The resulting avalanche killed four scientists and eleven observers.

In an article on techniques for curing that dry mouth feeling, *Self* magazine had this scientifically proven advice for sufferers: "Take frequent sips of water."

Turkish scientists conducted a study in 1981 to determine if disco music turned mice homosexual. It does, they concluded.

Scientists in Great Britain, who may have been colleagues of the researchers in Turkey, conducted a three-year study to determine whether fish feel pain when a fisherman gets them on the hook. Their conclusion: Fish do.

A grad student at Toronto's York University had his doctoral thesis, in which he analyzed the sociology of donut shops, approved.

In 1997 two Texas scientists built a six-foot, four-inch mousetrap. No six-foot mice have beaten a path to their trap.

In the 1600s English doctors prescribed tobacco as a cure for numerous diseases, including the plague.

In 1976 a swine flu scare swept through the United States. The government spent $135 million on a national vaccination program. Reacting badly to the vaccine, twenty-three people died, while hundreds of others had heart attacks or suffered paralysis. No swine flu was ever confirmed.

When DDT was created in 1939, its inventor received the Nobel Prize for developing an insecticide that would rid farms of mosquitoes and crop pests.

The Nobel Prize committee was as shortsighted as the inventor, who had failed to study DDT's long-term effects. Or perhaps they intended that the world should serve as their long-term study. DDT, they found out after enough sickness and death, was a worse solution than the problem.

In the 1970s a New York company packed twenty thousand tons of hazardous chemicals into leaking drums and buried them in a canal. A neighborhood was built on top of the canal, leading to birth defects and cancer for the little kids who lived there. The name of the dump: the Love Canal.

The United States Public Health Service conducted a thirty-eight-year study during which researchers told four hundred black men from Alabama that they were being treated for syphilis, even though they weren't.

The Health Service wanted to see what happened when syphilis victims were not treated. What happened? Many of the men died. All of them suffered.

No useful medical information was ever obtained. When the deceit was discovered, survivors and families of the victims received $9 million in settlement of a lawsuit against the government.

A Texas company will put your DNA samples on a rocket and shoot them into outer space. Why would you want to do that? According to the sales pitch: in case aliens are looking for human DNA to clone.

Scientists who tested and evaluated thalidomide decided it was such an effective sleeping pill that it could safely be sold over the counter without requiring prescriptions.

Somehow the scientists who developed the wonder drug missed the side effects. When taken by pregnant women, thalidomide caused horrible birth deformities, including babies born without arms and with flipperlike hands protruding from their shoulders.

Some eight thousand babies were born with these deformities before the drug was banned.

In 1984 in Bhopal, India, an insecticide plant storage tank containing methyl isocyanate sprung a leak, spewing poison gas over twenty-five square miles.

Even after the leak was discovered, it took two hours before the people of the town were warned of the danger. Two thousand of them died.

It took seven years to build the two-mile Tay Bridge in Scotland. The bridge was considered one of the great engineering marvels of its time, until it collapsed on December 18, 1879, during a storm eighteen months after it opened, sending a railroad train and eighty people to their death in the river below.

The people couldn't escape because the passenger cars on British trains were kept locked.

As for that engineering marvel, the engineer who had designed the bridge had failed to test for the effects of wind on the structure. He had also built it with inferior materials.

In 1963 cancer researchers at a Brooklyn hospital told twenty-three elderly patients they were going to take part in a new treatment program. Instead, they were injected with active cancer cells.

In the United States, the standard railroad gauge (the distance between the rails) is 4 feet, 8.5 inches. American track builders used that odd measurement because that's the way they built railroads in England. The

English engineers used the measure because the first rail lines were built by the same people who built the pre-railroad tramways.

Trams used that gauge because they were built with the same jigs and tools used for building wagons. The odd wheel spacing of wagons was designed to fit the wheels into the ruts of old English roads, which were carved into the dirt by Roman war chariots.

Civilizations may crumble, but specs never die.

Military researchers came up with an ingenious plan to train bees to sniff out land mines on battlefields. The scientists reasoned that chemicals from the mines would be leached into surrounding flowers and then could be detected in the bee pollen.

The research was immediately opposed by animal-rights activists, who reasoned that bees should not be forced into military service, since they're not U.S. citizens.

Puts the K-9 corps into a new perspective.

Dumb medicine can be practiced by patients as well as doctors. Take the case of a Belgian truck driver who thought he was following doctor's orders when he bought a bag of small nails at a hardware store. After dinner, the man swallowed several of the nails because his doctor had told him that he needed more iron in his diet. The metal cut into his stomach as he was rushed to the hospital.

In 1891 Isaac Cline, head of the U.S. Weather Bureau in Texas, told the Galveston newspaper that people shouldn't worry about hurricanes, even though the port city, which had been built only eight feet above sea level, had no seawall.

"It would be impossible for any cyclone to create a storm wave which could materially injure the city," the scientist asserted, further declaring that the concern expressed by other people was "simply an absurd delusion."

No defenses against storm or oceanic wildness were built. On September 8, 1900, a hurricane wiped out Galveston, killing eight thousand of its absurdly deluded citizens.

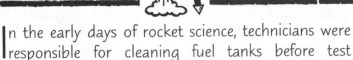

In the early days of rocket science, technicians were responsible for cleaning fuel tanks before test flights. Even small specks of dirt in a tank could alter the flight pattern and potentially destroy the rocket.

Before one launch, the technicians, dressed in clean suits, climbed down a ladder from the docking platform into the fuel tank and carefully cleaned the tank, eliminating every possible contaminant, wiping up every grain of dirt, every speck of dust.

When they returned to the control stations, remote instruments indicated there was still some contamination in the fuel tank.

So they reopened the hatch and pulled up the ladder.

TV minister Jerry Falwell announced in 1998 that computer programming problems resulting from the Y2K bug "may be God's instrument to shake this nation."

Falwell predicted that the problems of adjusting software to recognize code for the year 2000 could start a worldwide religious revival that would lead to Christ returning to take true believers to Heaven.

In preparation for this long-awaited event, Falwell stocked up on food and ammunition, although he did not make it clear why he would need ammunition on the way to Heaven. Or food for that matter.

Decades later, NASA spent only $125 million to send the Mars Climate Orbiter 416 million miles to study the red planet. Scientists, however, failed to spend a few bucks to check their math.

One team of scientists responsible for navigation used American measurements to calculate the orbit around Mars. But the other navigation team used the metric system. No one thought to make the conversion between the two numbering systems.

As a result, before the spacecraft could go into orbit, it crashed into the Mars surface and was destroyed. Taxpayers can take comfort knowing that it was one of NASA's inexpensive spaceships.

But it wasn't the first multi-million-dollar oops made by our rocket scientists, who proved that sometimes even rocket science isn't rocket science.

In 1962 *Marine 1* went off course and had to be

blown up before it crashed into the earth, at a cost of $18.5 million.

What went wrong? Someone put a hyphen in the wrong place in the directional computations.

When German university students took to saber duels in the eighteenth century, doctors had to stitch up their face wounds but not do a good job of it. Why did the injured students prefer bad stitching to competent repairs? Because the students were dueling for the scars. The more garish the scar, the higher a man's social standing.

Medical science during the Civil War lagged considerably behind military science. More than half of the 620,000 soldiers from the North and South who died in the war were killed not by bullets but by disease, or infections spread by army doctors.

One Union soldier wrote in a letter that, although wounded, he had refused treatment, thinking he had a better chance to survive on the battlefield than in the hospital.

Early European botanists called the eggplant "mala inana"—the mad apple—claiming that if you ate it—you'd go insane. Or maybe they were trying to convince their mothers that science said they didn't have to eat their vegetables.

An English doctor, James Salisbury, devised this unique cure for asthma in the 1880s: eating three, well-cooked beef patties a day with plenty of hot water.

The cure didn't work, but the hamburger-like entrée known as Salisbury steak stayed with us.

In prehistoric Europe, shamans attempted to cure epilepsy by cutting holes in the skulls of the sufferers. Such was their skill that people thus trepanned could survive the crude operations, and often returned for more treatments.

Oddly, trepanation made a startling return in 1962 when a Dutch doctor proclaimed that cutting away a small part of the skull would restore proper blood circulation to the brain, thereby raising consciousness.

The Dutch responded to this idea by putting the doctor in an insane asylum.

At least two of the doctor's English followers actually performed self-trepanation by drilling into their foreheads with electric drills and removing bone plugs from their craniums. Although neither had any medical training, they both survived the operations and opened an art gallery in London.

Ancient Romans didn't brush their teeth. Instead, following the advice of ancient Roman dentists, they prevented tooth decay by rinsing their mouths with urine.

The ancient Maori of New Zealand believed that God sneezed life into humans.

Taking the contrary view, many ancient European tribes believed that people could sneeze themselves to death by blowing the soul right out through the nose.

That's why we still say, "God bless you," when people sneeze, even though modern medical science does not suggest it as a preventive strategy.

In ancient Europe people were buried alive beneath the foundation of a castle or other major building because early engineers noticed that sometimes walls would shift and settle.

The engineers offered these people-bricks as sacrifices to gods of the earth to prevent the walls from crumbling.

Today's engineers prefer situation memos and team meetings as advanced techniques for ducking the blame.

In the Middle Ages doctors thought they could drive off a fever by putting a horse's head under a sick person's pillow. Probably the only way it drove off the fever was to drive off the sick person with it.

When scientists announced in 1954 that lung cancer among cigarette smokers was three to sixteen times higher than among nonsmokers, the number of smokers actually rose.

A Texas man suffered a fatal heart attack in 1995 when his pharmacist gave him high-blood-pressure medicine instead of an angina medication. The druggist couldn't read the handwriting on the doctor's prescription.

In the late 1800s, the English explorer Francis Galton turned his curious mind and considerable wealth to science, like his cousin Charles Darwin.

Among Galton's peculiar studies: a beauty map of Great Britain that he developed by counting the number of good-looking women he saw in each city (from London, pretty, to Aberdeen, ugly), the proper length of rope for hanging criminals, a pressure gauge for chair legs to determine to what degree people inclined toward their dinner companions, a quantitative evaluation of the dullness of lecturers, a sextant for measuring the figures of women from a distance, and his somewhat scandalous paper on the "statistical inquiries into the efficacy of prayer," which demonstrated, among other claims, that monarchs whose subjects pray for their long lives actually live shorter lives.

Galton was most infamous for promoting his science of eugenics, in which he proposed that only men from eminent families who exhibited the proper qualities of "health, energy, ability, manliness and courteous disposition" should be selected to form the breeding stock of England.

Idiots, criminals, and various other undesirables would be kept in labor camps and prohibited from breeding.

Another controversial geneticist, William Shockley, believed that his own children represented a "significant regression" in evolutionary intelligence from their father.

How had the Shockleys slipped? He blamed it on his wife's lack of high academic achievement.

Doctors in the nineteenth century locked patients inside a fever cabinet, in which high-intensity lightbulbs drove their temperature as high as 105 degrees, in an attempt to cure syphilis.

A British doctor devised the leech storm-warning system in 1851. His weather-analysis device consisted of a jar filled with leeches and a bell. When a storm approached, he predicted, the leeches would turn active, ringing the bell.

The doctor's idea was to establish a series of leech warning stations along Britain's coast. The government turned down the deal.

CHAPTER FOURTEEN

Dumb Things Famous People Said

If you want to be famous, start early with mouth-stretching calisthenics so that by the time reporters start writing down what you say, you'll be able to get the whole foot inside.

In the race to sound really dumb, the politicians may have an insurmountable lead.

President Calvin Coolidge: "When more and more people are thrown out of work, unemployment results."

Ronald Reagan, when asked what qualified him to be president: "I'm not smart enough to lie."

Marion Barry, Washington, D.C., mayor: "Outside of the killings, we have one of the lowest crime rates."

President George Bush: "I have opinions of my own, strong opinions, but I don't always agree with them."

Vice President Dan Quayle: "What a waste it is to lose one's mind. Or to not have a mind. How true that is."

President Warren Harding: "Progression is not proclamation nor palaver. It is not pretense nor play on prejudice. It is not personal pronouns, nor perennial pronouncement. It is not the perturbation of a people passion-wrought, nor a promise proposed."

Ronald Reagan, opposing legislation to protect our national forests: "A tree's a tree. How many do you need to look at?"

Chicago mayor Richard Daley: "Get this thing straight once and for all. The policeman isn't there to create disorder. The policeman is there to preserve disorder."

Senator Barry Goldwater while running for president in 1964: "Many Americans don't like the simple things. That's what they have against we conservatives."

President Eisenhower's adviser Howard Pyle: "The right to suffer is one of the joys of a free economy."

Senator William Smith, chairman of the government committee investigating the *Titanic* disaster: "Why didn't the passengers on the boat go into the watertight compartments and save themselves from drowning?"

Senator Smith missed the obvious: Anyone who took refuge in the supposedly watertight compartments would have either suffocated or drowned when the ship sank to the bottom of the North Atlantic.

Vice President Dan Quayle again: "It isn't pollution that's harming the environment. It's the impurities in our air and water that are doing it."

Governor Alf Landon on the campaign trail against FDR: "Wherever I have gone in this country, I have found Americans."

Senator Orrin Hatch: "Capital punishment is our society's recognition of the sanctity of human life."

Geography knows no boundaries when it comes to political foolishness, as French president Charles de Gaulle demonstrated: "China is a big country, inhabited by many Chinese."

Once more from Vice President Dan Quayle: "I love California. I practically grew up in Phoenix."

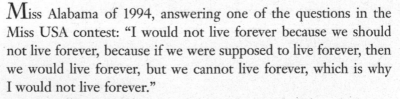

Ron Ziegler, President Nixon's spokesman, explained a common political paradox this way: "The president is aware of what is going on. That's not to say something is going on."

Βut the politicians have no monopoly on the phenomenon of people who can talk without requiring the use of a brain:

Wealthy philanthropist George Delacorte gave his money generously to benefit New York's Central Park. But he refused to give anything to fight poverty, explaining that "people are poor because they're dumb or because they're lazy. If you feed them, you just keep them in the same strata."

Miss Alabama of 1994, answering one of the questions in the Miss USA contest: "I would not live forever because we should not live forever, because if we were supposed to live forever, then we would live forever, but we cannot live forever, which is why I would not live forever."

Actually, she made a lot of sense compared to the others.

NBC executive Warren Littlefield about deleting discussion of orgasms from the TV show *Sisters:* "Corporately, we believe in orgasms."

Mort Naham, producer of the short-lived TV show *The Secret Diary of Desmond Pfeiffer:* "Although they were potentially painful and difficult periods in history, they were ripe for comedy."

The show was about slaves suffering in the American South. It was a sitcom.

Talk show host Phil Donahue: "I'd rather be called sleazy than to be identified as intelligent."

Violinist Zubin Mehta: "I don't think women should be in an orchestra. They become men. Men treat them as equals. . . . I think it's terrible."

Financier Ivan Boesky: "I think greed is healthy. You can be greedy and still feel good about yourself."

Wealthy industrialist John D. Rockefeller: "I believe that the power to make money is a gift from God."

Supermodel Beverly Johnson made this unique plea for everyone to join in the battle against poverty, no matter what Rockefeller and Boesky thought: "Everyone should have enough money to get plastic surgery."

Actress Brooke Shields offered this zen view on cigarettes: "Smoking kills. If you're killed, you've lost a very important part of your life."

Actor Telly Savalas evaluated who in history was the villain of villains: "A man worse than Hitler or Stalin, I'm speaking of Sigmund Freud."

Multimillionaire basketball star Shaquille O'Neal, when asked if he visited the Parthenon while in Greece: "I can't really remember the names of the clubs we went to."

Oakland A's owner Charlie Finley on the baseball commissioner in 1981: "I've often called Bowie Kuhn a village idiot. I apologize to all the village idiots of America. He's a national idiot."

National Hockey League president Clarence Campbell in 1974: "There has never been any violence in the NHL."

A happily anonymous book editor rejecting George Orwell's classic parable *Animal Farm:* "It is impossible to sell animal stories in the USA."

Writers often save their dumbest thoughts for each other.

Virginia Woolf described James Joyce's labyrinthine novels as "the work of a queasy undergraduate scratching his pimples."

Joyce's master scratch, *Ulysses,* was declared the best book of all time by a panel of scholars in 1998. None of Woolf's writings were on the list.

Leo Tolstoy evaluated the work of William Shakespeare this way: "Crude, immoral, vulgar and senseless."

Yes, but did he like it?

CHAPTER FIFTEEN

Idiotic Politics

"**S**uppose you were an idiot," Mark Twain ventured, "and suppose you were a member of Congress. But I repeat myself."

The connection between politics and stupidity is obvious to anyone who can bear to read the daily newspaper.

It makes you wonder: If politicians are so stupid, how do they ever get elected? Or does that answer the question?

Some politicians, by dint of working harder than others, manage to sink lower into the dumbing grounds of history.

While on a trip to Europe financed by taxpayers' money, Congressman Adam Clayton Powell studied work opportunities for American women in 1962 by visiting nightclubs and strip shows (all places American women could work).

Powell also charged taxpayers for his laundry, which he had cleaned in London and flown to Italy via diplomatic courier.

In 1971 Alabama governor George Wallace was awarded an honorary degree in the martial art of tae kwon do. You can't get an honorary degree in a martial art—fighting takes practice.

To save money, Congressman James Jeffords from Vermont moved out of his Washington, D.C., apartment and into his Capitol office. Congressmen in 1981 earned more than $60,000 a year.

Samuel Ferdinand-Lop ran for the presidency of France in the 1940s on the Lopeotherapy platform, which called for the elimination of poverty after ten o'clock at night and a unique way of improving the air in Paris: by relocating the city to the country.

More than 46,000 voters wrote in Edward Kennedy's name for U.S. senator in 1962. What's so dumb about that? These voters lived in Connecticut, while Kennedy was running in Massachusetts.

When the camp TV show *Batman* became popular in 1966, the Soviet government newspaper, *Pravda*, called the caped hero "a capitalist murderer." *Pravda* apparently preferred the more proletariat Joker and Riddler.

William Henry Harrison, elected to the presidency in 1840, wasn't stupid because he refused to wear a hat or coat to his outdoor inauguration in the middle of a March storm in Washington.

He was stupid because he was so in love with the sound of his own voice that he ran his speech for over an hour while everyone froze, including him.

Harrison droned himself into a serious head cold, which led to fatal pneumonia after only a month in office, making Harrison the first president to talk himself to death.

Hubert Humphrey wanted to be president so much that he agreed to serve as vice president under Lyndon Johnson. This was like a man who wants to learn to craft leather taking an apprenticeship with the Marquis de Sade.

As a politician, Johnson was an egotistical sadist who belittled Humphrey at every opportunity, once kicking him in the shins when the vice president didn't move fast enough to fulfill his boss's request.

"When I want your advice," Johnson told Humphrey, "I'll give it to you."

Despite his ignominy, Humphrey never got to be president. He lost the election to a politician who suffered even greater humiliations to get the job: Richard Nixon.

Harold Carswell, President Nixon's nominee to the Supreme Court, faced strong opposition. Democrats claimed that Carswell was not a distinguished enough judge to sit on the nation's highest court.

Senator Roman Hruska rose to a novel defense of Carswell's nomination.

"Even if he were mediocre," Hruska argued, "there

are a lot of mediocre judges and people and lawyers. They are entitled to a little representation, aren't they, and a little chance? We can't have all Brandeises and Frankfurters and Cardozos and stuff like that there."

Soviet dictator Joseph Stalin, whose reign of terror gave him the distinction of having killed more of his own people than rival megalomaniac Adolf Hitler, kept an entire nation in constant fear, wondering whom he would exterminate next.

Stalin once set the record straight by pointing out that "gaiety is the most outstanding feature of the Soviet Union."

General Joao Figueiredo, after being elected president of Brazil in 1979, showed an immediate flair for power politics.

"I intend to open this country up to democracy," he happily proclaimed, "and anyone who is against that, I will jail, I will crush."

In 1844 the Whigs ran against an obscure compromise candidate put forth for the presidency by the Democrats, with the insulting campaign slogan, "Who the hell is James K. Polk?"

Turns out Polk was the guy who beat the Whigs. Polk further distinguished himself by becoming one of the few, if not the only, presidents to fulfill every campaign promise he'd made. During his only term in office, these included winning the Mexican War and securing the Pacific Northwest for the United States.

As for Polk's taunting opponents, ask most students today and they'd answer, "Who the hell are the Whigs?"

Political expert Niccolo Machiavelli plotted a strategy for political affiliations in the afterlife that exposed the hypocrisy of most politicians.

"I desire to go to hell and not to heaven," he proclaimed. "In the former place I shall enjoy the company of popes, kings and princes, while in the latter are only beggars, monks and apostles."

President Richard Nixon held a White House dinner to honor jazz great Duke Ellington, then mistook singer Cab Calloway for the guest of honor, saying, "Pat and I just love your music."

Caligula, emperor of Rome, was so bloodthirsty that his own guards had to assassinate him to protect themselves from being next on his list.

In his lust for power, Caligula tortured and killed enemies and friends alike. He referred to Rome, whose people had made him emperor, as "the city of necks waiting for me to chop them."

President Ronald Reagan preached a great game of conservative economics, but didn't necessarily practice thrift when it came to spending money on what he wanted to spend money on. As an actor, Reagan knew that what you did could be covered up by what you said.

For his inauguration, Reagan spent more taxpayer money

than any president before him—at least $4 million by conservative estimates. How did Reagan defend his liberal spending policies? He simply proclaimed that no public funds were being used.

Such was his popularity that people believed him instead of the facts. Self-deluding responses encourage politicians to think they can fool the public enough of the time to have profitable careers.

When Warren Austin represented the United States in the United Nations in 1948, he offered a novel approach to settling problems in the Middle East, suggesting that Jews and Arabs settle their differences "like good Christians."

Richard Nixon's spokesman Ron Ziegler shed light on the president's position on the Watergate cover-up this way: "If my answers sound confusing, I think they are confusing because the questions are confusing and the situation is confusing and I'm not in a position to clarify it."

In 1998 a senatorial candidate from Oklahoma died a month before the primary election but still received 56,000 votes.

Maybe the electorate figured that a dead politician couldn't be any worse than a live one.

J. Edgar Hoover had FBI agents maintain a subversive file on poet Archibald MacLeish, who won the Pulitzer Prize three times and was Librarian of Congress.

What did Hoover come up with against the poet? Prior to World War II, MacLeish was "prematurely anti-Fascist."

Researchers tell us that nearly twice as many liberals as conservatives have gone skinny-dipping in their lives. Are liberals more daring? More prone to illegal activities? Or do they simply have better bodies?

Or perhaps conservatives lead equally wild private lives but keep them private by covering up their great, skinny-dipping bodies and not answering stupid questions asked by researchers.

Five-term congressman Sam Steiger of Arizona returned to politics after being out of public office for twenty-three years when he was elected mayor of the rustic town of Prescott in 1999.

Steiger grouchily accepted his victory, stating that the most interesting thing about the election was "that there were 96 people here stupid enough to vote" for his opponent.

How did it feel to be back in public office after such a long retirement? "It sucks," he explained.

President Gerald Ford declared that Poland was not under Soviet control in 1976, which must have come as a surprise not only to the Poles but also to the Soviets who controlled Poland at that time and had for many years.

To prove that there was no prejudice in the U.S. Army, President Ronald Reagan loved to tell the story about the black cook who shot down a Japanese Zero at Pearl Harbor. The only problem with Reagan's story is that it never happened.

Ironically, the U.S. Army was more integrated at the time than the rest of American society.

As for Reagan, he also campaigned against proposals for environmental protection by asserting that trees cause air pollution, which posed a threat to the nation's air quality because, according to Reagan, we had more forests in America now than in colonial times.

In 1927 incumbent president Charles King won the Liberian election with 234,000 more votes than his rival, which was odd because that was fifteen times the number of people who had voted.

George Washington's enduring popularity is fostered among schoolchildren by the tales of his chopping down a cherry tree but telling his father the truth because he could not tell a lie, and of throwing a silver dollar across the Potomac River.

While the stories have been made to serve educational purposes for years, they're lies, made up by biographer Mason Locke Weems in 1800 to sell more books.

In 1999 a politician ran for England's House of Lords on the platform of muzzling cats to prevent cruelty to mice and small birds.

CHAPTER SIXTEEN

Stupid Sports

They don't call them dumb jocks for nothing.

When Richard Nixon played football for Whittier College, he foreshadowed his approach to the presidency by being offside on nearly every play. There was only one thing the coach could do with his overeager player: bench Nixon.

The first four finishers of the 1900 Olympic marathon were disqualified for cheating. They left the race early, took a horse and carriage around the race path, and ran into the stadium ahead of the other runners.

The cheaters were easily found out because the real first-place winner had taken the lead early in the race, so he knew no one had passed him.

In basketball, power forwards are a breed unto themselves, which is probably just as well.

Utah Jazz power forward Karl Malone came up with this unshakable defense for the game's biggest showboat and fellow board monster, "Say what you will about Charles Barkley, when he tells you he is going to do something he'll either do it or he won't do it."

In 1998 Mark McGwire shattered the home run records of both Babe Ruth and Roger Maris, the greatest of the old, long-standing records. Even though McGwire didn't inch past the records but bombed them by hitting seventy homers, a sportswriter for the *New York Post* put the slugger down in seventh place in the ballot for most valuable player.

If you think football is rough now, ninety-five years ago it was played without helmets. Punching, kicking, and gouging were legal moves. During the 1905 college season, eighteen players were killed on the field.

Then there were the rules of a lacrosselike game played by the ancient Aztec and Maya Indians of Central America. The captain of the losing team was killed and his heart passed around among spectators for consumption.

When athletes make boneheaded plays, no one is particularly surprised that people nicknamed Daffy and Dizzy aren't always playing with a full helmet. But we expect an intelligent effort from the referees.

Track and field officials at the 1932 Olympics in Los Angeles set a world record for untracked minds. When Jules Noel of France broke the Olympic discus record, his winning throw was disqualified—not because of any infraction of the rules, but because all the judges who were supposed to be watching the discus competition had turned around to watch the pole vault instead.

During the 1972 Olympics, the United States basketball team won the gold medal in the final game against Russia. The horn sounded ending the game with the U.S. team ahead by a point.

Then an official overruled the clock, and gave the ball back to the Russian team. The Russians failed to make a basket, and time ran out again.

A second official overruled the clock again, and gave the Russians the ball again. This time they scored and were awarded the gold medal. The U.S. team boycotted the awards and their silver medals.

That incident remains the biggest blotch on the spirit of fair play, which the Olympics allegedly exemplifies, worse than athletes who use performance-enhancing drugs, worse than skating and gymnastics officials who favor certain competitions with subjectively high scores. Everyone saw the basketball officials make the wrong calls, not once but twice, until they got the result they wanted. No Olympics authorities responded to the protests.

At the Canadian rodeo in Edmonton, the game of cowboy poker became popular after being borrowed from a penitentiary rodeo event.

Four men sit at a table in the middle of the arena. They don't have to play cards and they don't need chips because they're gambling with their bodies.

The promoters select a nasty bull, who's let loose in the arena. When the bull charges the table, the last cowboy left sitting wins.

In November 1998, a bull smashed the poker table to shards, but the pot of $300 had to be split because two cowboys were still sitting there after the bull's charge.

Who says football stars don't make intelligent commentators on their sport? Consider this from ex-quarterback and TV expert Joe Theismann: "Nobody in football should be called a genius. A genius is a guy like Norman Einstein."

In the fashion of '90s athletes who use their bodies as posters, a USC tailback honored his mother by having her name tattooed across his chest.

He must have had a USC reverse on his mind, because he had her name tattooed Mabel, while Mom spelled it Mable.

Sports movies often look silly to sports fans because the actors are unconvincing as athletes. Most actors who start young in show business have no chance to play sports growing up; they're too busy going to rehearsals to try out for the team. So when they step up to the plate, they look like they've never swung at a live pitch before.

Then there was comic actor John Goodman convincing no one as the great Babe Ruth in the misguided baseball movie *The Babe*. Even worse than the actor was the writer, who had the Babe scoring an inside-the-park home run on an infield pop-up.

Something about facing a charging bull brings out the dumb ingenuity in certain matadors, including the man who tried to fight a bull from the back of a convertible Peugeot in 1901. Luckily, the bull didn't know it was a Peugeot, or he would have tossed the car.

Instead, the bull turned tail and ran, leaving the matador without a fight but a convenient way to beat his own hasty retreat from an arena filled with disappointed fans.

In 1897 a matador fought a bull from a bicycle. The bull was unimpressed, tossing man and bike over the wall. A bout between a bull and a matador on a motorcycle in Spain in 1932 ended in a draw, although not with the crowd, who showed enough disfavor that it wasn't tried again.

Ice brought out almost as many foolish athletes as bulls, including teams that played ice baseball in the late 1800s, a game in which sliding was not only allowed but unavoidable.

Other game athletes tried basketball on ice skates, while ice boxing had a flair of popularity in Cleveland at the turn of the century.

If they weren't sliding all over the ice, athletes were falling from their mounts as they tried football, boxing, and basketball while riding horses.

In the short-lived sport of water baseball, regulations required that infielders stand in the water up to their necks, the pitcher up to his waist, and the batter up to his thighs.

Other short-lived sports that required a certain adroitness but little brainpower: aerial golf, flagpole sitting, and goldfish swallowing.

In 1878 long-distance race walker Lyman Potter offered a $1,500 challenge to anyone who could push a wheelbarrow from San Francisco to New York faster than he could.

Amazingly, Potter's challenge was taken up by Leon Federmeyer, a forty-one-year-old French wheelbarrow pusher.

Loaded down with 133 pounds of food, clothes, and a tent, Federmeyer pushed that wheelbarrow across the desert, through winter storms, and over the mountains.

Six months later, Federmeyer shoved that wheelbarrow into New York City to claim the championship. His opponent—and the prize money—never showed up.

A broken Federmeyer tried to recoup by entering other long-distance walking (although wheelbarrowless) contests. Oddly, he raced slower without a wheelbarrow than he did with one.

Boxing hit a pre–Mike Tyson low when heavyweight great Muhammad Ali accepted a challenge bout for the "martial arts championship" of the world from Japanese wrestler Antonio Inoki.

Ali took care of the prefight publicity, while Inoki performed special martial arts training to strengthen his chin to withstand Ali's bee-stinging fists.

Inoki needn't have bothered with all the chin work. During fifteen rounds of attempting to prove that boxing didn't have to be a contact sport, he spent the match lying on his back, kicking at Ali anytime the boxer came near. Judges called the fight a draw.

The wrestler vs. boxer controversy was finally settled (or at least the huge wrestler vs. mediocre boxer controversy was settled) in 1976 when seven-foot-four wrestler Andre the Giant picked up journeyman boxer Chuck Wepner and tossed him out of the ring. Wepner stayed out, and Andre won, although both sports lost.

In the 1920s the Salem Trade School had the longest losing streak of any high-school football team in Massachusetts. After Salem played six years of losing football, league authorities discovered that there was no such school.

The team was composed of school dropouts who booked games with schools around the state for a share of the gate. The Salem eleven then made sure they lost so they'd be invited back again next year.

The ancient Minoans practiced a sport that defies modern athletes, at least those hoping to remain athletes for another day.

A young man or young woman would stand in the middle of an arena and face a charging bull. When the bull got close enough, the athlete had to grab the bull by the horns and somersault over the bull's back.

This sport may be one reason why there are so few Minoans left today.

✦

Tennis player Ilie Nastase set a record for dumb behavior, pro division. During various matches, he mooned a referee, spat at an opponent, forfeited after his opponent charged the net and attacked him for his behavior, and was disqualified during a match in which his opponent was leading but walked off the court in disgust because of Nastase's inclination to do everything but play tennis.

✦

In 1995 a man in India balanced on one foot for seventy-one hours and forty minutes. Foot-balancing is not a major money sport.

Other sportingly dumb attempts to get into the *Guiness Book of World Records* by people with more brawn than brains include:

1. A man in England who balanced one hundred bricks (weighing forty pounds) on his head for fourteen seconds.
2. A man who used his tongue to tie 833 cherry-stem knots in one hour.
3. Two men from Scotland who set the record for crawling (voluntary division) 31.5 miles on all fours.

That was the sprint event. For long-distance crawling, we look again to India where a man crawled 870 miles over fifteen months to demonstrate his religious devotion.

4. A British man who sliced a 12-inch cucumber into 264 slices in 13.4 seconds.

5. It took one of America's most prestigious universities to produce this mind-number: fourteen Stanford students who spent 244 hours and 43 minutes playing leapfrog. They covered 996 miles.

6. A Brit who walked seventy-two miles in twenty-five hours balancing a milk bottle on his head.

7. An American who rode a unicycle fifty-three miles and three hundred yards backward, looking over his shoulder the entire time.

In the 1976 Olympics, a Soviet army major competing in fencing, the sport of gentlemen, was disqualified for rigging his sword with a circuit breaker so he could register a hit on an opponent without actually making a hit.

King James IV banned golf from Scotland in 1491 for the simple noble reason that "it looketh like a silly game."

Later the king took up the game, and the law was changed so that golf was banned only on the Sabbath during the "tyme of sermons."

In 1967 K. V. Switzer became the first woman to run in the Boston Marathon. At least she ran until a race official tried to drag her off the course. Another runner stopped him.

After the race, Switzer was suspended from AAU competition for running longer than the 1½ miles permitted women and for running a marathon without a chaperone.

Thousands of women now compete in long-distance races annually, chaperoning themselves.

When it comes to team owners, George Steinbrenner of the New York Yankees is in a class by himself, primarily because no one else wants to be in that class.

After playing revolving doors with a series of managers, he announced in 1982 that "Bob Lemon is going to be our manager all year. You can bet on it. I don't care if we come in last. I swear on my heart he'll be the manager all season."

Steinbrenner then fired Lemon after fourteen games.

In the old days of bare-knuckle boxing, the rounds weren't timed. A round would last until one of the boxers was knocked down.

An 1871 bout between Jem Mace and Joe Coburn demonstrated the weakness of that rule. At the bell for the first round, the slugging Mace took up his stance in the center of the ring. But Coburn, a superior boxer, danced along the ropes. Neither man would alter his strategy.

The first round dragged on for seventy minutes without a punch being thrown, at which time police came and broke up the illegal fight, although how it could legally be classified as a fight no one could explain.

In 1912 a team of college all-stars played a football game against Gallaudet College, whose students were all deaf or hearing impaired.

The all-stars assumed that none of the opposing players could hear them, so instead of huddling to call a play they simply shouted out all their plays at the line of scrimmage.

The all-stars didn't realize that all of the Gallaudet players were expert at lipreading. Knowing every play the all-stars were going to run, Gallaudet blanked them 20–0.

Back before they had a shot clock in basketball, Illinois's Georgetown High School demonstrated why they needed one. After scoring a free throw early in the game, the Georgetown team stole the ball from their Homer High opponents, then stalled for the rest of the game.

Unable to break the freeze, the Homer players eventually sat down on the court, while the referee read the newspaper. When time ran out, Georgetown celebrated their 1–0 victory.

CHAPTER SEVENTEEN

Dumb Things You Can Waste Your Money On

If we bought all the things the ad agencies told us we needed, we'd be as dumb as they think we are.

But who exactly are they marketing this stuff to?

Thunderwear: a groin pouch for holstering your gun. The manufacturer advises that on large-grip guns, you should wear pants with a skoosh more room in them.

For dangerous ladies, there's a gun holster that attaches to your bra.

A couch-potato snack bowl that emits a crowd roar every time you reach for the chips.

A clear plastic tube bracelet that you fill with ants, then wear around your wrist.

Aspirin earrings. The pill-mounted drop earrings also come in Valium, Sudafed, and Pepcid AC.

They sell all kinds of souvenirs at the Mount Rushmore gift shop. Our vote for the one that makes the least sense for tourists who have come to observe mountainous images of famous presidents: the $7.99 baseball with fake autographs from presidents George Washington, Thomas Jefferson, Abraham Lincoln, and Theodore Roosevelt.

Washington and Jefferson never even heard of baseballs, much less the concept of autographing them.

A gold-plated slinky for $129.95.

An inflatable rubber airplane.

An electric tongue cleaner.

A phone shield designed to prevent electromagnetic fields from seeping into your ears when you talk on the phone.

Air bags built into your underwear. The air bags deploy when you fall, to prevent hip injuries.

A sneezing doll.

A sneaker-shaped bed, under which you can put your bed-shaped sneakers.

Dog owners seem to be heavily identified by marketers as a target audience for all kinds of junk designed for consumers with their brains on a short leash.

How about edible greeting cards for dogs? Since your dog can read, maybe you should get him a book to go with the card, okay?

Or Rover might prefer a dog shampoo that smells like baby powder. Why baby powder? Because dogs have become the babies of the family.

Minivans with built-in TV sets. Just what drivers with car phones, car faxes, and satellite mapping systems need: something else to distract them from focusing on the road.

A souvenir A-bomb that goes off with a bang and a flash, and produces a mushroom-shaped cloud of smoke. It's made in Japan.

Rock 'n' roll pants that connect to a stereo system. for good trouser vibrations.

Sparkling mineral water for plants.

T-shirts with fake sweat stains under the arms.

See-through underpants for men.

Psychic perfume blended to enhance your ESP abilities.

An executive door closer so busy CEOs can use a push button to hydraulically shut the office door in your face.

CHAPTER EIGHTEEN

The Business of Stupidity and Vice Versa

Hewlett-Packard once came up with the bright idea of removing all the doors from its offices to encourage open communication among management and staff.

Any time, any day, you could look out into the parking lot and see scores of people in twos and threes huddled among the cars, having the private conversations they couldn't have in their door-less offices.

But surely all corporations can't be run by people with their brains on permanent break time. Or can they?

Pacific Bell sent a multipage phone bill to customers even if they only had one page worth of charges. Many light phone users received a second page of their bill upon which were printed only two words: *blank page.*

When the Gillette company started selling safety razors in 1902, men by the hundreds bought them, then threw them away, claiming the razors wouldn't shave their beards.

Gillette officials found out that the dissatisfied customers weren't removing the paper wrappings before shaving with the blades.

Car companies spend millions researching the names for new models. Chevrolet came up with Nova, then found they couldn't sell it in Latin America because *no va* in Spanish means "doesn't go."

You know how hard it can be to find what you're looking for in a big department store, especially if you've never been there before. Perhaps that's why a California store posted this sign: SECOND FLOOR: UPSTAIRS.

British Rail was having trouble keeping its InterCity express trains running on time in 1998, but executives solved the problem without a major overhaul of equipment or systems enhancement.

They simply redefined "on time." Now trains run on time if they arrive within an hour of schedule.

In 1990 an American was reading the operation manual for his new VCR and noticed that the date used as an example of how to set the VCR's timer was December 7.

The VCR was made by a Japanese manufacturer. December 7 was the date of the Japanese sneak attack on Pearl Harbor that triggered America's entrance into World War II.

A California consultant sold corporations on a teamwork training program called Kindergarten for Grown-Ups, in which executives built forts and strung noodle necklaces.

At least this program worked. It made them better managers by keeping them out of their employees' hair for a day.

Once matches became the common way to light cigarettes, soldiers learned that it was not safe to share matches during wartime.

That's how the superstition against lighting three cigarettes on a match began. Hold a match in the darkness for that long and an enemy sniper has time to aim and fire, making it unlucky to be the third on a match.

Match manufacturers exploited that sensible precaution by turning it into an international superstition that had nothing to do with surviving a war.

The result: People wouldn't share matches in peacetime, when no snipers threatened them, which increased the number of matches used and the profits of match makers.

Mark Twain, who was about as smart as Americans get, had the chance to invest his money in Alexander Graham Bell's new telephone company. He turned down the offer and sunk his money in a new kind of typesetting machine. That company lost everything and declared bankruptcy.

An English shipping company paid $2 million in damages to South Pacific islanders in 1998 when its giant freighter destroyed the island's coral reef while maneuvering too close to shore.

Why did the ship venture out of the channel? The skipper wanted a closer look at the island's topless women.

The tasty, sweet crust of that Black Forest ham comes from caramel. Unless you're in Canada, where meat processors received government permission to replace the expensive caramel coating with rust. Rust, the experts say, is cheaper, sticks to the ham better than caramel, and is safe for human consumption.

A worker in an Alexandria, Virginia, company was unhappy with his annual job-performance rating. He called his manager to complain. Than he called again, and again.

After the fiftieth complaint, he was arrested for harassment, convicted, and sentenced to thirty days in the county lockup.

What was his complaint? He felt he should have been rated outstanding. What had his manager rated him? Highly successful.

Perhaps complaining is a trait of highly successful, but not outstanding, people.

For several months, nurses were baffled to find a patient dead in the same bed every Friday morning at a South African hospital.

There was no apparent cause for the death. An

extensive search for possible bacterial infection failed to reveal any clues.

Officials finally discovered that every Friday morning a cleaning lady would enter the ward, remove the plug that powered the patient's life support system, plug her floor polisher into the outlet, then wax the floor.

When she had finished her chores, she would plug the life support machine back in and leave, unaware that the patient was now dead.

A Ukrainian businessman, who had bought pagers as gifts for each member of his staff, was so alarmed when all fifty of them went off at the same instant that he drove his car into a lamppost. After he checked himself for injuries, he checked the messages on the fifty pagers. They all read: "Congratulations on a successful purchase!"

In 1997 you could spend $7 for a polo shirt from a discount mart, or you could buy a designer shirt for $49. *Consumer Reports* magazine tested both for durability and general workmanship. Guess which came out on top? Yep, the cheapie.

Japanese women were sold on Infidelity Detection Cream, an invisible gel they could spray on their husbands' clothes. If he disrobed during the day when he was supposed to be at work, the clothes would change color.

The most noticeable result of the promotion: More Japanese men started washing their own clothes.

A sign outside a secondhand shop: WE EXCHANGE ANY-THING—BICYCLES, WASHING MACHINES, ETC. WHY NOT BRING YOUR WIFE ALONG AND GET A WONDERFUL BARGAIN?

Message on a leaflet: "If you cannot read, this leaflet will tell you how to get lessons."

Spotted in a toilet in a London office: "Toilet out of order. Please use floor below."

After helping to disgrace the presidency by having an affair with a married president while interning at the White House, Monica Lewinsky tried to capitalize on her infamy by selling purses through the Internet, each one bearing the curious label: "Made especially for you by MONICA."

Ms. Lewinsky really wanted her own lipstick line. "I'd like to have a lipstick," she told *Marie Claire* magazine. "I think it could be a neat thing, something that would be fun and lucrative and a respectable decision. Um, I'd like to be using my head again."

How about the Emeryville, California, restaurant that changed its name from Bavarian Village to Sushi Village. What's dumb about that? It was a Chinese restaurant.

Keenly aware of the new businesswoman's need to save precious seconds in her day, *New Woman* magazine offered this suggestion: Save time by "seeing several friends at once."

Pennsylvania farmers in the nineteenth century weren't going to be easily hoodwinked when oil was discovered on their land and business tycoons offered them a percentage of the profits in exchange for drilling rights.

Some farmers rejected the oil company's offer of ½ the profits and held out for ¼ because 4 was larger than 2.

For thirty-two years, a dentist in northern China collected 28,000 diseased teeth that he had extracted from his patients' mouths.

What did he do with so many rotten teeth? He built a tower with them, eight feet four inches high, to raise awareness of dental hygiene.

The plague of the fourteenth century had one unexpected result: the birth of the workers' movement.

When France was faced with a labor shortage because the black death had claimed so many peasants, surviving peasants went on strike for workers' rights.

The French nobles responded in true management fashion: They massacred the strikers and tossed their bodies in the rivers with the plague victims.

The looting of the New World by adventurers from the Old was more of a business venture than a military campaign. It's just that Spanish conquistadors found it a sensible business practice to slaughter the natives of South America as a convenient way of investing in Aztec gold.

Occasionally, the Spanish businessmen had trouble organizing their transportation divisions.

In 1520 Cortés and six hundred of his business associates arrived in the Aztec capital of Tenochtitlán and proceeded to acquire vast amounts of gold and jewels through the trading practice known as killing the other party.

But the city was an island in a lake, with only one way off: a long series of bridges. When the Spanish tried to conclude their transaction and depart, Aztec warriors destroyed some of the bridges, then attacked in canoes from both sides.

The Spaniards could have escaped if they had brought boats or had dropped their loot and run for it. But weighed down by gold, half the Spanish investors were killed.

Fortunately for Cortés, the Aztecs killed so many gold-heavy Spaniards that their bodies falling into the lake formed a bridge that the rest could run across, and flee to invest again another day.

When coffee was introduced by Venetian traders working the Arab routes, it was banned by the Italian clergy as the drink of infidels, until Pope Clement VII had a cup. Suddenly, coffee wasn't so evil. He pronounced it a moral drink for Christians.

One of the Western world's first dictionaries, the *Manipulus Vocabulorum*, written in 1570, had a unique approach to helping people understand the meaning of words: Instead of listing words alphabetically, the authors arranged them by the spelling of the final syllable of each word.

In Venice, prostitutes in the sixteenth century took to wearing shoes so high they were more like low stilts. The government eventually made prostitutes' shoes illegal, not on moral grounds but because too many women were falling off their shoes.

When Sir Francis Drake returned to England in the late 1500s, he brought back his New World discovery: pipes and tobacco. When he lit a pipe to show Queen Elizabeth how to smoke, a royal servant threw a bucket of water on Sir Francis, assuming he was on fire.

The next time you're trying to help a smoker quit, you might want to try the Elizabethan approach.

In the 1630s Dutch farmers started speculating wildly in tulips, driving up the price of bulbs into the thousands of guilders.

The spiraling speculation eventually bankrupted thousands of Dutch businessmen when investors realized that tulips had no inherent value that made them worth so much money, a lesson today's baseball card and Beanie Baby collectors have yet to learn.

In the 1950s an engineer was asked by an electronics manufacturer to improve push-button tuners for radios so they wouldn't lose contact with the station and slip into static.

His solution called for buttons that you could pull and also turn to fine-tune the station. His idea was rejected—not because it didn't work (it did), but because the company didn't want their radios to look different from everyone else's, which all performed poorly using push buttons.

Consumers become so accustomed to having things a certain way that improvements often have to be abandoned or disguised.

Take the QWERTY keyboard, which was designed to slow down typists by putting the most frequently typed letters under control of the weakest left-hand fingers. The nineteenth-century machines weren't mechanically trustworthy enough to keep up with fast typists.

Now word processors can go much faster, but the old slow-down keyboard arrangement remains the same because no one wants to learn a new one.

The British manufacturer Ariel produced a superior design for their motorcycle by moving the fuel tank to the rear of the frame. Designers then had to add a fake tank up front because riders were uncomfortable without it, even though they didn't need it.

The Sydney, Australia, Opera House is one of the city's most recognized landmarks, with its flamboyant design evoking the images of sailboats.

That fantastical design ignored engineering realities, resulting in nine years of construction delays that ran up the budget 1,400 percent. Engineers still couldn't solve enough of the design problems to avoid a $75 million, ten-year rehab project only sixteen years later.

Tin cans were a marvelous invention in 1810, allowing the preservation and transportation of food far from its source—particularly useful for armies on the march.

The only problem: No one invented a can opener for forty-eight more years.

Until then, soldiers used knives and bayonets to open the tin cans—and if that didn't work, they shot them open.

One food manufacturer included these operating instructions on his tin cans: "Cut round on the top with a chisel and hammer."

When the Chevrolet Monza was first designed, you had to remove the entire engine just to replace two spark plugs.

When Ford was approached by one of its designers to produce the first minivan in the 1970s, the company not only turned him down, they fired him. He went over to Chrysler, which then cornered a market that no other car manufacturer thought existed.

IBM turned down the chance to manufacture the first office copiers in the 1960s because IBM execs thought there would be no market for them.

The Gerber company made a fortune selling baby food in tiny jars. But the company flopped big time in the 1970s when they tried to sell single-serving food for adults in the same baby food jars.

Among ancient Assyrian traders, no business deal was finalized until the seller gave the buyer a single shoe.

The exploration of remote and remotely understood territories was risky business. Choose intelligently and you could bring home the gold—or at least the corn and tobacco.

Then there was nineteenth-century English explorer John Franklin, whose crew of 129 ill-fated men did not come home at all.

As Franklin struggled through the vast icy regions of the Arctic territory, his men lugged along a clothes brush, a tin of button polish, a backgammon board, and books.

They neglected to bring along their rifles, which would have enabled them to shoot game along the way. Instead, they all starved to death.

When Hungarian millers developed a more efficient grinding process for turning wheat into flour in the 1850s, they discovered that the new mills removed the nutritious bran and germ from the wheat, leaving the bread flour white.

To solve their marketing problem, they promoted a campaign to convince people that the white bread made from devalued flour was better than whole wheat bread because white was the color of nobility.

Movie theater owners in the 1920s barred patrons from eating popcorn during the show, thus depriving themselves of vast profits. Once they switched positions, theater operators learned that they made more money off snacks than movie tickets.

Ice cream sales in Japan plummeted during World War II because people feared they would be identified as traitors if they ate the American novelty. What they didn't know was that ice cream was invented by Italians, Japan's allies during the war.

New Coke.

All right, that's too easy a slam. It's not a brainless mistake for Coke to try a new formula. But it was a soda blooper of economy-size proportions for a company to spend two years on research, taste tests, consumer awareness studies, and focus groups, and then come up with a yecchy pop that everyone immediately hated. That $4 million wasted on New Coke left a bad taste in plenty of mouths when it was introduced in 1985.

A decade later, the Coca-Cola company announced they were developing a soda vending machine that could sense changes in temperature so it could raise prices when the weather got hot and people got really thirsty.

Americans spend two billion hours mowing their grass each year. None of them enjoy the chore. All of them know they wouldn't be mowing it if they weren't growing it. Yet they never stop growing it, so they never stop mowing it. For this dubious privilege, Americans spend millions of dollars on seed and mowers, only to end up with lawns that don't look as good as their neighbors'.

When soda pop was invented in the 1880s, it was sold as a medicine. Now people who drink too much of it may have to take medicine to counter the calcium-depleting effects of soda.

On the Pacific island of Alor, natives developed a monetary system based on drums and gongs that were never played and were spent only to buy pigs and wives.

Among natives of the Admiralty Islands, dog teeth were the currency exchange for wives, while on the isle of Yap the currency took the shape of twelve-foot-tall carved stones that weighed over a ton, which at least prevented them from getting shortchanged.

In 1911 the *Ladies' Home Journal* fired fifteen women for the shocking transgression of dancing the turkey trot.

A tired mother, Marion Donovan, invented the disposable diaper in 1951 by cutting up a plastic shower curtain. When she tried to sell the idea to American manufacturers, they told her it would never become popular enough to make money.

When Bette Nesmith invented Liquid Paper to correct typing mistakes in the 1950s, manufacturers turned her product down, convinced no one would want it.

Forced to finance production herself, she made a fortune.

Cheap, disposable paper dresses enjoyed a brief fad in 1966, until women found out that the dresses fell apart in the rain and caught fire easily. They were also uncomfortable.

Out of a job but not out of ideas, adman Gary Dahl sold over a million Pet Rocks in 1975. A Pet Rock was a rock in a box. They made Dahl a millionaire.

Trying to cash in on the blue jeans craze in 1974, American Motors put out an edition of its Gremlin and Hornet upholstered in denim. The cars didn't sell. The company missed the essential idea: that people wanted to wear jeans, not drive in them.

Four million women in the 1970s spent $40 million on mail-order breast enlargers that didn't work.

When airlines began commercial flights, passengers were not allowed to buckle their own seat belts. Stewardesses were required to buckle up each one of them.

An actual tip from a Silicon Valley electronics company's *Environmental, Health and Safety Handbook for Employees:* "Blink your eyelids periodically to lubricate your eyes."

From the 1983 edition of the employee manual from Morgan Guaranty Trust Company: "Avoid saying hello. This elsewhere pleasant and familiar greeting is out of place in the business world."

Let's end with just a few product-label instructions:
1. On Nytol sleep aid: "Warning: May cause drowsiness."
2. On a hairdryer: "Do not use while sleeping."
3. On Chinese-made Christmas lights: "For indoor or outdoor use only."
4. For a Rowenta iron: "Do not iron clothes on body."
5. On a pudding package: "Product will be hot after heating."
6. On a bag of Frito chips: "You could be a winner! No purchase necessary. Details inside."

CHAPTER NINETEEN

Advertising How Dumb We Are

Dumb advertising is an industry built upon a simple premise: They're smarter than we are.

Ad agencies think of consumers as fools who can be tricked into buying any swill they sell. If there's a truth that works, fine, advertise that. If not, lies will do the trick just as well.

That explains the old gasoline ad that showed Our Brand producing clean exhaust, while Their Brand produced black, sooty exhaust. Was Our Brand really a cleaner gasoline, good for your car and our mutual air? Or did the ad provocateurs simply use a car with a dirty motor for Their Brand of gas?

Oddly, this is not just the view of a cynical age. Decades ago, when advertising was a fledgling, uncertain influence on mob-buying persuasions, advertisers still took our forefathers, not to mention our foremothers, for idiots. Consider these ancient advertisements:

A 1910 ad for Gillette razors: "You don't have to take a correspondence course to learn how to use it. Just buy it and shave."

From a 1930 ad for Drano liquid cleaner: "I can feel his eyes accusing me every time the bathroom drains slow up. He'd look at me as much to say, 'Your fault!' And it was."

From a 1918 ad for corsets: "Women play a most important role in the affairs of the world. It's not only their privilege to represent the highest type of beauty, it's their duty to do so."

An ad for Lestoil household cleanser shows a pretty model in a space suit and the pitch: "Women of the future will make the moon a cleaner place to live."

From a 1944 ad from the American Meat Institute: "Human nature's yen for that good meat flavor is one of the most consistent manifestations in the history of food."

Who could resist this pitch for soda in 1962: "7UP stimulates your mouth's natural moisture"?

In 1928 Lucky Strike sold cigarettes to women with aviator Amelia Earhart's endorsement through the intriguing slogan: "For a slender figure, reach for a Lucky instead of a sweet."

If you reach for enough of them, you could end up with a figure as slender as a coffin nail.

The Modess sanitary napkin offered its revolutionary "silent purchase plan" to women suffering through the guilt years of the 1950s.

The plan turned out to be a coupon a woman could cut out of the magazine and hand to the pharmacy clerk so she wouldn't be embarrassed by having to ask for Modess out loud.

Dumb advertising existed even before there were dumb ad agencies.

Soldiers in the nineteenth century needed strong teeth to rip open rifle cartridges. Enterprising dentists harvested teeth from the strong young dead at the Battle of Waterloo and turned them into strong dentures, which they promoted as "Waterloo teeth."

A real estate ad in the hot housing market of Phoenix, Arizona, featured a photo of a woman realtor, who was slightly over the hill, posing with her pet poodle below the headline, "Top dog again this year." And smiling about it.

Dumb ads don't have to be created by professional ad agencies. Amateurs working newspaper classifieds can come up with doozies like these:

"Snowblower for sale. Only used on snowy days."

"Do something special for your Valentine: Have your septic tank pumped."

"Two wire-mesh butchering gloves: one 5-finger, one 3-finger."

A New York ad agency that represented several toy companies devised a new business pitch by sending stuffed toys and ransom notes to the executives of companies they were hoping to sign up.

In true kidnapping fashion, the notes were composed of words cut out of newspapers. The notes read: "We're holding your kid for ransom. We have their favorite stuffed animals. The kidnappers."

A cautious corporate executive passed one of the notes on to the FBI. Investigators determined that the note wasn't actually an extortion threat, just another ill-conceived idea by an adman who wasn't going to win a new account.

A California ad agency decided to treat potential clients to doughnuts, representing all the goodies the agency promised businesses if they signed up.

The agency demonstrated their sharp business sensibilities by sending the doughnuts through the mail. By the time prospective clients received the pitches and opened the boxes, they were treated to smashed doughnuts covered with mold, one of the few examples of truth in advertising.

Paris turned to an ad agency to convince dog owners to clean up after their pets. One ad shows a blind man with his white cane covered with dog excrement, as the announcer comments: "You're right not to clean it up. He does it very well for you."

Why are such ads necessary? Because Parisian dogs deposit ten tons of excrement on city sidewalks each day, and six hundred people end up in the hospital each year from slipping on it.

No wonder Paris is the City of Lights. Without the lights, no one would be safe walking there.

Designers for the wealthy are now promoting two-kitchen homes. One kitchen is for the family to gather for that old-time, around-the-stove, happy family meal.

What's the second kitchen for? That's where your cook does the actual cooking, as you wouldn't want her getting in your family's way.

In 1986 the ad agency for Gallo wines came up with a unique way to sell a new wine cooler. The agency created two fictitious farmers, naming the homey pitchmen Frank Bartles and Ed Jaymes (because James looked too ordinary).

Gallo ran a series of folksy TV ads with the two actors explaining that they had to take out a second mortgage on Ed's home to go into the wine business. The ads always concluded with Frank saying, "We thank you for your support."

When Frank announced in one commercial that he hoped people would buy more wine coolers because they needed the money, people actually wrote to the giant wine corporation, offering financial assistance to help cover the balloon payment on Ed's mortgage.

In 1883 a farm machinery manufacturer outraged veterans of the Civil War (and families of casualties) by promoting their reaper with a poster that depicted the Battle of Gettysburg interrupting a farmer at his harvest.

In 1954 a model demonstrated the dangers of live advertising on television when she was unable to open the door of a Westinghouse refrigerator to show off how easy it was to use.

Quaker Oats came up with a unique promotion in 1955: Buy some cereal, get a deed to land in the Yukon Territory — one square inch of it.

The cereal manufacturer bought 21 million of these miniplots from the Canadian government for $10,000. When the promotion didn't pan out, Canada took the land back for $37 in back taxes.

In 1964, when Pepsi's ad agency came up with the slogan "Come alive, you're in the Pepsi Generation," they didn't hire the best translators for international sales.

In German, the slogan became "Come alive out of the grave." In Chinese it was worse: "Pepsi brings your ancestors back from the dead."

The Marlboro Man, who rode tall in the saddle as he smoked his way through Marlboro Country, started out as the Marlboro woman.

Marlboros were originally marketed in the 1950s as a woman's cigarette, "mild as May," according to their less-than-successful ad slogan. The soon-to-be tough guy's cigarette even came with a red filter so the woman's lipstick wouldn't show up on the butt.

When that ad campaign flopped, Philip Morris simply switched horses in midstream and created a symbol of manhood out of a failed symbol of womanhood.

In the United States, opinion pollsters conduct 20 million interviews a year to find out what we want in our products—from cars to soda to political candidates. After all that research, they still don't know what we want—and neither do we.

Not content to put ads on the outside of buses, the inside of toilet stalls, projected onto the sides of buildings, video-displayed on gas pumps, and printed on the linings of airplane dinner trays—now they're sticking milk ads on the outside of bananas. When you prepare your morning cereal, the ads will remind you that if you've only got cereal and bananas in the bowl, then something's missing.

A Georgia high-school boy was suspended for wearing a Pepsi shirt on the school's Coca-Cola-sponsored "Coke in Education Day," during which students were requested to line up on the field for a photo and, in marching-band formation, spell out the word *COKE*.

Before W. C. Fields became a famous comic actor on stage and in movies, he worked as a juggler/drowner on a tourist pier in Atlantic City. When business was slow, he stopped juggling and waded into the ocean, where he pretended to drown.

The idea was that Fields's dramatic rescue by lifeguards would attract a crowd, so pier barkers could sell refreshments and Fields could go back to juggling. When business was slow, he drowned four times a day.

The pervasive influence of advertising allows for the transformation of anything into a sales tool. One man's art becomes an adman's pitch.

Consider this observation from writer William Burroughs about the free spirit who named the Beat Generation and the way marketers took advantage of the Beat vision of personal freedom: "[Jack] Kerouac opened a million coffee bars and sold a million pair of Levi's to both sexes."

The Ford Motor Company missed a chance at greatness when they turned down an endorsement offer, which came in the following letter: "While I still got breath in my lungs, I will tell you what a dandy car you make. I have drove Fords exclusively when I could get away with one."

The letter and the promotion offer came from Clyde Barrow, of the notorious, Hollywood-lionized bank robbers, Bonnie and Clyde.

Ford passed up another chance at uniqueness when the company was having trouble naming their new car in 1958. Executives got so desperate that they hired the poet Marianne Moore to come up with poetic names for the car.

She suggested several: Utopian Turtletop, Andante con Moto, Pastelogram, Intelligent Bullet, and Bullet Cloisonne.

Instead, Ford went with the Edsel, and the rest is history.

Famed adman Jerry Della Femina was in a brainstorming session, trying to devise a campaign slogan for his agency's electronics account, the Japanese manufacturer Panasonic.

Della Femina suggested the following headline for their ad: "From those wonderful folks who gave you Pearl Harbor."

It didn't fly, but Della Femina did make the gag work—as the title for his book about advertising.

In some businesses the surest way to lose business is to offer your merchandise at a reasonable price.

Helena Rubenstein, who made a fortune selling her own brand of expensive makeup, understood that you can't sell cosmetics to women unless you overprice it. "Some women won't buy anything unless they can pay a lot," she explained.

Our final thought on the foolishness of advertising comes not from a businessman but from Arctic explorer Vilhjalmur Stfansson, who was not easily dazzled by bright lights.

"Unethical advertising uses falsehoods to deceive the public," he pointed out. "Ethical advertising uses truth to deceive the public."

CHAPTER TWENTY

Dumb Crime

We never learn much about the clever criminals who get away with their crimes because they're smart enough not to tell us how they fought the law and won.

Then there are the dumb crooks:

A Detroit burglar took his dog with him on a 1968 break-in. When the cops showed up unexpectedly, the burglar ran off, leaving his dog behind.

The police caught up to the crook through a simple act of detection: They said to the dog, "Home, boy."

Police busted a San Antonio woman for possession of pot after an auto mechanic found eighteen packages of marijuana stashed inside the engine compartment of her car.

How did the mechanic stumble upon the grass? The woman had brought the car in for an oil change and didn't know that the mechanic would raise the hood to change the oil.

When a construction worker robbed a Fort Smith, Arkansas, convenience store, he didn't get caught because he was using a toy gun. The police caught him because he wore his hard hat during the robbery with his name written across the front.

☞☜

A Tampa, Florida, man handed a bank teller a note demanding cash. The police had no trouble catching up to the bank robber because he wrote the stickup note on his own pay stub, right below where his name and address were printed.

☞☜

The robber holding up a restaurant in Newport, Rhode Island, in 1975 was nervous and unpracticed at stickups. To stuff the money into his pocket, he used his gun hand. The gun went off, and he killed himself.

☞☜

A Texas man who killed his mother-in-law offered this novel defense: He thought she was a large raccoon.

☞☜

In Salinas, California, a woman was convicted of stealing credit cards to feed her addiction to Beanie Babies. "It was like a drug," she claimed. "Once I started, I couldn't stop."

How did she get started on a life of crime? Working at McDonald's, where her job exposed her to the larceny-inducing risk of stuffing the give-away toys into Happy Meals for kids.

A gang of eleven professional thieves pulled off one of the most successful robberies in history when they held up Brink's Boston headquarters in 1950, taking more than $2 million from the vaults, although they left behind another $800,000 in cash by mistake.

The crime went unsolved for years. Then eleven days before the statute of limitations was to expire, one member of the gang spilled everything to the police. Why? He felt cheated on his cut.

Thus, the perfect crime was thwarted by petty stupidity, a method of detection that has brought down more criminals than the superior intellects of any real-world Sherlock Holmes.

A defendant in a 1986 Illinois murder trial attacked his attorney in court, then punched the judge. After his conviction for murder, he appealed on the grounds that the attack had prejudiced the judge against him.

In 1978 a computer whiz manipulated a software program to steal $10 million by electronically transferring the money from a Los Angeles bank to his own bank account in Switzerland.

The only reason he got caught: He told someone what he'd done.

While on bail for the original crime, the electronic thief made a second illegal transfer, this time stealing $50 million. Authorities were watching him. He was sent to prison for both crimes.

In New York City each year nearly three times as many people are bitten by other people than are bitten by rats. These attacks prove not only that people are more dangerous than rats, but that rats have better taste.

Right up there with the bungling burglars of the world are people who think they are safe-guarding their houses by installing burglar alarms.

The top six reasons burglar alarms are set off:

1. Homeowners trip the alarms by mistake.

2–5. The alarms are set off by temperature changes, forgotten windows left open, pets, and insects.

6. They're set off by party decorations such as helium balloons.

After all of those false alarms, burglars come in seventh.

Maybe after police solve the helium-balloon problem, they'll be able to do something about the burglary problem.

In Virginia in 1998 a woman called the town jail and told officers that the prosecutor had dropped the charges on a man being held, so he should be released.

When officers explained they'd need that order in writing, the woman faxed a handwritten note alleging to be from the prosecutor. The note contained several misspellings and grammatical errors and was sent on a hand-drawn letterhead.

The police tracked down the sender through the fax number and arrested the girlfriend of the guy already in jail.

Singer Bobby Brown, Whitney Houston's husband, was allegedly drunk when he went into court to surrender so he could serve time for drunk driving.

Dumb crooks don't stop being dumb just because they're put in prison. That's where dumb crooks become dumb jailhouse lawyers, lawsuit-happy inmates with too much time on their hands.

These frivolous lawsuits came from New York convicts in 1998:

A burglar sued for $35,000 because he was served stale Pop-Tarts for prison breakfast.

An inmate alleged cruel and unusual punishment when he was denied deodorant while in solitary confinement.

A jury in the Los Angeles Superior Courthouse got into a fight during a break while they were watching Jerry Springer's guests fight on TV.

Playing with handcuffs, an Arizona man locked himself up, then couldn't find the key. Instead of calling a locksmith, he called the police to set him free.

While the cops were getting him loose from the hand-cuffs, they made a routine computer check, then arrested him on an outstanding warrant.

☞☜

A bank robber was busted after passing a Florida bank teller a stickup note written on the back of his parole card.

☞☜

Shooting for thief of the year award was the man who broke into a car, found a camera inside, and posed for pictures, which his girlfriend took, of him brandishing the screwdriver he used to break into the car.

It was a cheap camera, so the thief left it in the car. When the car was returned to its owner, he developed the pictures and found the ones of the car thief, who then posed for one more picture: a police mug shot.

☞☜

Two young men were charged with second-degree murder, attempted murder, and armed robbery of a Florida jewelry store. The men reportedly planned the job to raise money to pay their tuition at the Palm Beach Community College Police Academy.

☞☜

In Peoria, Arizona, Mom and Dad didn't want to drink and drive after a two-day binge. So they handed the car keys to their daughter and told her to drive them home.

Their daughter was eleven years old at the time. She crashed the car into a house. Her mother broke an ankle and some ribs in the crack-up, and both parents were charged with child abuse.

❦

A woman forger was arrested in Phoenix in 1998 for passing checks she'd stolen along with the victim's purse. She got caught when she misspelled the name on the checks she passed. Not only that, she misspelled it twice, wrong in two different ways, while she had the name right in front of her.

Also, the forger was in her twenties and handed over the victim's ID to cash the check. The victim pictured on the ID was twenty years older.

❦

In Florida a burglar was caught and convicted based on fingerprint evidence left at the scenes of the crimes.

The burglar was surprised because he'd been careful to wear gloves during each theft—golf gloves, the kind without fingertips.

❦

In Tukwila, Washington, a grab-and-run thief hustled out of a Target store with a stolen VCR. When employees followed him outside, they found that the thief couldn't start his van because he was out of gas.

The thief carried the VCR over to a gas station to buy gas. When police arrived, he was still filling up his van, with the stolen VCR under one arm.

An Ohio woman was sentenced to jail for two months over magazine subscriptions. The woman's crime? She got mad at three people in her town and forged their names to magazine subscriptions: 350 times.

ᘔ

A Wisconsin man was arrested for firing a weapon illegally when he dragged his washing machine down the stairs and shot it three times with his pistol.

An original counterfeiter was arrested in Wichita, Kansas, for trying to pass two $16 bills at a hotel.

An Alabama Girl Scout leader was busted for stealing $700 in cookie money in 1982.

ᘔ

In 1981 New York City's creative thieves came up with a new specialty: subway-token sucking. These thieves, who may have flunked pickpocketing, would place their mouths around subway turnstiles and suck the tokens back up out of the slots.

Police estimated that a competent token sucker could make about $75 a day.

A navy veteran was convicted of first-degree murder for killing his wife, who had filed for divorce. In his novel defense, the man admitted that he stabbed her multiple times, but said he didn't kill her because she was already dead.

The husband claimed he stabbed his dead wife to prevent their son from finding out she had committed suicide.

♂🕭

An off-duty Baltimore police officer, who worked in the antidrug unit, was out shopping for a car. On a test drive, he was surprised when the car salesman asked him to stop at one of the city's outdoor drug markets. He was even more surprised as he watched the salesman buy drugs from a known dealer.

When they returned the car to the dealership, the cop arrested the salesman, describing the arrest as "the most bizarre bust I've ever heard of."

♂🕭

The famed English barrister F. E. Smith trapped a con man who sued over an alleged arm injury during a bus accident.

The plaintiff painfully demonstrated that he could raise his injured arm only to shoulder level. Smith asked him how high he could lift his arm before the accident. The man demonstrated by raising his arm over his head, winning Smith's case for him.

♂🕭

Sadamichi Hirasawa convinced the clerks of a Tokyo bank to take some medicine, telling them that he was the bank doctor. The medicine was cyanide. As they died, he robbed the bank of $700.

When caught in 1948, Hirasawa got a life sentence instead of execution because lawyers convinced the judge that since Hirasawa knew he would be executed, the bank robbery was actually his way of committing suicide.

Japanese officials couldn't execute him, since their constitution prohibited suicide. Hirasawa was released from prison in 1980.

☙❧

One final thought on crime: It costs so much to keep thieves in prison that if we gave them the money we spent to house them, they wouldn't have any reason to steal.

CHAPTER TWENTY-ONE

Avoidable Catastrophes

Planes are risky. Ships sink. Accidents happen—too often to too many people who had nothing to do with the cause but everything to do with the effect.

Then there are the avoidable accidents that happen because the people who were supposed to be in charge were asleep at the wheel of their brains.

The history of plane crashes usually involves a strange set of circumstances: bad weather, unexpected events, equipment problems. Same story for trains, ships, and industrial disasters.

But the pattern of unfortunate circumstances changes when augmented by mind melt. Then we suddenly become the bugs on their windshield.

The burning and sinking of the excursion steamship *General Slocum* in 1904 was caused by idiocy compounded by stupidity, resulting in the death of 1,031 people in New York's East River, most of them children on board for a Sunday school picnic.

The ship was seriously overloaded because of company greed. The bosses wanted the ticket money.

A fire started in a locked room in which flammable materials were stored in violation of safety regulations and common sense.

The fire hose didn't work because it had been sealed to prevent water leaks. When the seal was knocked loose, the hose burst under the water pressure because it hadn't been replaced or inspected in years.

The lifeboats were so tightly lashed to the decks that they could not be loosened. Some of the ship's life jackets had been nailed to the walls so customers wouldn't steal them.

Many of the life jackets wouldn't have done much good anyway, since they were stuffed with sawdust instead of cork. Some of these life preservers had been fitted with cast-iron bars so that instead of keeping the children afloat, they pulled them to the bottom of the East River.

The captain of a Portuguese sailing ship, the *St. James*, killed 450 passengers when he rammed the ship directly into a reef off the Cape of Good Hope in the late nineteenth century.

The captain never should have been anywhere near that reef. He had the ship running before a strong wind—at midnight, when he couldn't see the reef that the crew kept telling him was directly ahead of them.

The captain compounded his stupidity by deserting his foundering ship and its passengers in the one good lifeboat.

When the captain returned safely to Portugal, he was given another ship—which he rammed into another reef. This time he went down with the ship. If he hadn't, the officials in charge of astoundingly bad decisions would certainly have given him a third.

The owners of a grand new Chicago theater, the Iroquois, advertised in 1903 that it was fireproof. The city inspector agreed with them. However, the editor of a fire-prevention magazine warned them that the theater was a firetrap. He was ignored.

On December 30, a fire started onstage at the Iroquois and spread into the auditorium. People sitting in the orchestra section rushed out the fire doors to discover in midstep that the street was four feet below them. The first rush resulted in many broken bones, but these unfortunates served to break the falls of the people who came after them.

The balcony was the scene of the real tragedy. There were no exit signs. Most of the exit doors were locked and secured with iron grates. The doors that could be forced open led to fire escapes that had no ladders.

The fifteen-minute firestorm inside the theater killed 591 people, all of whom could have survived what started as a small stage fire if any sensible precautions had been taken.

Workers in a Russian collective in 1929 decided to celebrate the anniversary of the abdication of Czar Nicholas by getting drunk and watching a movie.

They had no theater, but commandeered a small factory room, although the factory manager told them it was too danger-ous to pack so many people into a room where gasoline had been spilled on the floor.

They ignored him. The film was accompanied by a drunken accordion player, who tossed a cigarette onto the flammable film stock that piled up on the floor because the substitute projection-ist didn't know how to run a projector.

The nitrate film ignited, which in turn set the gasoline-soaked floor ablaze in an overcrowded room, and 120 people died.

As for the factory manager who had tried to warn everyone off, he was beaten and killed by the survivors.

In a French disco called the Cinq-Sept Club, one of the main doors was locked once the crowd was inside. The other door was always sealed shut. One unlit fire exit was hidden behind the bandstand. The other exit door was blocked by stacked chairs. The club had neither fire extinguishers nor a telephone.

When a fire started in the club, all these dumb mistakes fed the blaze that killed 146 disco dancers in 1970.

Many of the early dirigibles crashed, but the most brainless crash can be pinned on politicians who ordered the Shenandoah to fly over a series of midwestern towns in 1925.

The ship's captain warned against taking off because of bad weather conditions. But local politicians convinced the Secretary of the Navy to order the dirigible into the air, against the captain's advice, so they could impress voters.

The Shenandoah crashed, killing fourteen crew members.

In 1957 the pilot of a chartered airplane crashed it, killing seventy-seven people aboard. Amazingly, the pilot had previously been fired by another airline for intentionally flying a plane into the ground—an incident that miraculously resulted in no deaths.

Under psychiatric care, the pilot had been declared unfit to fly. Although his record was known, the second airline hired him anyway.

In 1987 a ferry collided with an oil tanker in the Philippine Sea. Some three thousand people were killed in the explosion or drowned.

How did the ferry captain miss seeing the tanker in open water? He had given the bridge to an unqualified seaman because he wanted to take a break to watch a videotape and drink a beer.

CHAPTER TWENTY-TWO

Intelligent Thoughts About Stupidity

Amazing how smart people are when they're talking about how smart people aren't.

The Persian poet Saadi outlined the paradox of intelligence: "A stupid person should keep silent. But if he knew this, he would not be a stupid person."

President Woodrow Wilson countered with this practical advice: "If a man is a fool, the best thing to do is to encourage him to advertise the fact by speaking. It cannot be so easily discovered if you allow him to remain silent and look wise. But if you let him speak, the secret is out."

Cowboy wisdom: "Never miss a good chance to shut up."

The twentieth century's most celebrated genius, Albert Einstein, noted: "Only two things are infinite, the universe and human stupidity, and I'm not sure about the former."

Author Elbert Hubbard agreed: "Genius may have its limitations, but stupidity is not thus handicapped."

Biologist Luther Burbank put man's wars, and the probable victor, in perspective: "Men should stop fighting among themselves and start fighting insects."

Transcendentalist Henry Thoreau observed man's ability to learn and grow: "Every generation laughs at the old fashions but religiously follows the new."

Feminist writer Erica Jong interpreted the relationships between men and women: "You see an awful lot of smart guys with dumb women, but you hardly ever see a smart woman with a dumb guy."

Austria's absurdist author Franz Kafka evaluated man's chances to improve his plight: "In a fight between you and the world, bet on the world."

Psychologist Carl Jung reflected upon his life's work: "Show me a sane person and I'll cure him for you."

Psychologist Havelock Ellis ranked his hope for man's improvement: "The place where optimism flourishes most is the lunatic asylum."

Social observer and humorist Will Rogers offered a solution to the Great Depression: "Stupidity got us into this mess. Why can't it get us out?"

Rogers also pointed out the undeniable: "Everybody is ignorant, only on different subjects."

British bicycle designer Mike Burrows, on a tour of America, came to an understanding of the American class system: "Marin County [California] was wonderful. The community was idyllic and the people were just beautiful. The whole town had nothing but beautiful people. I think there must have been an ordinance banning stupid and ugly people within city limits. Then I came to Las Vegas and realized what they had done with them all."

German philosopher Immanuel Kant grasped the difficulties of shaping man's fate: "From such crooked wood as that which man is made, nothing straight can be fashioned."

Attorney Clarence Darrow put the issues of his time into perspective: "History repeats itself. That's one of the things that's wrong with history."

Isaac Newton, one of the greatest scientific minds mankind has ever produced, didn't think much of mankind's achievements: "I do not know what I seem to the world, but to myself I appear to have been like a boy playing upon the seashore and diverting myself by now and then finding a smoother pebble or prettier shell than ordinary, while the great ocean of truth lay before me all undiscovered."

Sigmund Freud, father of psychoanalysis, probed the human mind until he came to this conclusion: "I have found little that is good about human beings. In my experience most of them are trash."

Upon further reflection, he added: "In the depths of my heart I can't help being convinced that my dear fellow men, with a few exceptions, are worthless."

Italian dictator Benito Mussolini also wasn't impressed by the good deeds of others: "The history of saints is mainly the history of insane people."

Writer Mark Twain faced up to our no-escape clause: "April 1, this is the day upon which we are reminded of what we are on the other 364."

Twain also observed: "It is better to keep your mouth shut and appear stupid than to open it and remove all doubts."

Acerbic author H. L. Mencken matched Twain's insight: "A man may be a fool and not know it. But not if he is married."

Humorist Dave Barry worked on newspapers long enough to realize: "If editors were so damned smart, they would know how to dress."

The life of the aristocracy has its pitfalls, as the duke of Gloucester pointed out: "The absurd thing about being a duke or a prince is that you are a professional ignoramus."

> The witty Oscar Wilde soothed his wits with this observation: "We are born in an age when only the dull are treated seriously, and I live in terror of not being misunderstood."

Writer Edith Sitwell put a blunt edge to similar feelings: "I am patient with stupidity, but not with those who are proud of it."

Novelist Alexandre Dumas chose sides with a clear mind: "I prefer the wicked rather than the foolish. The wicked sometimes rest."

Henry IV, a sixteenth-century king of France, was listening to a pompous dignitary make a dull speech when a donkey started to bray. The king turned to the donkey and said: "Gentlemen, one at a time, please."

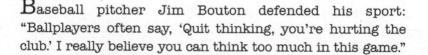

Scientist Arthur C. Clarke was smart enough to take a pragmatic approach to the workings of his own mind: "It has yet to be proven that intelligence has any survival value."

Medical researcher Oliver Sacks put life in perspective: "Nature gropes and blunders and performs the cruelest acts. There is no steady advance upward. There is no design."

College professor Frank Easterbrook countered a prevailing homily with this thought: "Some men achieve insignificance. Others have insignificance thrust upon them."

Star running back Knute Rockne took a common-sense view of his game: "The only qualifications for a [football] lineman are to be big and dumb. To be a back, you only have to be dumb."

Baseball pitcher Jim Bouton defended his sport: "Ballplayers often say, 'Quit thinking, you're hurting the club.' I really believe you can think too much in this game."

Playwright George Chapman found this truth for the ages in the sixteenth century: "Young men think old men are fools. But old men know young men are fools."

Writer Don Marquis outlined the dangers of intelligence: "If you make people think they're thinking, they'll love you. But if you really make them think, they'll hate you."

High-tech entrepreneur Guy Kawasaki contrasted smart craft with smart advertising: "Many expensive products are not indulgent—they are simply stupid—while some very inexpensive products are surprisingly indulgent. For example . . . a $20 haircut in Tokyo involves five attendants, a full upper-body massage, shaved eyebrows, four heated shampoos, and a parting gift."

Boston University president Daniel Marsh made this prediction in 1950: "If the television craze continues with the present level of programs, we are destined to have a nation of morons."

Biologist Stephen Jay Gould illuminated another side of intelligence: "Really bright people tend to be very modest in some overall cosmic sense, because they know how intensely ignorant we are about everything."

In 1776 economist Adam Smith saw clearly the effects of the industrial revolution on the human soul: "The man whose life is spent in performing a few simple operations of which the effects too are, perhaps, always the same or very nearly the same has no occasion to exert his understanding, or to exercise his invention. He generally becomes as stupid and ignorant as it is possible for a human creature to become."

In *Fiddler on the Roof*, the wise but poor Tevye observes: "If you're rich enough, no one will call you stupid."

The final word, but only for now, comes from an anonymous poem written in 1929 that makes the case for the equivocal nature of self-awareness: "See the happy moron. He doesn't give a damn. I wish I were a moron—my God, perhaps I am."

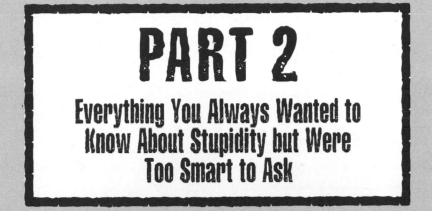

PART 2

Everything You Always Wanted to Know About Stupidity but Were Too Smart to Ask

Everything You Always Wanted to Know About Stupidity but Were Too Smart to Ask

Exactly how stupid are we?

We'll never know because we're exactly too stupid to figure it out. Unfortunately, we're just intelligent enough never to stop wondering about it.

Isn't intelligence the culminating achievement of nature?

If it were an achievement. But accidents don't count to our credit.

Nature has no long-range goals, no mission statements, no preference policies. Intelligence, the ability to fly, or a talent for chewing your way through dirt, it's all the same to nature—the coordination of millions of unrelated events running wild on an overoxygenated planet.

"There are six thousand species of mammals, none of which—outside the order of primates—is threatening to become a powerfully conscious species," biologist Stephen Jay Gould points out in the annoying manner of someone who knows what he's talking about.

"If intelligence was meant to be, you'd think it would have evolved convergently in lots of other lineages. It's just a weird invention that developed in one odd species living on the African savannas a couple of million years ago."

Who's dumber: primitive people or us?

Primitive people solved their problems. The solutions to the problems of civilized people only create more complex problems. We're short-term thinkers in a world of long-term consequences.

Primitive people were short-term thinkers too. But they lived in a short-term world.

Find food and survive pretty much encompassed the mental requirements of the ancient nomads, before they became attendants to the seed.

When these hunters, and their sidekicks the gatherers, came upon a hill, they went around it. They moved on with their lives.

We see a hill: We clear-cut it, strip-mine it, zone it, build a shopping mall on it. Later we moan about deforestation, soil erosion, air pollution, lousy shopping.

Then we try to move on through the twelve-step process of recovering hilloholics.

When primitive people got cold, they built a fire. We build atomic power plants.

Despite evidence to the contrary, we think we're more intelligent than our primitive ancestors. Still, the odds remain high that civilization's only lasting achievement will be the destruction of civilization.

Won't technology save us?

Science, the style of thinking practiced by people who are good at passing tests, is a complex machine for the production of poisons that nature could not produce in sufficient quantities herself.

Science examines our efforts to destroy the air, water, land, and everything that moves upon it, and devises clever ways to measure how we're doing.

Smart people might say: We're poisoning ourselves. Let's stop.

Scientists say: We're poisoning ourselves 4.78 percent less this year than we were doing last year. Let's issue a press release.

Is intelligence an independent attribute, or does it depend on what school you went to?

In 1982 two psychologists had a little fun, which in itself is news. They retyped, word for word, articles written by psychologists from Harvard, Princeton, and other top universities.

Well, they probably had their secretaries retype the articles. Or their grad students.

They changed the authors' names and institutions to colleges of less prestige, then resubmitted the articles to the same journals that had already published them.

Eight of the twelve articles were rejected as being not up to publication standards.

What would it be like if we were all smart?

Finland.

Every Sunday, we'd watch the National Curling League. Taco Bell would sell instant muesli. We'd have traffic jams on the bike paths to work each morning. Rival gangs of teenagers would hang out on street corners offering contrasting views on Hegelian philosophy in monotonal exhortations of blank verse.

Why are we so stupid?

We have to be. Nature designed us this way, the same way she designed gazelles to be quick and tigers to be terrifying.

If people weren't stupid, there goes cigarettes and triple bacon cheeseburgers, not to mention designer water and Brooklyn.

Civilization depends on masses of people making decisions that smart individuals thinking for themselves would never make.

Without dumb habits, we would all be living with the Amish, and the world would be run by people with sensible shoes. We'd go see big summer movies like *Nonlethal Tool, Live Easily,* and *Titanic Lessons in Proper Boat Safety.*

Are smart people dumber than stupid people?

The Chernobyl disaster in 1986, in which a Ukrainian nuclear reactor attempted to turn Europe into the ultimate New Jersey, was not a dumb error committed by dumb people.

It was a dumb error committed by smart people.

Operators ignored safety regulations under the theory that the reactor wouldn't explode because it hadn't exploded before.

Chernobyl's technicians frequently violated safety rules because they knew the rules had some built-in flexibility. Without this systematic stretch, the reactors would explode the second someone crossed the safety line.

So they played with the leeway and lost.

Dumb operators would have stuck with the rules. They wouldn't have been smart enough to think that the rules could cut them some slack.

Ask any army officer if he'd rather fight a battle with a squad of dumb soldiers or smart ones.

Smart soldiers will question orders because they know how often the orders are stupid and who's going to pay for bad decisions. Those confrontations are fine for movie dramatics, but a great way to get your squad shot to pieces in an actual firefight.

Dumb soldiers will follow orders to their death because they think they have to.

In the Civil War battle of Fredericksburg, wave after wave of Union soldiers charged across an open field and were mowed down by Confederates firing in safety from behind stone walls.

Some twelve thousand Union soldiers fell in those charges before the Rebel line was breached. You'd never find twelve thousand smart soldiers to follow those orders.

Scientists set up systems, like atomic reactors, that are far more intricate and unclear than operators can handle. We are clever enough to devise technology we're not intelligent enough to use.

We think we're as smart as our systems. We're not. Chernobyl wasn't an accident. It was an inevitability.

At least we learned our lesson from Chernobyl: Be careful; work smarter from now on.

Yeah, right.

Take the chain reaction set off by mistake in a Japanese nuclear fuel plant in 1999. Human error again. Fuel workers mishandled the enriched uranium they were processing and set off a chain reaction, resulting in radiation leakage that could have been disastrous.

Company execs blamed the uranium handlers, labeling them blunderers who took shortcuts so they could get off work early.

But these were veteran uranium workers, trained, aware of proper safety procedures. Why did they take shortcuts?

Because they could, same as Chernobyl.

Investigators accused company execs of encouraging workers to ignore correct procedures in order to speed up production.

It was Japan's sixth nuclear-handling accident in three years.

Is there any way our foreign policy could be more idiotic?
Apparently not, or our politicians would be voting it into effect right now.

American national policy since World War II has been based

on the School-Yard Bully theory of diplomacy: If you know we can beat you up, you won't force us to do it.

This approach might work if other countries weren't run by leaders as dumb as ours, people who base their national policies on the Oh Yeah? theory of government. When they meet up with a school-yard bully, they figure they'd better test him out to see if he's as tough as he says he is.

Our military and CIA carry out our bully policy around the world through a simple strategy: If we kill you now, we won't have to kill you later.

Which is the smarter choice: draft beer or Genuine Draft Beer?

Seems like a question of taste rather than of intelligence. But nothing is simple in an age where your share of the advertising costs more than your share of the beer.

Real draft beer is better if you like good beer. Genuine Draft Beer is better if you want to marvel at how marketers can make millions by continually lowering the bottom of the barrel we live in.

Draft beer comes from a barrel. You hold the glass up to the tap, and the beer falls out. Makes for better beer, as any English pubster can explain, if you're buying.

Genuine Draft Beer comes in bottles or cans, the opposite of draft beer. They can legally call nondraft beer draft beer by the international law that states: If you can make big money out of a lie, go ahead.

First, the boss says: Let's go for quality—as long as it doesn't cost more, take more time, or drag me away from my golf game.

Then the marketing masters step in and make the beer better through the use of better words.

And sometimes pictures.

Particularly pictures of sexy young women, who if they actually drank the nondraft draft beer would turn into fat blowsy women, the kind men drink beer to forget.

Are hard workers dumber than bums?

Consider the bum: no money, no place to sleep, no food, no lovers, no season tickets, no prospects. Yet there must be something attractive about the proposition, or so many people wouldn't be entering the profession.

There is a lure: no work.

That's the only advantage a bum life has to offer—and it's enough.

As the rest of us rush off to work too fast every morning, fight the traffic, get steamed by coworkers who don't do their share and bosses who know less than the idiots who had the job before them; as we put in too much time making the owners rich, only to fight the traffic to get back home, only to do it all over again the next day—they don't.

Not working seems to balance out all the alleged benefits that work provides.

Has it always been the worker vs. the shirker? Let's trace the progress of the career man.

Prior to civilization, there were unlimited opportunities for all men, women, and children to work. The job was called survival.

The basic job skills: Find something to eat; keep warm; don't get hit on the head with a rock.

Sounds simple enough. But all jobs have drawbacks: bosses, saber-toothed tigers, cubicle psychology, the tendency of other people in your field to look for the same warmth or the same food to kill rather than share.

Still, compared to the job insecurities that comprise civilization, those were the good old days.

Because people followed where dinner led, companies remained small and competitive, clan-sized operations. There were no prehistoric corporations insisting that we wear the badger tie with the mammoth skin suit on the daily hunt.

Civilization brought with it the first curse of mankind: farming.

Farming was hard work and a slow way to produce dinner; although once it did, it also produced lunch and breakfast.

The working farmer was obligated to stay in one place, as anchored to the cubicle of his farm as we are to our desks.

Stationary dinners gave rise to the second curse of the working class: the nonworking class.

These people recognized early on that there was no point in everyone doing the same hard work if someone else was going to do the hard work anyway.

They became kings, priests, and thieves, the nonworking class.

Thieves led to defense. Defense led to offense. Offense led to armies. Armies led to bigger armies. Bigger armies led to generals. Generals led to corporations, and that's how we got into the mess we're in today.

That fantastic structure of nonwork rests on the back of the little turtle down at the bottom of the stack: the Yertle worker. The cannon fodder, mill fodder, PC fodder.

The worker always gives more than he gets to the company he works for. If he got more than he gave, he wouldn't be a worker. He'd be the boss.

Meanwhile, the bum contemplates our folly without worrying that he will be down-sized. He will not be replaced by someone half his age willing to be a bum for half the pickings.

The bum has the one thing workers can never have: job security.

But surely we're smarter than we used to be?
Regular people in the tenth century could muddle through their entire lives without meeting a smart person. They never felt dumb by comparison.

Perhaps they couldn't figure how to shut out the drafts in the winter or grow enough turnips to give themselves that well-fed feeling, but neither could anyone else they knew.

To them, the world was just a drafty place with insufficient turnips.

They knew no one who wore Gore-Tex while they shivered damply, or who dined at five-star restaurants while they ate at Turnip King.

Now we live in the green age of jealousy. We're envious of movie stars who have sexier lovers than we do, software kings who have more money, and politicians who get away with better lies than we would dare tell at the corner bar.

People who score 550 on their college entrance exams feel they're smart enough. They'll be going to the same school as the brains they made fun of in high school.

They don't get it. They're being let into college so they can finance the education of the smart kids. Colleges need their tuition money so they can give scholarships to the brains.

If they only let smart kids into college, America would be able to get by with a half dozen universities. The rest of the schools could open NFL franchises.

What do those 550 scorers learn in college? How to throw keggers without throwing up.

The lowest score anyone can get on an SAT is 200. Why not zero? Because the college board doesn't want people to think they have zero intelligence.

Who is smarter: your boss or you?

You are.

The boss has money, the power and perks, the authority to act like he knows what he's doing when he's actually wondering how long till people find him out. He's got membership in the rich guys' club, where they sit around trying to top one another with ways to torture employees in the name of human resource development.

But the bosses don't have the brains.

We can prove that in three ways:

1. During the boss's absence, any secretary in the world could fill in and do the job better. But no boss could do their secretary's work.

2. On the average, 60,000 Americans have the good sense to quit their lousy jobs every day. But bosses only have enough sense to fire 12,000 people a day. Bosses are too dumb to fire 48,000 people who hate their jobs and are getting ready to prove it.

3. If your boss was smarter than you, he'd make sure you liked him. Only stupid bosses create resentful employees.

But bosses don't care about being liked because they are the new royalty. The goal of this elite is not to make a better product, or a better world, or even a more profitable company. Their goal is to make the process so complex that only they can operate it.

It's like basketball. You may be the best player at the Y on Saturday morning, hitting a high percentage of your shots, playing smart D. When you see film from the NBA as the game was played forty years ago, you say to yourself, "Man, they were slow and clunky back then. I could play better than that."

Probably you could. But the game has been raised to such a

complexity of height, speed, and agility that you would be run off the court, even by the Los Angeles Clippers.

That's why those arrogant, loafing players make millions. They have successfully specialized the game to the point where only they can play it.

The elite are doing the same thing to us everywhere.

Eventually, we'll all be asking them, "You want fries with that?"

We've been stupid for so long, can we still find original ways to do something dumb?

Absolutely. We're doing it all the time.

In southern California, a man gazing through a telescope from his house overlooking the beach spotted a pink Corvette on the sand. The car was about to be swamped by waves from the incoming tide. Worried that someone might be incapacitated inside the car, he called the police.

The cops couldn't find a car on the beach—pink, Corvette, or otherwise.

When they went up the bluff to the man's house and looked through his telescope, they figured out what the man couldn't: He had the scope trained on a toy car a kid had left in the sand.

Who's dumber, men or women?

Only men are dumb enough to ask that question.

Women simply look at what men have achieved with their dominion over the world and know there's no way they could have messed it up as badly.

Still, if women are so much smarter than men, why haven't they taken over?

Perhaps the answer is hidden in this separation statistic: After divorce, 58 percent of the men say they're happier; but 85 percent of the women say they're happier.

Are religious people smarter than the nonreligious?

Most religions agree upon the worship of a supreme God who created the universe and demands of His people high moral standards of behavior.

In the name of this one God and our high moral standards, the devout of all religions have slaughtered one another for centuries.

Everyone calls for this spiral of slaughter to stop in the name of God.

It never stops.

Peace is a temporary cease-fire during which the various sides reload.

How can we account for this persistence in the endless slaughter of the children of God in the name of a loving God who demands the end of slaughter?

Comfortably, it turns out.

It's the difference between the true religion of the one God fighting against the evil heathens of the false god.

Ours is the former. Theirs is the latter.

It's true throughout history and from all sides toward the middle. We are all someone else's heretic.

Is there a one-religion race in another galaxy, where aliens know God and celebrate the universe in some way other than trying to destroy it?

Not if God made them like us.

Is the lottery the dumbest possible way to get rid of excess money?

No, we'll invent something dumber as soon as the Bright Boys get through with their research.

Meanwhile, lotteries combine two of our most popular mental weaknesses: gambling and advertising.

Does every state lure the gambling-positives with the same slogan logic: "You can't win if you don't play"?

As with most advertising, you'd be better off betting against the pitch. The only truth about the lottery is that you can't lose if you don't play.

Odds on winning big in the lottery are so bad you'd be better off taking all the money you have, putting it in a sock, giving that sock to the first stranger you meet on the street, and saying, "Here, if by some chance you make $10 million with this money, find me and give me $1 million, okay?"

You don't even have to be good at math to know you can't win the lottery. The state lottery is run by the government. When was the last time you beat the government at anything?

If you could make money through the lottery, then rich people would play and they don't. They fly off to Vegas, where they also don't make money, but at least are made to feel important. When was the last time the mini-mart made you feel important for blowing the milk money on a few lottery tickets?

Who's dumber, the judges or the attorneys?

We leave that tough call to Judge Thurman Arnold, who resigned from the U.S. court of appeals and returned to private practice, saying, "I'd rather have to talk to a bunch of damn fools than listen to them."

Is it a smart idea to take advice?

Here's the only advice you should ever take: Don't ever take advice.

Sounds like advice, but it's not advice. That's a paradox, and the whole point of a paradox is that you can't follow it.

Actually, there could be some advice worth taking. Unfortunately, it's not the kind people give out.

Nearly everyone who knows what they're doing keeps it to themselves. If they shared it, then everyone would know what they knew and it wouldn't work anymore.

Who's smarter: dumb beasts or dumb men?

President John Tyler buried his favorite horse with these words inscribed on the tombstone: "Here lies the body of my good horse, the General. For 20 years he bore me around the circuit of my practice and in all that time he never made a blunder. Would that his master could say the same!"

People frequently honor their laudable pets and other beasts of our burdens. No animal has left an epitaph for a man.

Is it smarter to try try again or quit while you're ahead?

When we say quit while you're ahead, we really mean quit while you're behind but not by too much.

In reality you're never ahead. All life is 6–5 against, as Damon Runyon once pointed out. That's why realists invented the moral victory and the close one, in hopes of slowing down the rate of failure.

However, if you try try again, you're more likely to sink deeper by finding new ways to lose than if you had quit when you weren't too far behind. There are always more ways to lose than to win.

There is one strategy that can bring victory: Encourage others to try try again, then observe their failures.

When it's your time to step up, you will know what to avoid and have a better chance to get ahead early, at which time you should offer your opponents a chance for a moral victory, so they will feel good about quitting while they're not too far behind.

When you leave defeated opponents happy, they are more likely to accept a close defeat next time.

Finding enough people who are satisfied with moral victories is how you get on a winning streak.

Who's dumber: a moron or an idiot?

The moron is the guy who speeds past you recklessly on the right, while the idiot is the guy in front of you going too slow, forcing you to pass him on the right.

Or is it the other way around?

We have become so accustomed to thinking of idiots and morons as everyone who gets in our way that we forget that they were once technical terms.

The idiot was an adult who had the brains of a three-year-old kid. The moron was doing much better; he had the brains of an eight-year-old.

Look around you. If you find enough morons with the brains of eight-year-olds, you're probably living in a college town.

What about Harvard and Stanford? Doesn't get much smarter than that, does it?

Or so they'd have us believe.

As an experiment, we sent the following letter to one hundred Harvard professors and one hundred Stanford professors:

"I'm writing a book about stupidity/intelligence and thought you might like to participate by answering the following question:

What's the stupidest thing you've done?

My theory is that really intelligent people are exceptional in their dumb moments also."

We got back the following responses:

Harvard: 2

Stanford: 1

From Harvard professor J. H. H. Weiler came this reply: "Answering this E-mail would be way up on the list."

From Stanford professor Tom Wasow:

"In 1982 I was invited to give a talk to the International Congress of Linguists in Tokyo. I also agreed to give several other talks at Japanese universities.

"The night before I was to leave, my wife asked if I needed a visa for Japan. I was certain I didn't.

"The next day, when I checked in at the airport, the clerk informed me that I couldn't board because I had no visa. She told me I had to get to the Japanese consulate in San Francisco that afternoon (it was Friday, and the consulate would be closed over the weekend) and convince them to give me an expedited visa.

"Since I would miss my flight, I would also have to go to the airline office and rebook. On reflection, I decided that the chances of being able to accomplish all this in one afternoon were so slim that I should give up on the whole trip.

"I walked out of the terminal in a daze and got on the bus. When the bus reached the freeway, it turned north (toward San Francisco), not south (toward my home in Palo Alto) as I had expected.

"Once in San Francisco, I figured I might as well see whether I could get the visa and the ticket changed. Much to my surprise, I was able to do so that afternoon, and I made it to Japan a day late.

"This incident could be taken as illustrating one thing about my life that has been extraordinary: my luck. Here I did two really stupid things (not getting a visa and taking the wrong bus), and they more or less canceled each other out!"

From Harvard professor Nikolaas J. van der Merwe:

"I grew up in South Africa and have done fieldwork on most continents. One colleague has described me as the best person to have in a nasty spot in a foreign place, but not everybody will agree. However, I am an instrument-rated pilot, have cruised the upper Amazon and Orinoco (and Okavango swamps) in dugout canoes, and know from experience which vehicles can cross Africa from north to south with a reasonable chance of success (hardbody Land Cruiser, Hi-lux 4WD, Land Rover 109).

"So here I am living in a house hidden in the trees near Concord, Massachusetts. My mailbox is a quarter mile away, and I have to drive across the neighbors' land to get there.

"One Sunday morning last winter, I put the coffee on, and went down the driveway to pick up the *New York Times*. This involved getting in my dressing gown, shoes untied, into the four-wheel-drive Mazda pickup.

"At the mailbox, I find the *Times* lying on the ground, so I turn the pickup around in the road and stop next to the paper, headed back up the driveway. I open the door and lean out to pick up the paper, *with my feet on the clutch and brake.*

"I fall out the door. The pickup, its engine on fast idle in the cold, takes off by itself. It takes down about fifty feet of my neighbors' fence, then heads across their lawn and ends up in their stream, its engine stalled.

"Meanwhile, I'm running after the vehicle, but the wet earth near the stream sucks my shoes off. Eventually, I find my shoes and get in the vehicle.

"At this point, the four-wheel-drive becomes properly useful for the first time in its life, and I pull out of there, pick up the paper, and go home.

"I had to explain the problem to the neighbors. That was okay; money fixed the damage. But my field-working colleagues were not nearly so accepting. *You had your feet where?*"

Apparently, 197 other learned professors at these top universities have never done anything stupid. Or hope we'll believe that.

Why are people who have careers invested in intelligence afraid to admit their foibles, follies, and failures? Do they worry that if we think they're human, it will devalue their brain stock, as the rich fret over money when they already have enough?

This experiment wasn't meant to embarrass the few professors who participated, or even those many who participated by not participating.

The confessions of the brave are intended to comfort the rest of us with the realization that intelligence and stupidity are not mutually exclusive but fully compatible.

If the brightest among us can pull dumb stunts, then the rest of us shouldn't be so quick to kick ourselves for our own screwups.

Instead, we should think about applying for teaching positions at Stanford and Harvard.

Is it smarter to tell people how you really feel, or to keep it to yourself?

When people say, "Tell me how you feel," what they really mean is, "Sit still while I tell you how I really feel."

Sharing your innermost thoughts is only smart if you're in a college psych class and are trying to turn it into a rap session so you can get a good grade without having to write another term paper.

Feelings are like body odors. Everyone has them, but we'd rather you covered yours up.

Whining, however, makes a lot of sense.

Moaning and groaning are strategies that fit almost every occasion. Unlike feelings, complaining has a definite upside: The more you whine about how terrible everything is, the longer God lets you live because He sees that you get it.

In the face of so much evidence to the contrary, why do we insist that we're smart?

We need to feel smart because it makes us feel safe, as if we will have the wits necessary to deal with life's daily dangers.

Despite childproof caps on our medicine and insurance agents with giant soft hands, we are not safe from a world with more dinks than caresses.

If we did not feel smart enough to cope with assistant managers, ozone depletion, and phone solicitors, civilization as we want to know it would crimble, which is what happens when something isn't even smart enough to crumble.

A sense of intelligence works as a security blanket. If we were smarter, we'd realize that there is no security, that civilization is like a bus shelter: It may keep you dry in the rain, but you can't stay there forever.

In fact, we're only intelligent enough to fool the only people we have to fool: ourselves.

We live in a complex world. Isn't complexity a sign of intelligence?

All the great religions and spiritual traditions of the world guide us down the path of simplicity. Many of them state quite clearly that you cannot know enlightenment until you rid yourself of all worldly obsessions. Yes, that includes your remote control.

Aren't you confusing wisdom with intelligence?
Only a society without wisdom would insist on its intelligence.

So it's smart to be wise?
Not if you work for a living.

Corporations prefer people who are good at pushing buttons and having their buttons pushed.

Businesses do not want their employees pursuing wisdom, unless the pursuit of wisdom is listed in the goals and practices section of their mission statement, probably subgoal 47.3 (see your supervisor for details).

Then there are companies that pursue wisdom?
There are companies that pursue wisdom consultants because they already have run through management consultants, time-utilization consultants, problem-solving consultants, and even consultant-coordinating consultants.

They turn to wisdom consultants if they have funds left over in their consultant budget, because they realize that if they turn the extra money back into the company's general fund, they will get less funding in next year's budget.

But don't these consultants teach wisdom?
You cannot teach wisdom. You can only learn it.

Any coach can tell you how to hit a baseball. But you will never get a hit until you step up to the plate and start swinging for yourself.

No one likes living in overcrowded cities, yet millions do it in the world's densest: Manila, Shanghai, Cairo, Paris, Bombay. Why aren't they smart enough to move?
They're waiting for everyone else to smarten up and move out. Then their cities won't be so unlivable.

Paris, ah, the City of Lights. It's such a beautiful city, surely we can jam another million people in there.

But won't that make it miserable for everyone?

Not if we keep telling them: Paris, ah, the City of Lights.

In this way we counter any smart move we make simply by making too many of them. There's nothing good we can't dumb down.

Overpopulation is not just a global problem. It's a marketing solution.

Was America founded by the brains or the jerks?
The first European who stumbled upon America thought he'd found India, so we didn't get off to a great start.

The next group of laterally mobile Europeans were called explorers because no one erects statues to looters, which is an Indian word for "here come those lost guys in their big ships to steal anything we haven't nailed down, and isn't it a shame we didn't invent nails before they got here?"

The natives—smart and stupid—had been living quietly in America (or Our Place, as they mistakenly called it back then), not needing nails to deal with one another.

They psychically floated back to Europe the notion that the earth was flat in hopes of keeping the Europeans from falling into their laps.

Didn't work. The quest for loot was simply too strong. The explorers were willing to risk falling off the end of the world because that was still better than being poor in Europe.

Looting is a sign of intelligence, recognizing that a system of governance isn't strong enough to stop looters, in which case the looters are going to become the new system of governance, so you might as well get what you can, or they're going to erect a statue to the next guy.

These early looters took their stolen wealth back to Europe because the natives had neglected to set up shopping malls in America.

Returning to Europe was not a sign of intelligence, as rent was higher and very few looters were able to keep their loot once they got back, where they found that even smarter looters were waiting for their return. But they had to go back to the Old World because at the time there was simply nothing to buy in the new one.

If there had been, the early explorers would have stayed, everyone in Europe would have assumed they'd fallen off the edge of the world, and Americans would now be eating at McGeronimo's and watching the NLF (National Lacrosse Federation) on the tube every Sunday instead of the NFL.

The next group to come to America were our four fathers: the British, the Spanish, the French, and the Miscellaneous.

These people were definitely brains because they devised a more efficient method of looting: Stay in the New World and steal its resources without giving the stay-at-home looters a share. The colonial spin doctors called this business theory the American Revolution.

The natives were too smart to do all the back-breaking work this kind of strip-mining and deforestation required because they'd been getting along just fine without doing it.

So the bosses had to import a labor pool, which they did by persecuting the poor of Europe, in an attempt to make their lives so miserable that they'd leave.

This plan had limited success. Turned out that many poor people were used to being miserable and preferred to be persecuted in their own hometowns, rather than drown on the way to America.

When the bosses couldn't get enough European poor to exploit the resources of America, they kidnapped a work force from Africa and gave them minimum-wage jobs in America, the minimum wage being a plate of bad food a day.

Now that slavery has been abolished, the minimum wage for lousy jobs is just enough money to buy a plate of bad food a day.

So the answer is, America was settled by brains and jerks and plenty of them.

What's the smart thing to do about crime?

There are thousands of armed robberies in the United States every year. This field of work is getting so crowded that armed robbers are often forced to rob one another.

In Iceland there has been only one armed robbery in the country's history.

We need to educate America's armed robbers so they grow smart enough to move to Iceland, where there's no competition.

Is it stupid to keep a gun in the house?

Depends. Were you also planning to keep bullets?

Three Americans are killed by guns in the house every day. That's three houses today where people now realize they would have been smarter to get rid of their guns.

On the other foot, one American a day dies in bathtub accidents. So we would be smart to get rid of baths too.

Is it smarter to marry for love or for money?
Some of America's native tribes had a smart system: Anyone rich and powerful was forbidden to marry anyone from another rich family. Instead, the rich had to marry someone from a poor family.

Using that system, there was no tribal CEO making one thousand times what everyone else made, and people at the bottom knew they weren't going to stay there forever.

These sensible tribes were wiped out by Europeans, who came to America preaching freedom, which they achieved by annihilating everyone else.

The Europeans had a system of marriage that has become the world standard: The rich and powerful can marry anyone they want. The poor and powerless can marry anyone the rich don't want.

Back to you.

If you marry for love, your condition can be cured. People who are in love eventually won't be.

Therefore, it's smarter to marry for money, as long as you remember the first rule of successful prostitutes: Get the money up front.

As surely as you marry for money, you will be traded in for the same reason. Being rich means never having to say: "Can I afford the new model, the one with the shinier gadgets?"

While marrying for money is smarter than marrying for love, it's not much smarter. If you marry for love, you're doomed to fall out of love. If you marry for money, you're doomed to be kicked out.

There must be a smarter system, and there is—because you can't get divorced unless you get married first.

Without marriage, you can fall in love as much as you want and not worry about whether this is the one person you should marry. There is no one you should marry, only someone you do marry.

If the person you're in love with insists on getting married, stall like crazy. Stalling is a strategy of intelligence, a prime way to solve problems. Eventually, you'll fall out of love, and the question will become moot.

As for money, if you're so smart, don't marry for it. Go out and get some of your own. Then you'll know what it's like to have someone want to marry you for your money.

Should you try to improve yourself? Or are self-help programs just a waste of time?
Everything is a waste of time.

Half a million Americans a year try cosmetic surgery to improve their looks.

Look around you. You won't see half a million better-looking people each year.

Can dumb people still enjoy life?
You have to be dumb to enjoy life. If you get too smart, you see the flaws in the plan.

Death, that's a big one, gets in the way of any kind of sustained fun.

Disease, injury, depression, oppression, repression, regression, obsession, and group sessions—all flaws in the plan of life, which when originally designed was: Run free; find pleasure.

You don't need intelligence for that.

Intelligence will always impede enjoyment because the brain would rather be analyzing: What is enjoyment? What is true enjoyment? How can I tell if I'm really enjoying myself, or only think I'm enjoying myself? What do I mean by enjoyment? What do I mean by life? What do I mean by what do I mean?

Meanwhile, that dumb jerk next door is riding his muscle car across someone's meadow with his arm around some bunny babe, and his brain is going right along with his arm.

Are people growing smarter or dumber?

Smart people are getting smarter, which causes the rest of us to get dumber by comparison. As the bar gets raised higher, we're turning into a nation of limbo brains.

Smart people used to swallow hemlock for the good of the idiots in society. They used to let morons burn them at the stake, failing to convince the fire-happy dummies that just because they could think it didn't make them heretics.

Then smart people wised up. They packed us into overcrowded cities so we would be more reluctant to start bonfires.

They convinced us to pay for their scholarships to Stanford and MIT, so they could make easy livings as engineers and lawyers.

They run the corporations that run the world. They are no longer heretics because they now control the computer program that controls the heretic-labeling apparatus.

How did the smart ones turn the tables on us, transforming themselves from the persecuted into the princes of the world?

They learned the art of pacification.

People who are not too bright are generally contented when left alone in an emotionally neutral muddle. The smart ones learned how to mass-produce muddle the way Henry Ford mass-produced cheap cars.

In the Dark Ages, the world's princes pacified the none-too-bright by slaughtering them. With the Enlightenment, the smart ones who couldn't manage slaughter effectively came up with better diversions: gadgets.

They pacify us with VCRs and SUVs, with Prozac and the Internet, with spectator sports and shopping malls.

Big Dumb Lunks used to take pleasure in crushing the necks of smart guys. Now BDLs take pleasure in using their remote controls to channel surf. TV turns a BDL's hovel into a realm, and the remote gives him control of that magic kingdom, the most controllable realm he'll ever get his hands on.

Hands busy massaging buttons won't be crushing scrawny necks.

Now and then Big Dumb Lunks rise up and need to hit something. So the smart ones have invented ways to neutralize their muscle by killing them from a distance, where strength and courage are no longer required.

Back in sword days, the world was ruled by stout shoulders and big biceps, while smart weaklings cowered in the corner calculating the varying degrees of unfairness in approaching death.

But the head brains got revenge by learning how to slaughter muscle heads by the thousands with the push of a button. They didn't actually need a button. Could have used a lever. But levers require a biceps.

As for evolution of the intelligence of Big Dumb Lunks, it's carefully monitored by the brains. Anytime they see the threat of a breakout, they release another gadget to pacify the restless.

We get compact disc players, mobile phones, Net-surfing computers—all issued with user guides that undermine the efforts of BDLs to rise up by proving to them that they'll never understand how anything works. They'll have to be satisfied to sit back and push the buttons.

As soon as the brains invent a button that gives instant orgasms, the BDLs will never rise up out of their La-Z-Boys again.

Who's smarter, Democrats or Republicans?

Democrats know the rich won't vote for them, except for confused movie stars. Republicans know the poor won't vote for them, except for one guy in Cleveland who hasn't figured it out yet.

So they both work the middle.

The Republicans try to convince the middle that unless they have Republicans in office, the Democrats will turn them into poor people; while the Democrats try to convince the middle that no one will turn them into rich people, ever.

Therefore, the only intelligent politicians—Democrat or Republican—are the ones who lose the election. Once they're out of office, they'll leave you alone, and that's about as intelligent a result as we can ask for.

Doesn't coping with a difficult world imply intelligence?

Cavemen didn't have day planners. Or lawyers.

You might think that makes us smarter—dealing with incredibly complex lives day after day.

But barbarians didn't have therapists either. No one thought of encouraging Attila the Hun to get in touch with his feelings. Attila and the Huns expressed themselves all too clearly.

Because we can operate computers and negotiate the labyrinth of self-improvement, we assume that takes superior brains.

You think it was easy to operate a horde of screaming Huns so you could conquer half the world?

We're still screaming like barbarians as we charge down the circuits of our control chips and master complex ways to simplify our lives so that we can feel good about ourselves from 2:40 to 3:05 every other Thursday.

Knowing which buttons to push doesn't make us smart. It just makes us better at pushing buttons.

What's the stupidest thing mankind has done to itself?
Invent guns and use them. Guns made killers out of losers.

Before guns, when you wanted to kill someone you had to get within counterstrike range, which required courage, skill, strength, and luck.

Guns changed the basic premise of killing from Thou shalt kill if thou can, to If you can reach them from farther away than they can reach you, then you can kill them before they kill you.

Now we have pilots who sit a mile up in the sky and kill thousands of people they never see, then go home and have dinner that was cooked in a factory ten thousand miles away, get up in the morning, and kill a few more thousand faceless people who will soon have no faces.

Human beings can see problems coming and figure out ways to solve a crisis before it strikes. Doesn't this unique predictive intelligence make us special?
In the same way that having long necks makes giraffes special. Everyone stares at us, but that doesn't mean we're going to beat the odds in the long run.

For all our abilities to analyze and prepare for disasters, we have equal talents for misanalyzing.

We take disaster-aversion maneuvers that shift us directly into the path of a worse disaster. We create new crises that never would have come about if we hadn't been trying to preempt the crisis we thought was coming.

The best analytical minds of the early 1900s assured us that if we banded together and defeated Germany in World War I, we would put an end to war.

This predictive, crisis-aversion strategy succeeded in creating an even more destructive war twenty-five years later.

When we read in the Bible that the meek shall inherit the earth, we, in our inexhaustible vanity, assume that we're the meek, even though the human race is the most arrogant killer the life force has ever devised.

The truly meek, who will inherit the earth by surviving us, cannot predict the future and have no need to. Look under your heel. They scurry in the dark and are surprisingly hard to stomp out.

If cockroaches could laugh, or had any reason to, they would be laughing at us.

But the human race has produced Plato, Shakespeare, Emerson. How can you say we're not smart?

Emerson? Didn't he play for the Red Sox? Good trivia question, man. How many points did we score?

Consider that 99.9 percent of the race that produced these great thinkers have never heard of them, read their writings, or thought about their ideas. Yet they manage to live their existences of brutish pain and brutish pleasure without having any reason to seek the advice of philosophically committed nonbrutes.

If the greatest minds the human race has produced serve any purpose, it's to distract teenagers with college. Without college, students would be forced into the cold world, where they'd suffer like their parents, who are too busy thinking that no matter how hard they work they can't keep up, to worry about whether they're heeding the timeless wisdom of Plato or the enlightened advice of Emerson.

Exactly how did Einstein make a living and does he have any good stock tips? If Plato had pondered the realities of the investment portfolio, then he would have been of some worth to his fellow human beings.

Are stupid people stupid? Or just differently intelligent?
While our society pays lip service to the notion of equality, lip service is generally as far as anyone in power cares to go. There is no promise of equality of brains.

However, stupid people are almost as smart as smart people, but that's only because smart people aren't as smart as they think they are.

Fortunately, stupid money is just as good as smart money. Politicians and marketers assume they can separate stupid people from their money easier than they can smart people, which is easy enough.

Plenty of political careers have been built around cornering the stupid vote and letting the brains fume over lost opportunities. Advertising is at its most effective when campaigns are pitched to the stupid psychographic segment of the buying public.

Remember that commercial about the guy so dumb he has to write his shopping list—he wants a soda—on the back of his hand because he gets so dazzled by the merchandise that he always forgets what he went into the mini-mart for?

Then, uh oh, he sticks his hand in the cold soda barrel and the ink washes off. Now he's stuck. But not to worry. He'll feel right at home in our store.

Are stupid people going to ruin it for the rest of us?
Not a chance. Smart people will.

Stupid people should take comfort in their moral superiority because nearly all of the really horrendous travesties throughout history were perpetrated by smart people.

It takes superior brainpower to build atomic bombs that can destroy everyone we're mad at, along with everyone we like and everyone we've never met, then decide that that's not enough, we need variety in our self-annihilative devices, so let's also design chemical and biological weapons that can do the same job, only leaving behind, when all the humans get radiated into the next plane of existence, less of a charred mess, because it's well known that cockroaches do not care to sweep up.

If dumb people wanted to destroy the human race, they'd grab a brick and go around hitting everyone over the head, which would take several centuries to get the job done.

Smart people can wrap it up in a couple of hours. Intelligence may turn out to be nothing but efficiency attached to motivation.

How can I tell if I'm stupid?
You can't.

If you are stupid, then you're too dumb to know it.

If you're smart, then you are no doubt smart enough to doubt yourself.

When your mother says, "What a smart boy you are," ask for a second opinion. She'd probably say the same thing if you were a blabbering idiot, which you may be for all you know, since it's impossible to know.

You certainly can't trust the experts. If they say you're stupid, they may be too stupid themselves to make the call.

If they say you're smart, they may be lying. That's what smart people do. If someone tells you you're smart, hang on to your wallet.

Colleges are the perfect example of the smart-telling strategy. Each year thousands of teenagers receive letters like this:

"You are one of the chosen few smart enough to be admitted to our college. Please send $40,000 to cover your book deposit for the first semester."

How smart are people who pay $40,000 a year to get an education that will qualify them for jobs that command a salary of $20,000 a year?

If I'm stupid, should I feel bad about it?
Absolutely not.

Being stupid shares many characteristics with being in love, primarily that you never have to say you're sorry. Also five years later, you will wonder how you ever could have been that dumb.

The friar never apologized for coming up with the brilliant idea of having Juliet pretend to be dead so Romeo would then kill himself and she would wake up and kill herself too—and neither should you.

Aren't prisons full of stupid criminals?
Half right. You'll find two kinds of popular criminals populating our prisons: the stupid and the unlucky.

Prison wardens typically divide inmates into the dangerous and the slightly less dangerous. Enlightened prison wardens divide them into smoking and nonsmoking sections.

They're all missing the point. Prisons should be divided into a stupid section and an unlucky section.

When stupid and unlucky criminals are mixed together, the smart but unlucky ones educate the stupid ones, turning them into smarter thieves. When they come out of prison, they are less stupid and, therefore, more successful crooks.

If we separated them, the stupid ones would be educated by other stupid criminals and come out even dumber than when they went in. They would be more likely to be caught when they commited their next crime, approximately an hour and a half after getting released.

246 Everything You Always Wanted to Know . . .

Meanwhile, the smart but unlucky ones would spend their time surrounded by other unlucky criminals, which would compound the frustration of their own intelligence.

So they would be more likely to be caught when they committed their next clever crime, precisely an hour and a half after getting out of prison. When you're unlucky, the smarter the crime the better the chance you're going to get caught.

If we can't avoid stupidity, is there anything we can do to lessen the impact?
Choose your stupidity wisely.

Two hundred years ago, Benjamin Franklin, a man who flew kites in thunderstorms, advised people who complained about the government imposing taxes that "we are taxed twice as much by our idleness, three times as much by our pride, and four times as much by our folly."

Following Franklin's formula, the wise man would choose idleness over pride or folly as his preferred form of stupidity, thus dramatically decreasing his rate of taxation.

Are scientists brilliant? Or just vain enough to think they're brilliant?
"Had I been present at the Creation," King Alfonso of Spain said in the twelfth century, "I could have given the Deity some valuable advice."

So could we. Don't create kings of Spain, for example.

Alfonso was one of the first of the modern scientists, making significant advances in early astronomy when he wasn't trying to push the Moors out of Spain.

With his offer to work as a retroactive deity consultant, King

Alfonso postulated a scientific theory that would be proven popular over the next seven centuries: that because scientists come to some basic understandings of how our universe operates they can play God just as well as God can.

Actually, scientists rarely discover anything. Mostly they stumble upon something that has existed all along. Their talent for taking credit for good fortune tends to go to their heads, where they convince themselves that they have a right to do whatever it is they're capable of doing.

That's why scientists will turn a theoretical understanding of atomic interaction into atom bombs, which they engineer for the future good of the race, the insect race if not the human race.

Martin Klaproth didn't "discover" uranium. It was there all the time, happily ignored by all sorts of people who didn't need Klaproth coming along to give them good advice about new and better ways to die.

Are successful people smart or just lucky?

The exceedingly rich John Paul Getty pointed out the best way to get rich: "Rise early, work hard, strike oil."

If you follow step 3, you can skip steps 1 and 2. As a perk of being exceptionally adept at step 3, you are entitled to encourage other people to work hard while you sleep late.

We have all defied incredible odds by succeeding at life. We exist. A million-to-one shot at best.

We may make a mess of our lives, but if we last till the end of this sentence, then we have stayed alive longer than the odds say we should. While you've been reading this, millions of other life forms with as much claim to existence as you have died. Millions more never got a shot at staring at a starry starry night or eating a pint of Ben & Jerry's.

Could have been a different planet, a million different histories, several thousand different genes.

Anyone who tops a successful existence by succeeding at what they attempt should put good luck high on their résumé. The best fortunes are made with good fortune.

But people who succeed tend to be the kind of people who like to take credit for their accomplishments.

They don't write many books about people who take credit for their failures.

The successful people want you to think there's no such thing as good luck. They already have it and don't want you to get any, which might diminish their share.

Getting born into a family with brains, with money and connections: luck. Getting a good education, the right job, the breaks: all luck.

The rest of us are left with lottery tickets. We keep an eye out for that bag of money someone's got to drop in the street sometime, somewhere, don't they?

But good luck can be cultivated, like any other talent. How? Through inexhaustible hard work.

Which means if, unlike John Paul Getty, you have yet to strike oil, you must get up early and work hard until you do.

Once you pass that stage, you will be able to tell everyone how smart you were to find oil where no one else thought to look, and you can remind yourself in your quiet moments that good luck is a silent partner.

Look at all the marvelous tools and conveniences we've invented. Surely that shows our intelligence?

We are clever, aren't we, restless inventors, ceaseless tinkerers. But why so restless?

We wouldn't need this constant reinvention of the screw, the screwdriver, the toaster, the car, if we had got them right the first time, or even the hundredth time.

Inventors look around at the objects in their lives and think: Hmm, that doesn't work as well as it should. What if we made it better?

But if it ever did work as well as it should, they wouldn't have to make it better.

Wait a minute. Didn't we invent the airplane, the TV dinner, and cable TV?
No, we didn't. They did. The smart ones. The deviants.

We took the airplane and added bombs so we could destroy ourselves in more efficient ways than ever before.

We took the TV dinner and filled the tray with globby matter only idiots would confuse with food.

They gave us the potential for watching hundreds of TV channels. We filled those channels with mental globby matter not worth watching.

The unique features of human intelligence—genius and idiocy— exist side by side in rough harmony. The guy driving the Rolls and the guy behind the wheel of the exploding Chevy can drive through the same pothole.

The smartest people do the dumbest things because they are clever enough to attempt things that are beyond the average dummy.

But we're making progress, aren't we? We've gone from the buggy to the car?
Car crashes, air pollution, traffic jams. More successful bank robbers.

We've moved from huts to skyscrapers?
City jams, urban blight, ennui, alienation, $10 hamburgers.

Ships, airplanes, spaceships?
Without ships, we wouldn't be able to take cars from Germany, bring them to the United States, then fill the ship up with American cars and send them to Germany.

Planes enable the rich to bomb the poor without having to clean up the mess afterward.

Spaceships? Maybe, but we've gone twice as far in science fiction movies as we have in real life.

Life-saving medicine?
People can now live long enough to grow into feeble prisoners of their own age, nursing-home inmates who can't leave, hate the bad food, are shoved around by stressed-out attendants, and sedated by vegetative drugs, thus confusing the elderly with the criminally insane.

Are disasters accidents, or the result of stupidity?
The concept of human error is the great PR job of civilized man.

Every time a pilot drives a plane into the ground, a train engineer ignores signals and crashes on the wrong track, a mine operator violates safety regulations and blows the shaft—and a few hundred people who thought they were doing something else find out what Heaven is really like—we call it human error, operator mishap, pilot mistake.

We have procedures and standards, regulations and codes, that say: "Don't do that." We train them over and over again: "Don't do that." Then they go and do that.

But not to worry. That's why we have company PR experts.

We don't put morons with their minds on empty behind the wheel. If you thought we let idiots run our cockpits, why would you ever fly with us again?

It's not stupidity. That's scary. It's human error. You don't have to worry about human error because we'll put in new procedures, higher standards, stricter codes. It won't happen again—until next time.

But we have so much more than any generation before us. Isn't that a sign of our progress?

The more we have, the more failure to go around.

Everything we make is failure-based. Take any common product—this book, for example. It looks like a thousand other books you've seen, other than the title and the words.

But it probably doesn't fit in your pocket for easy transport. When you are through reading a page, you have to turn to the next one. If you're reading in bed, you have to hold it open. It may contain words or ideas you wish it didn't. It may not contain words and ideas you wish it did. It is not the perfect book. No book is.

Neither is the light that shines on the book, the chair you're sitting in, the room the chair is in, the house the room is in.

Our faults abound. What's amazing about the human race is how easily we live with our faults.

You can go through life with your pantry half stocked and get away with it. The stupid elk is quickly an ex-elk. The stupid person has friends, family, social welfare, low standards, and good luck to sustain him.

Our inventions are inspired by the faults of the inventions that went before. The new stuff we rush onto the market contains enough faults to inspire another round of inventors to design and produce more faulty merchandise.

They can make fortunes on things that never quite work right because consumers will always trade new frustrations for old.

Anytime the user's manual is more than ten pages thick, that's a sign of bad engineering. They didn't get it right inside the machine and they're counting on you to make up the difference.

But we've solved so many problems?
Within each solution is the promise of strange problems never foreseen. Take the common paper clip. Brilliant little device for holding papers together. Problem solved.

But studies show that only one out of every ten paper clips is used to hold papers together.

The other nine are lost in paper clip–shaped crevices, used to clean teeth, fingernails, and ears, and to hold ties to shirts, turned into game chips or weapons, or twisted into garbage to relieve nervous tension.

People waste money, break fillings, poke out eardrums, with a problem-solving device that was designed for none of its more popular uses.

Won't learning how stupid we are have a negative effect on us?
Bound to. So relax, settle back, and feel those IQ points melting away.

IQ points? What a waste of numbers.

Intelligence is the most overrated of human quirks because it's rated by people who have a vested interest in rating intelligence highly. It's their ace in the hole.

Tigers don't rank themselves by intelligence. But the next time you're standing within fang range of a tiger, ask yourself why, if you're so smart, he's not afraid of you.

IQ points? No one ever looked at a tiger and said, "His claws are only 97 percent as sharp as the claws on this superior tiger over here."

Points are meaningless. Any tiger is sharp enough to get the job done.

How is the stupid future shaping up?

Just because we think the human race has made a mess of this opportunity for life on a dinky planet, it doesn't mean we're pessimists.

What would it take to get us to change our idiotic ways? To stop killing one another, to clean up the air, water, and New Jersey? To switch from a misery-based system to happiness mode, in which we spent more of our lives enjoying peace, harmony, and strong beer, and less time in mess-deepening activities?

Obviously, intelligence isn't going to get the job done. It's our brains that got us into this mess in the first place.

But here's where our optimism jumps in—we're just stupid enough to stumble our way out of the mess we stumbled into.

If anything is going to see us through, it's pure dumb luck. That's one resource the human race has yet to deplete.

So how do we get out of this mess?

Got to walk that 12-step path to nirvana. While intelligence is a disease, it is curable.

Step 1: Admit who you are. I'm going to do it right now, so stand up and say it with me: "Hi, my name is Bob, and I'm an idiot."

There, don't you feel better? Unless your name's not Bob, of course.

Step 2: Repeat: "Every day in every way I'm trying to be not quite as dumb as I was the day before (which I think was a Thursday but maybe it was Tuesday)."

Steps 3–10: Don't make lists.

Step 11: Repeat step 12.

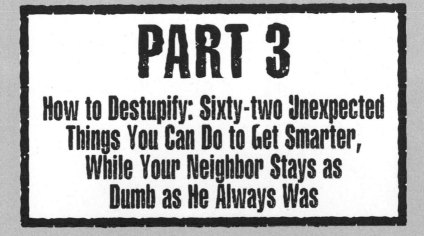

PART 3

How to Destupify: Sixty-two Unexpected Things You Can Do to Get Smarter, While Your Neighbor Stays as Dumb as He Always Was

How to Destupify:
Sixty-two Unexpected Things You Can Do to Get Smarter, While Your Neighbor Stays as Dumb as He Always Was

1. Set your goals high and deep.

Even if you don't fulfill your dreams, you'll accomplish more than if you aim low. Short goals leave no room for constructive failure.

Consider these goals of remarkable people, which have little to do with common notions of success:

Scientist Albert Einstein: "I want to know how God created the world. . . . I want to know his thoughts. The rest are details."

Artist Pablo Picasso: "I'd like to live like a poor man with lots of money."

Social critic Simone de Beauvoir: "I wish that every human life might be pure, transparent freedom."

Writer Logan Smith: "For me, there is one thing that matters—to set a chime of words tinkling in the minds of a few fastidious people."

Artist Salvador Dalí: "At the age of six, I wanted to be a cook. At seven I wanted to be Napoleon. And my ambition has been growing steadily ever since."

Drummer Ringo Starr (about why he joined the Beatles): "I always wanted to play with better bands. My aim wasn't to be big and famous. It was to play with really good people."

Writer Damon Runyon: "You can keep the things of bronze and stone and give me one man to remember me just once a year."

2. Don't let the rules stop you.

Every time we think there are rules to what can and cannot be done, someone smart succeeds by completely ignoring them.

Before Ibrahim Pasha became a great eighteenth-century general, he was an observant boy in the Egyptian court, watching his father test his generals to see who was smart enough to protect the nation.

The king placed an apple in the center of a vast carpet, then challenged the generals to pick up the apple without stepping on the rug.

When none of the generals could solve the problem, the young Ibrahim asked for a chance. He walked to one side of the room, rolled the carpet up toward the middle, then reached over and picked up the apple.

3. Exploit your weaknesses.

Nearly everyone has liabilities that can lead to success as soon as you view them as assets.

"Some people have youth, some have beauty," said the old, ugly actor Edward G. Robinson. "I have menace." He turned that menace into a long career playing gangsters on the big screen.

4. Get your own cheetah.

"I just use my muscles as a conversation piece," bodybuilding movie star Arnold Schwarzenegger said, "like someone walking a cheetah down Forty-second Street."

5. If you're only half smart, be half smart twice.

Most people are not exceptional at any one thing. But they're okay at a couple of things. The trick is to find two things you're pretty good at and put them together.

"I know my limitations," cartoonist Berke Breathed said. "I

could never make it as a writer, and I could never make it as a fine artist. Thus, the world of cartooning was waiting for me to come along. I have plenty of partial ability."

6. Don't be great. Do great things.

If people do something brilliant, they get labeled as brilliant people. Don't believe your own press clippings.

In subsequent endeavors, these brilliant people may do stupid things, and frequently.

Truly great people concentrate on what they're doing, not on what they're called.

"I am not a great man," Sigmund Freud, who pioneered modern psychoanalysis, admitted. "I have made a great discovery."

7. Challenge pretensions.

Ingyo, a fifth-century Japanese emperor, was troubled by too many families filing false claims to titles of nobility. He announced a divine solution to the problem: All claimants would have to sink their arms into pots of boiling water.

The gods would protect only those with genuine claims to nobility, Ingyo explained. They alone would not be burned.

On the day of the test, only a few men showed up. Ingyo awarded them all titles without requiring immersion in the boiling water to judge their sincerity.

The unsure and the unfaithful had eliminated themselves from contention.

8. Develop an outrageous sense of confidence.

"I have no use for humility," Jackie Gleason, the TV star who styled himself the Great One, explained. "I am a fellow with an exceptional talent."

9. If you're going to be humble, also be great.

"Sometimes I amaze myself," boxing promoter Don King admitted. "I say this humbly."

"We are all worms," Winston Churchill, who guided England through World War II, admitted. "But I do believe that I am a glow-worm."

"I'm fifty-five, I'm overweight, I'm bald-headed, I'm corny," TV personality Willard Scott said, "and I'm on top of the heap."

10. Become a smarter idiot.

You only have to be smart at one thing. Just about everyone is.

People often dismiss what they're good at as being unimportant. They discount their own intelligence if it applies to something like cooking or welding. We guarantee you there are college professors out there who would give away a degree and a half if they could fix their cars without having to call in an expert.

"There is a proper dignity and proportion to be observed in the performance of every act of life," the philosopher Marcus Aurelius observed two thousand years ago. "Love the little trade which thou hast learned, and be content therewith."

Find out what you're smart at. Pursue that thread until you weave it into a rope.

11. Fake it.

Soldiers learn that if you are not naturally courageous (few people are), you can fake it by pretending to be brave.

In the heat of battle it doesn't make much difference whether your courage is authentic or well faked.

It's the same with intelligence.

Few people can tell the difference between true brains and someone acting smart. Those who can tell will be kind to those who strive.

"You gain strength, courage, and confidence by every experience in which you really stop to look fear in the face," the inspirational Eleanor Roosevelt wrote. "You are able to say to yourself, 'I lived through this horror. I can take the next thing that comes along.' . . . You must do the thing you think you cannot do."

As long as it moves you forward, it works.

12. Take a job you hate.
Working a lousy job will spur you on to do something you don't hate, and that's a step closer to something you might love, which is the intelligent way to work.

It worked for movie star Paul Newman. "I wasn't driven to acting by an inner compulsion," he admitted. "I was running away from the sporting goods business."

13. Know what you really want.
Naturalist John Muir once declared that he was richer than millionaire E. H. Harriman because "I have all the money I want and he hasn't."

14. Pray sufficiently but keep working.
Confederate general Edward Porter Alexander, one of the reasons the South almost won the Civil War, wrote this about his experiences: "It is customary to say that Providence did not intend that we should win, but I do not subscribe in the least to that doctrine. Providence did not care a row of pins about it. If it did, it was a very unintelligent Providence not to bring the business to a close—the close it wanted—in less than four years of most terrible & bloody war. . . . It was a weakness to imagine that a victory could ever come in even the slightest degree from anything except our own exertions."

15. If you can't leap, take many small steps.
You may not be able to jump up to a higher level of intelligence. But you can climb that ladder one rung at a time.

"You learn to steer your way around your own shortcomings," physicist Steven Toulmin said. "The world is made up of getting a little better at things."

16. Use the steam.

Harvey Firestone, who founded a rubber and tire company that successfully challenged the giants Goodyear and Goodrich, advised, "Nervous energy is all right if it is expended in constructive action, in doing real things. But you have to be sure that the nervous man isn't the kind that simply stirs himself and everybody around him into a turmoil. He sets the water to boiling, but he doesn't do anything with the steam."

The clever trick in any enterprise is to harness whatever steam you produce and use it to move cogs, turn wheels, go forward.

17. If you can't stop making dumb mistakes, make them faster.

Everyone screws up. But smart people don't wallow in their mistakes. They move on.

The Burpee Company ran a small mail-order poultry business in the late 1800s. They added seeds to their product line so customers could raise the food for the chickens they bought.

Few customers wanted to buy chickens through the mail. Mail-order ducks? Are you kidding? What a stupid idea. You must be an idiot.

But Atlee Burpee didn't beat himself up over his mistake. He simply switched directions and made a fortune selling seeds for flowers and vegetables, which people were happy to buy through the mail.

18. Challenge yourself the way you would a rival.

Put yourself in circumstances tough enough to force you to think your way out of them.

As science writer Robert Ardrey wrote, "We are bad-weather animals, disaster's fairest children. For the soundest of evolutionary reasons man appears at his best when times are worst."

Trust in your genes. We have the power to think better than we think we can think.

19. Restructure your time.

Look at what you do best and what you love to do the most. They should be the same thing. Count the time in a week you spend doing that. Then find ways to increase that amount of time each week. You can accumulate your intelligence quantitatively.

As Frank Deford, one of *Sports Illustrated*'s best writers, wrote, "I try never to forget that the ultimate skill is to learn what best you do, and then to try and seek to pass as much time as possible in that endeavor."

20. Take it outside.

Leave the city. Find the wilderness, what's left of it. Find some big open solitude and let your mind fill it.

Writer Edward Abbey had a wilderness explanation for the madness of poets, a kind of dark stupidity that strikes down the too intellectual.

Abbey wrote, "Our suicidal poets (Plath, Berryman, Lowell, Jarrell, et al.) spent too much of their lives inside rooms and class-rooms when they should have been trudging up mountains, slogging through swamps, rowing down rivers. The indoor life is the next best thing to premature burial."

21. Make better mistakes.

Smart people make mistakes too, but not the dumb ones that mess up so many lives. We're a mistake-ingrained race. When you upgrade the level of your mistakes, you may come out looking clever.

Pianist Josef Hofmann found himself in a dumb situation at a concert. With the orchestra waiting for him to start, he turned to a woman in the front row and asked to see her program.

"I forget what comes first," he explained.

Another musician seeking to avoid embarrassment would have sat there fretting his brain to remember the first piece.

Hofmann solved his slipup in a direct, ingenious way. Instead of being humiliated by his mistake, he became a musical legend.

22. Try strange connections.

Peanut butter and chocolate? Who would have guessed it until someone tried it and made a tasty fortune?

Jokes often make us laugh by connecting the ordinarily unconnectable.

"Waiter, what's that fly doing in my soup?"

"I think it's the backstroke."

Swimming in soup. Absurd. But a successful, if old, joke.

"Nonsense and beauty have close connections," the writer E. M. Forster remarked, contradicting common sense to find an uncommon sense.

Or as the master of nonsense, Lewis Carroll, wrote in *Through the Looking Glass:* "Sometimes I've believed as many as six impossible things before breakfast."

That's how to get an early start on everyone else. Wild connections can lead to poetry, romance, or the Pet Rock fortune.

23. Give up.

Don't fight it. Cut loose. Drift, daydream.

All the best artists and writers do.

Consider poet Emily Dickinson's clear advice: "To make a prairie it takes a clover and one bee, one clover and a bee, and revery. The revery alone will do, if bees are few."

Creative thinkers unfocus from their problems. They let their minds wander until the subconscious makes itself heard. The answer comes like a dream, almost unearned, always valuable.

24. Ask someone smarter than you are what to do.
If you can't solve a problem, perhaps Socrates or da Vinci or Einstein could. They're not available? No problem.

Curl up in a cozy room by yourself. Read their writings. Close your eyes, ask them your question, and listen to what comes into your mind.

That's Socrates talking. You say it's not? Then who is it? Just you talking to yourself? Well, that's a start, the basic trick that writers use.

Have you ever had a dream where some famous person appeared? That was you too, and yet it was also them.

"To know is nothing at all," the wise writer Anatole France said. "To imagine is everything."

25. Shoot the brave ones.
During the Civil War a Confederate general ordered his men not to fire at a particular Union officer because he showed such courage on the field of battle.

Later, Gen. Stonewall Jackson explained the error of this strategy: "Shoot the brave officers," Jackson commanded. "The cowards will run away and take their men with them."

26. Test for idiocy.
When confronted with Robert Browning's poem *Sordellow*, the writer Douglas Jerrold could not follow it and confessed, "I am an idiot."

When his wife read the poem, she declared it gibberish. "Thank God," Jerrold replied, "I am not an idiot."

27. Violate proverbs.

When Lyndon Johnson was the majority leader of the Senate, he pushed the other senators into long, overtime sessions. "What's all the hurry," one of them asked. "Rome wasn't built in a day."

"No," a fellow senator replied, "but Lyndon Johnson wasn't foreman on that job."

28. If you can't sell it, give it away.

When painter Joszi Koppay couldn't get a commission from the wealthy publisher Adolph Ochs to paint a portrait of Ochs's daughter, Iphigene, Koppay offered to do the painting for free.

Along with the finished portrait, Koppay sent a bill for $1,000. Ochs reminded the artist that he had agreed to paint Iphigene for free.

"Your daughter has such a beautiful face, it was a joy to paint it," Koppay explained. "But the body was dull and bored me. It is for this that I charge you $1,000."

29. Fool your rage.

Anger blocks intelligence. Strong anger obliterates otherwise sensible intentions.

A member of President Lincoln's cabinet was having trouble with a subordinate. Lincoln suggested that he write the troublemaker a nasty letter expressing his rage.

When the cabinet officer had written the letter, Lincoln further advised him, "You don't want to send that letter. Put it in the stove. It's a good letter and you had a good time writing it and feel better. Now burn it and write another."

30. Switch hit.

Train yourself to be ambidextrous. Leonardo da Vinci could draw with one hand while writing with the other. President James Garfield wrote Greek with one hand while writing Latin with the other. Switch-hitting baseball players cut down the pitcher's advantage.

The effort involved with teaching yourself to go left if you always go right is a difficult and, therefore, liberating experience. Liberation smartens.

31. Develop the portion of the brain labeled ESP.

People of rational intelligence claim ESP does not exist, while others think they've been using it productively for years.

The thirteenth-century monk Roger Bacon left writings that accurately predicted automobiles, airplanes, modern ships, gunpowder, bombs, the telescope, and the microscope—hundreds of years before the technology to develop such machines was conceived.

32. Work outside time.

We rush around by the minute, charge by the quarter hour, rely on nanosecond technology, as if that timing was truly important to a life intelligently lived.

Devotion to time is a trap that dulls the mind, like the obsession with money. Artists cannot approach inspiration until they stare off into space, not into time.

How important are those seconds and minutes by which we monitor our lives? Clocks didn't even have minute hands until 1687. The hour hands were sufficient because no one had to be any more accurate than that.

If you hear that ticking, it's not just the clock but your life that's ticking away. The trick is not to listen to the tick.

33. Find a sacred cow and bet against it.

Holding something sacred exposes a weakness. But because it's considered sacred, most people are reluctant to take advantage of it.

Not the ancient Persian king Cambyses II. He broke the siege of the Egyptian city of Memphis in the sixth century B.C. when he discovered that the Egyptian defenders held the cat to be sacred.

Cambyses simply had his soldiers gather up all the stray cats they could find in the surrounding villages and throw them over the city walls.

Horrified at such heresy but powerless to stop it, the Egyptians ended the sacrilege the only way they could: They surrendered.

34. Move to a stupid state.

If you move from California or New York to Arizona or Arkansas, your IQ will automatically go up 50 points.

Or move to a college town, where brains aren't something you get punished for.

As the actor Wally Cox lamented, "When I was a kid in the Midwest I got straight A's in school, and I spent thirteen years on the psychiatrist's couch paying for it."

35. Evaluate your talents accurately.

It's incorrect to discount your abilities. It's not ego if you're right.

"I'm young, I'm fast, I'm pretty," Muhammad Ali said during his undefeated years, "and I can't possibly be beat."

Ali was often put down for bragging. But he was rarely put down inside the ring. Not only was he correct about his talents, but he advanced the art of outmouthing your opponent to get a psychological edge (and pump up gate receipts).

36. Steal from the best.

You don't always need creative ideas if you know how to steal from creative people. As Dale Carnegie, the inspirational author, admitted, "The ideas I stand for are not mine. I borrowed them from Socrates. I swiped them from Chesterfield. I stole them from Jesus. And I put them in a book."

37. Develop a strong inner drive.

People who are intrinsically motivated push deeper than people who are motivated by the rewards and punishments imposed by society or authorities.

As a child Blaise Pascal locked himself inside his room for several days and refused to come out. When his parents finally got him to open the door, the young Pascal, who was to become a brilliant mathematician, had figured out all of Euclid's geometrical propositions on his own.

38. Don't stop.

Losers might become winners if they didn't quit early. Inner greatness takes commitment, more than most people think appropriate.

Hokusai, the eighteenth-century Japanese painter whose work influenced the Impressionist movement in Europe, painted all his life. On his deathbed at eighty-nine, he said, "If heaven had granted me five more years, I could have become a real painter."

That's the kind of effort we're talking about. Too much? Do you have something better to do with your life?

Persistence requires that you go on after you think you've been persistent. It worked for Albert Einstein.

"I think and think for months and years," he said. "Ninety-nine times the conclusion is false. The hundredth time I am right."

39. Do what you haven't done before.

You're already smart enough to do what you know how to do. To get smarter, take on new challenges.

This takes courage, which comes from effort. How do soldiers find the courage to carry on against certain death? They fall back on training. They do what they were taught to do. They don't overthink. They charge.

If soldiers can find fortitude under such daunting conditions, you can find the courage to take risks in ordinary life.

If you don't try something difficult, you will fail by default. It's smarter to fail by daring. Fail going forward so you learn something that may make the next charge successful. But keep something in reserve. Failure can sap energy. Save enough firepower to start over again.

40. Study outside your main field of endeavor.

The great English scientist Isaac Newton was known for his work in physics and the promotion of scientific experimentation at a time when the scientific method was not an accepted course of action.

Newton was also a secret student of more arcane studies. After his death, it was found that he'd written extensively on the occult, astrology, and alchemy.

41. Develop a backup plan in case your first brainstorm doesn't play out.

Siam's king Prajadhipok bought a revolution insurance policy in 1935. When he was usurped while on a visit to England, he simply stayed in Britain, living lavishly on his unique form of unemployment compensation.

42. Identify the real competition.

Ballet star Mikhail Baryshnikov was driven to greatness by trying to match the toughest competition of all.

"I do not try to dance better than anyone else," he said. "I only try to dance better than myself."

43. Sharpen your critical judgment without having to intellectualize your reactions.

Movie mogul Harry Cohn knew exactly how to tell if a film was any good. "If my fanny squirms, it's bad. If my fanny doesn't squirm, it's good."

44. Make your weaknesses flamboyant.

"I don't remember anybody's name," said Zsa Zsa Gabor, a woman who became famous for being famous. Instead of letting her shortcoming embarrass her, she turned forgetfulness into an essential flair.

"Why do you think the 'dahling' thing started?" she explained.

45. Keep a dream journal.

When you go to bed, set a notebook and pen on the night table and tell yourself that when you wake from a dream you will write it down.

Record everything you remember from the dream and any thoughts you may have about it.

Repeat for twenty-one nights.

On the twenty-second night, before you go to sleep, ask yourself a question about a problem that's been occupying your mind. Ask for a solution to come in your dream. Even if it doesn't, something interesting will.

Your subconscious mind knows many things that you don't know consciously. Once your subconscious realizes that you're listening through the dream journal, it will flood you with information (dreams, daydreams, inspirations) that you didn't have before.

46. Ask too many questions.

As they used to say in the Chicago newspaper racket, "If your mother says she loves you, check it out."

Or as Ann Landers put it, "Don't accept your dog's admiration as conclusive evidence that you are wonderful."

47. If you can't convince yourself, convince others.

Most intelligent people appear to know what they're doing. But you don't have to know what you're doing as long as people think you know what you're doing. If civilization teaches us anything, it's to keep up appearances.

The great filmmaker John Huston drew story boards for every scene of his masterpiece, *The Maltese Falcon*, which he directed early in his career.

He didn't draw the story boards because he needed them to visualize scenes before he started shooting. He drew them because he thought the people working with him thought he needed them.

"I didn't want to lose face with the crew," Huston explained. "I wanted to give the impression that I knew what I was doing." He's given that impression to anyone who's ever seen the movie.

48. Flex your brain.

When you find yourself thinking there's only one way to do something, that's a sure sign that there's another, and probably better, way to get the job done.

"I am a man of fixed and unbending principles," the politician Everett Dirksen claimed, "the first of which is to be flexible at all times."

49. Free yourself from outside expectations.

Don't expect much from society. Relying upon the system makes you soft. Intelligence is a hard thing.

If you get your priorities straight, it simplifies matters and leaves you time to think.

The Irish writer Brendan Behan had his priorities clearly in line. "I respect kindness to human beings first of all, and kindness to animals. I don't respect the law. I have total irreverence for anything connected with society, except that which makes the roads safer, the beer stronger, the food cheaper, and old men and old women warmer in the winter and happier in the summer."

50. Help your enemies outsmart themselves.

Florida police set up a clever trap. They put up a sign on a highway frequented by drug runners that said: "Narcotics Inspection Ahead."

Then they hid by the sign. Anytime a car made a sudden U-turn, they stopped it and searched for drugs.

51. Learn how to learn from criticism.
General John "Blackjack" Pershing, one of the toughest leaders of World War I, expected as much from himself as from others.

As Gen. George Marshall, who served under Pershing in that war, commented, "He could listen to severe criticisms, just as though it was about a man in another country."

52. Fool yourself first.
When Theodore Roosevelt was a boy, he suffered from severe asthma and other crippling problems. "There were all kinds of things of which I was afraid at first," he said. "But by acting as if I were not afraid, I gradually ceased to be afraid."

Later in life Roosevelt was the most active man anyone knew. Although he loved to hunt, even African safaris did not offer enough engagement for his restless mind. So he took a hundred books along with him. Every moment he wasn't hunting, he was reading.

53. Focus on the deeper goals.
Writer Sherwood Anderson put goals in perspective. "Try to be humble," he advised. "Smartness kills everything. . . . The object of art is not to make salable pictures. It's to save yourself."

54. Look for paradoxes.
Self-canceling ideas can open your mind instead of shutting it down.

As philosopher Daniel Dennett said, "There is a good strategy to adopt whenever there is a stagnation in science: Find the thing that everybody agrees on; deny that and you probably break through the self-evident truth that turns out to be false, however self-evident. One should always look for paradoxes, because they tend to be breakthroughs."

55. Don't give up at quitting time.
It's easy to give up. When the going gets tough, the reasonable try again. But after a few failures, they usually move on.

Poncélet, a French mathematician, was forced to fight in Napoleon's army in the disastrous invasion of Russia. Captured by the Russians, he was locked in a prison for two years.

Without paper or writing instruments, Jean Poncélet put his imprisonment to use, solving math problems. He scratched formulas on the walls of his cell with pebbles, solving all the axioms of projective geometry.

If he could do that, what can we do if we don't give up?

56. Break the TV habit.
TV is a habit-forming drug, ruining more minds than marijuana or heroin. According to the Annenberg Public Policy Center, kids spend an average of $4^1/_2$ hours watching TV every day. That's 1,642 hours a year or 642 more hours than they spend in school.

TV shows demand disconcentration. TV teaches the dismissal of focus, disengagement from the thinking process, and a reliance on easy answers to misstated problems.

TV shows are so simpleminded, they reward our not paying attention. We almost always do something else while we watch their shows: eat, fold the laundry, balance the checkbook, do homework.

Then we carry that skill of vague focus into other parts of our life, where sharp focus is required.

Modern cars are built like TV systems: comfortable chair, no outside noises, easy to drift. How many car accidents occur because people are paying only vague attention to their driving?

Focus doesn't mean nervous attention. Focus requires relaxed concentration on the matter at hand, the way a great shortstop fields his position. They don't teach that in school. They should.

57. Show confidence in your doubts.

Field Marshal Bernard Montgomery, who led Britain's military, was speaking of the quality of great leaders when he said, "He must radiate confidence, even when he himself is not too certain of the outcome."

That quality applies also to intelligence. Uncertainty is a component of most rational analysis. To turn halting analysis into successful action, confidence in a dubious outcome is required, and is often sufficient unto itself.

58. Improve your reading.

Everything you need to know is available in books. Some of the finest minds educated themselves by reading their way through the public library.

But some 36 million American adults read below the eighth-grade level, leaving their minds to starve when a wealth of intelligence is set before them.

59. Slip by authoritarian roadblocks.

You don't have to agree with authorities. They're only authorities because the people who quote authorities need someone to quote.

As the high-tech entrepreneurial maverick Guy Kawasaki writes, "If a person with the right credentials says something can be done, then it probably can be done. If the person says it can't be done, then probably it still can be done."

If you think it can be done, then find a way to do it.

60. Learn plumbing.

John Gardner, former secretary of the Department of Health, Education and Welfare, put the skill of thinking in perspective: "The society which scorns excellence in plumbing because plumbing is a humble activity, and tolerates shoddiness in philosophy because philosophy is an exalted activity, will have neither good plumbing nor good philosophy. Neither its pipes nor its theories will hold water."

Find something you do well, then practice until you do it better. You will strengthen your skill, which fosters intelligence.

After you have learned plumbing, learn carpentry. Stop when you have run out of things to learn.

61. Read poetry.
Poems will stimulate your thinking in ways that nothing else can. There are hundreds of inspirational poets out there who can stir your mind. Keep reading till you find them.

Consider this from poet and physician William Carlos Williams: "It is difficult to get the news from poems. Yet men die miserably every day for lack of what is found there."

Or as practical philosopher Daniel Dennett said, "If you want to remember something, it's useful to make a rhyme out of it. . . . Maybe it's better still to turn it into a song, because songs stick in the memory in a way that mere spoken words don't. Poetry sticks much more readily than prose."

62. Watch whom you kiss.
No matter how dumb you feel at times, you will never seem quite so stupid if you just remember one thing: Never kiss a rattlesnake on the mouth.

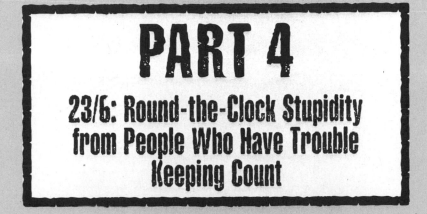

PART 4

23/6: Round-the-Clock Stupidity from People Who Have Trouble Keeping Count

CHAPTER TWENTY-THREE

Egos of the Knuckleheaded:
Disinfecting the Common People

Can you really make yourself dumb? Oh yes. It's practically the only way.

But in a world of egotistical Yertles, you might be surprised to find out who wanted to be called His High Mightiness.

Although with competition from spitting llamas and silver dollar–tossing Texans, we might narrow it down by asking: Who is *not* His High Mightiness?

●●●

Queen Henrietta of Belgium trained her pet llama to spit—but only at commoners.

To prevent assassinations, most royalty treat their personal bodyguards decently. Then there was the nineteenth-century king of Haiti, Henry Christophe, who ordered all his bodyguards to march off a cliff to their deaths. Any guards who refused were executed.

●●●

What does a parent with a big ego do when his kid's shelf piles up with soccer trophies, Little League trophies, swim trophies?

According to a woman who runs a California trophy-making business, the proud dad (proud of himself, anyway) orders her to make up some old-looking trophies with his name on them so he can regain household bragging rights.

●●●

When eccentric millionaire Ted Turner bought the Atlanta Braves, he experimented with putting their nicknames on the backs of the uniforms. If a player didn't have a nickname, Turner made one up for him.

Pitcher Andy Messersmith was given the nickname Channel. Why? Because his uniform number was seventeen, and channel seventeen was the number of Turner's Atlanta TV station.

●●●

Michael Jackson used to visit Disneyland three times a week dressed in wigs, fake beards, hats, and fake noses to blend in with the crowd.

Eventually, Jackson gave up the disguises. Instead, he went to the amusement park in a wheelchair so he could be pushed to the front of the lines and get in first.

James Gordon Bennett, a fussy editor of *The New York Herald*, had some strange newspaper rules. For example, he insisted that all his reporters use the word *night* instead of *evening* because "*night* is a more exact term."

Bennett was finally shown the error of his ways when a reporter filed a story that included a description of a society woman who "looked ravishing in a pink silk night gown."

● ● ●

Calouste Gulbenkian made a vast fortune in the early 1900s through Iraqi oil. He spent his money on European mansions and castles, which he stocked with harems.

He passed the remaining fortune on to his son Nubar, along with this advice for maintaining manageable harems: Get rid of the women after they turn seventeen, when they become impossible to manage.

● ● ●

Nubar Gulbenkian took his father's eccentricities a step further, dressing in Edwardian style throughout the 1950s, wearing top hats, spats, and brocaded jackets to dinner parties.

He also owned a thousand handcrafted canes, which meant he could walk for about three years without having to repeat a cane.

● ● ●

Edith Rockefeller inherited a family fortune, then doubled it by marrying the wealthy Harold McCormick. Edith maintained that she had been an Egyptian queen in a past life—but then who hasn't?

She kept one servant whose sole job it was to convey her orders to the other servants so she wouldn't be obliged to speak to them.

Edith also kept four butlers to serve her personally at mealtime because one or two butlers simply couldn't get the job done right.

●●●

Eccentric eighteenth-century British aristocrat Edward Montagu had diamonds sewn all over his clothes. For formal occasions he wore a wig made of iron.

He also had a penchant for getting married indiscriminately. When he died in 1776, he left behind one hundred widows.

●●●

The president of Communist Romania, Nicolae Ceauşescu, liked to present himself as a man of the people. This was a tricky business since he also had a phobia of catching germs from other people.

So before Ceauşescu ventured out into the streets to be photographed shaking hands with common people, his secret police would first disinfect the chosen ones.

4 Rulers Who Could Have Given Nicolae Ceaușescu and Donna Summer Ego Lessons

1. As a young boy, Ivan the Terrible, who would become czar of Russia, amused himself by throwing dogs off the roof of the Kremlin.

2. Henry VIII put Thomas à Becket on trial for heresy. Becket didn't take the witness stand in his own defense because he had been dead for 300 years.

3. Zingua, seventeenth-century queen of Angola, kept male concubines. If she really liked one of her love slaves, she had him crippled so he couldn't run away. Zingua felt that such precautionary motivation would make the men better lovers.

4. When Selim I, sultan of Persia, was advised by royal doctors to stop his drinking or he would ruin his health, he ordered the doctors hanged.

    His new doctors made the startling medical discovery that drinking was actually good for the health—theirs.

Donna Summer explained one little-known secret of God's plan: "God had to create disco music so that I could be born and be successful."

●●●

If you're fabulously wealthy, what can you do with so much money? Any wacky thing you want.

Millionaire shipping magnate Aristotle Onassis had the bar stools on one of his yachts covered with a unique kind of leather made from the skin of a whale's penis.

●●●

Vastly entertaining are the unintended consequences of stupid actions. Michael Romanoff was a con man extraordinaire who so delighted the people he fooled that he eventually ran a successful restaurant in Hollywood, where his pretense of being a Russian prince made his place popular.

Before going into the restaurant business, Romanoff lived the high life by pretending to be rich. In 1931 he impersonated a famous illustrator, Rockwell Kent, which made the artist happy. Romanoff was so winning as Kent that he sold more of Kent's art books than the real artist did.

●●●

Polish opera singer Ganna Walska had one of the all-time worst voices in opera. But she had a talent for attracting rich men and getting them to support an almost-career on the stage.

She married millionaire Harold Fowler McCormick, who gave her whatever she wanted: money, houses, jewels, her own opera company. But any time Ganna was scheduled to sing, something would come up to cancel her performance.

In 1920 she was scheduled to open in Chicago but sailed to Europe instead, claiming the company director had insulted her in rehearsal.

McCormick chased after Ganna, promising to buy her a new opera company. Instead, she insisted that her husband have an operation in which monkey glands were implanted in his body to improve his sexual prowess.

He went through with the dangerous operation, and she still threw him out of the mansion.

●●●

Texas oilman James Marion West Jr. amused himself by tossing fistfuls of silver dollars around the streets of Houston. He liked to watch people rush after inconsequential money.

West joined the Texas Rangers and designed his own special badge, highlighted with diamonds. He kept ready to take on criminals by toting a .45 in a golden holster and outfitting all his cars with rifles, shotguns, and machine guns.

●●●

In the seventeenth century the British elite developed an unusual passion: employing ornamental hermits to live in caves and hollow trees on their estates. The aristocracy felt that quaint mystics injected a proper mood of melancholy into the life of the shire.

Charles Hamilton of Surrey advertised in English newspapers for a prospective hermit. The job requirements:

1. The hermit must never cut hair, beard, or fingernails.
2. He must remain for seven years within the confines of the Hamilton estate.
3. He must never converse with the servants.

If the ornamental hermit lasted under those conditions for seven years, Hamilton would pay him 700 pounds.

The man chosen for the job lasted three weeks.

•••

The Greek leader Herostatus had nothing against the goddess Diana, yet he burned down her temple at Ephesus in the fourth century B.C. Why? So history would never forget his name.

•••

Everyone knows that billionaire Howard Hughes was a tad eccentric and a hypochondriac of legendary proportions. He refused to discard his urine, saving it to be analyzed for new diseases attacking his body. He saved flakes of his skin for the same reason.

Hughes became convinced that good health could only be maintained by drinking gallons of orange juice, all of which had to be squeezed in his presence. Hughes believed that if the juice was thirty minutes old, it lost all its health-giving qualities.

King Louis XIV of France threw the courtier Francis Seldon into prison, where he remained in solitary confinement for seventy years. Seldon's crime? He'd made a joke about the king being bald.

●●●

After he was chosen to be our first president but before the position's title had been decided upon, George Washington suggested that a president should be called His High Mightiness.

Many of the men who have held the position since Washington have also taken that attitude, if not that title.

CHAPTER TWENTY-FOUR

Resurrecting the Furniture and Other Dumb Moves in the Face of Fate

Step 1: Stare fate directly in the eye.
Step 2: Take the flakiest possible disadvantage of your golden opportunity.
Step 3: Welcome to history. You're in.

●●●

The paintings of Amedeo Modigliani weren't worth much while he was alive. But after the artist's death, their value shot up.

Many Parisian café owners, who had traded Modigliani drinks for paintings, suddenly were able to cash in.

But one café owner lost a fortune because his wife had scraped the paint off Modigliani's paintings so she could use the canvas to cover beds and sofas.

● ● ●

A Navy mechanic stationed in Spain in 2003 wanted to check the fuel level in a jet fighter, but he didn't have his flashlight. No problem. He simply borrowed a buddy's Bic lighter.

Amazingly, he survived and became a Navy legend.

● ● ●

The Dutch mystic John Roeleveld collected animal bones for forty years, believing the animals that once surrounded the bones would be resurrected on Judgment Day.

He also collected broken furniture and busted machines, believing God would resurrect them too.

● ● ●

Anna Edison Taylor was the first person to go over Niagara Falls in a barrel, a plunge she survived in 1901. What makes her a candidate for legendary stupidity: She couldn't swim. If that barrel hadn't held together, she wouldn't have either.

● ● ●

Buy a few lottery tickets—there's always a chance you'll hit the jackpot. Take a trip to Vegas or Atlantic City—win a little, lose a lot.

But it's not such innocent pleasure when you consider this startling stat: Americans lose over $22 billion each year by gambling.

Someone's getting rich off all that gambling, but it's not the gamblers.

Despite these gargantuan losses, 39 percent of Americans think that buying a lottery ticket is the best way to get rich. And we wonder why telemarketing works.

•••

William Miller, a nineteenth-century preacher, was a convincing prophet. When he declared that the world would end on April 3, 1843, hundreds of his followers killed themselves. They wanted to be the first of the faithful taken up to heaven.

Other Miller converts tried to launch themselves into heaven by running off hills with homemade wings strapped to their backs—making Miller was one of the first preachers to specialize in the spiritual needs of morons.

Despite the repeated failure of these efforts, when Miller announced a new date for the end of the world, July 7, 1843, thousands of his followers who hadn't already killed themselves dug graves and sat in them on that day, waiting for deliverance.

But not before they made Miller rich by purchasing at a special, one-time ascension rate his you-can-take-it-with-you heavenly robes.

•••

An anonymous critic once sent a letter to preacher Henry Ward Beecher. The letter contained a single word: "Fool."

No minister ever received a better setup line, and Beecher made the most of it.

"I have known many an instance of a man writing a letter and forgetting to sign his name," he told his congregation that Sunday.

"But this is the only instance I've ever known of a man signing his name and forgetting to write his letter."

•••

When war correspondent and TV newsman Edward R. Murrow was a boy, he bet a friend that he could duck faster than the friend could fire a BB gun. He lost the bet. The pellet hit him between the eyes.

Murrow survived to become one of the most intelligent men on TV, although it's questionable how far TV gets you up the IQ scale.

•••

William Pitt was prime minister of England in the early 1800s. A doctor advised him that drinking a bottle of port each day would maintain his health.

Pitt did the math and reasoned that if he drank six bottles of port a day he would be six times as healthy. He drank himself into the grave at the age of forty-six.

•••

Joseph Gould came from a wealthy family and graduated from Harvard. Then he showed his true mad colors by traveling to North Dakota on a self-inspired research mission to measure the heads of five hundred Mandan Indians and one thousand Chippewas.

After completing his work for the science of physiological irrelevancy, Gould moved to Greenwich Village in the years prior to World War I, where he became the first Bohemian poet.

He once submitted a book review to a small magazine, which wouldn't publish it because the review itself ran two hundred pages long.

Gould became known throughout the Village as Professor Seagull because he would imitate the birds for drinks from tourists. He proclaimed himself the world's leading expert on seagull language.

●●●

John Cleves Symmes was a decorated officer who fought for America in the War of 1812. Then he retired from the military and decided that the earth was hollow.

Symmes tried for years to raise money for an expedition that would enter the hollow earth at the South Pole and emerge at the North Pole.

Other people have postulated a hollow earth, but Symmes's reasoning was particularly interesting: that God would create hollow planets because he was frugal. The Lord would not waste so much matter making solid planets when He could as easily make planets hollow so people could live in the centers.

Symmes actually found support for his theory in Congress, an institution that has extensive experience with hollowness. Two ships set sail for the South Pole in 1829 to prove his theory correct. They were never heard from again.

●●●

When radios reported the Japanese attack on Pearl Harbor on December 7, 1941, people across the country assumed it was another radio hoax, like Orson Welles's scare of invading Martians. This time they weren't going to be so easily fooled, so they laughed it off.

But it didn't take long for the laughing to stop.

Even when people stateside believed the attack on Pearl Harbor was real, they didn't all have a patriotic reaction. *Life* magazine reported that while the attack was still going on, an Arizona newspaper received a call asking for the score in the football game between the Cardinals and the Chicago Bears.

The caller complained: "Aren't you getting anything besides that war stuff?" No, and not for a long time to come.

• • •

To celebrate the Fourth of July 2001, a man in Kansas City put fireworks in his oven and blew up his kitchen.

He survived the explosion, giving him something to celebrate, but no more fireworks to celebrate with.

• • •

The People Who Miss It Entirely Award goes to the *Chicago Times* for complaining about a lousy presidential speech.

The paper ranted: "The cheek of every American must tingle with shame as he reads the silly, flat and dishwatery utterances of the man who has to be pointed out to intelligent foreigners as the President of the United States."

Yes, the *Times* was slamming Abraham Lincoln for his Gettysburg Address.

Four Curious Final Gestures
That Defied the Way
the World Usually Works

1. British Army Major Peter Labelliere, who died in 1800, had a clear view of the muddled world. He insisted in his will that he be buried vertically, headfirst. Why?

    "As the world is turned topsy-turvy," Labelliere explained, "it is fit that I should be right at last."

2. Eccentric British philosopher Jeremy Bentham believed that people shouldn't be buried. He recommended that they be mummified, then placed as statues around the garden so children would never lose touch with their ancestors.

    Are you guessing he had this process performed on his own body when he died?

    Dressed in his favorite suit, Bentham was totally varnished, then displayed in a wooden cabinet in University College in London.

3. For some now-forgotten reason, after composer Joseph Haydn died in 1809 his head was separated from his body.

    The severed head was stolen by phrenologists (the bump specialists) who wanted to study the head of a genius.

    Years later, Haydn's head was put on display at the Vienna Academy of Music. But it wasn't until 1954 that someone wondered, what are we doing with the head of a dead composer? What a travesty and sacrilege. Haydn's head was finally returned to be interred with the rest of his remains.

4. In the Philadelphia College of Physicians' Mutter Museum, they keep all kind of strange displays. One of the strangest: a woman who died in 1792 and was buried in earth full of chemicals that turned her body into soap.

The first time Bizet's opera *Carmen* was performed, critics condemned it as obscene. Audiences shunned it. The humiliated composer died three months later.

Now *Carmen* is recognized as a great opera and one of the most popular.

•••

Actor James Earl Jones was honored with a plaque that was supposed to read: "Thank you, James Earl Jones, for keeping the dream alive." But the engraver made an odd mistake, etching in the name "James Earl Ray" instead. Ray was the man convicted of assassinating Martin Luther King Jr.

Jones said he occasionally gets introduced as James Earl Ray. We have so many famous names in our heads, they trip over each other.

•••

In the 1950s, parents throughout America were worried that their kids would catch polio. When a vaccine was developed, the government set up a program to vaccinate children across the country. But the program quickly ran out of supplies.

Oveta Culp Hobby, the federal official in charge of the program, explained that the government didn't have enough vaccine because "no one could have foreseen the public demand."

No one, that is, except for everyone in the country not working for the federal government.

John Mytton, a nineteenth-century British aristocrat, devised an unusual method of curing his persistent hiccups. He set his clothes on fire. After his servants saved his skin by putting out the fire, Mytton shouted with joy, "The hiccup is gone, by God!"

●●●

The German airline Lufthansa offered "nostalgia" rides over London in 2002. The English survivors of World War II could revisit memories by riding in old German bombers, the planes that bombed London during the war.

●●●

First, Congressman James Traficant of Ohio was convicted of bribery, tax evasion, and racketeering in 2002. Then he was kicked out of Congress.

Then he really embarrassed himself by threatening TV cameramen: "If you don't get those cameras out of my face, I'm gonna go 8.6 on the Richter scale with gastric emissions that'll clear this room!"

●●●

Ines de Castro was crowned queen of Portugal in 1357. Nothing stupid about that. Well, one thing: She was dead at the time of her coronation. But a dead ruler probably gave her subjects less grief than a live one.

Tough-guy actor John Wayne made scores of Westerns, which apparently qualified him to interpret the history of the Old West this way: "I don't feel we did wrong in taking this great country away from them. There were great numbers of people who needed new land, and the Indians were selfishly trying to keep it for themselves."

Wonder if the movie star felt the same way about his own estate.

CHAPTER TWENTY-FIVE

Food for Thoughtlessness:
The All-Turnip Diet and Other Loony Meals
at the Mindless Café

What do you do with a $300,000 bottle of wine? How should you serve flamingo brains? And what's the best dessert to finish off a good meal of Leviticus?

These culinary questions present no problems if you're among the people who don't fire up on all four burners. Here's an extra helping of the incredible eating habits of really weird people.

When King Mausolus of Turkey died in 353 B.C., his wife had his body cremated. She then mixed his ashes into a glass of wine and drank him.

●●●

For odd diets, few people can compare to Menelik II, emperor of Ethiopia in the late 1800s, who ate the Bible for health reasons.

Book eating is an acquired taste. A man from Zanzibar named Dubash Meghji ate an entire Koran. Took him thirty years to do it.

●●●

Roman Emperor Elagabalus was a bird brain eater. He preferred flamingo and thrush brains, but was also known to sup on parrot heads.

●●●

Some people develop strange eating habits for the good of science.

A California high school teacher in 1993 wanted to demonstrate to his students that what people ate was simply a matter of cultural habit. So he stood up in front of the biology class and ate live mice.

●●●

In 1989 a wine merchant proudly held a news conference to display his new acquisition: a 1787 bottle of Chateau Margaux worth $300,000. A minute later it was worth nothing at all—after he dropped the bottle on the floor.

Writer George Bernard Shaw, who was painfully thin, met writer G. K. Chesterton, who was painfully corpulent.

"Looking at you, one would think there was a famine in England," Chesterton pronounced.

"Looking at you," Shaw countered, "one would think you caused it."

●●●

Coming soon to a Japanese restaurant near you: female tables.

In Manchester, England, a Japanese restaurant hoped to start a trend by serving teriyaki, yakitori, and sushi on the bodies of two nude women, who worked as living tables.

"Exquisite food and female beauty combine two essential ingredients that make up the Japanese culture," the restaurant owner explained. Warm those chopsticks, please.

●●●

Coming soon to a Ukrainian restaurant near you: a delicacy invented by a Ukrainian candy company—chocolate-covered pork fat.

Will the treat marketed as Fat in Chocolate catch on in the United States? Or will health-conscious Americans demand the Diet Fat in Chocolate?

●●●

Chickens were first raised for consumption in India five thousand years ago. Until then no one had any idea of what other meat tasted like.

Wine was invented six thousand years ago. Beer has been brewed for four thousand years. So the odds are good that civilization as we know it was first conceived by a couple of guys sitting around drunk one night, and one of them said, "Hey, I've got a crazy idea."

Don't you wonder what our distant ancestors might have come up with if they weren't drunk?

•••

Although opera singer Enrico Caruso depended on good health for his fortune, he ate seven large meals a day, chain-smoked, and consumed garlic, whiskey, and ether to protect his voice.

•••

Horace Fletcher, a nineteenth-century author, wrote influential books on nutrition. He advanced the theory that good health could only be derived if you chewed each bite of food seventy times before swallowing.

You may not be surprised that Fletcher's notions fooled many uneducated people, but he also convinced the famed psychologist William James and the writer Upton Sinclair to sit at table counting their chews.

•••

William Gladstone, prime minister of England for Queen Victoria, didn't fall for such nonsense. He kept his health by chewing every mouthful of food precisely thirty-two times.

Six Cheeses That Sound Too Dumb to Eat

1. Bgug: an Armenian sheep cheese.

2. Bra: a salty Italian cheese.

3. Hay: a French cheese.

4. Leather: a German buttermilk cheese.

5. Potato: a German cheese mixed with mashed potatoes during the processing.

6. Rayon: a Swiss cheese not made of a polyester material.

Oxford professor William Buckland had an extraordinary and universal appetite. Among the things he bragged of dining upon: hedgehog, crocodile, elephant trunk, porpoise head, panther, slugs, earwigs, and dirt.

●●●

Actress Ally Sheedy explained the higher consciousness of food in 1987: "If someone's not being a vegetarian, they might be working out some karma, meatwise."

Either that, or they're having dinner.

●●●

If health food keeps you healthy, it may eventually lead you to a dilemma described by comedian Redd Foxx when he said, "Health nuts are going to feel stupid someday, lying in hospitals dying of nothing."

●●●

On the other side of the health food debate, almost a million Americans drink Coca-Cola—for breakfast. Soda has no known nutritional value.

●●●

In Arizona there's a roadside restaurant designed to look like the skull of a longhorn steer that died and dried in the desert. You enter through what would have been the cow's nose.

The poet Lord Byron may have been mad, bad, and dangerous to know, but he was also vain, maintaining a slender figure to attract the ladies he madly pursued.

To keep his looks, the poet's meals consisted of a single potato or, for variety, a small bowl of rice or a few crackers with water.

Not satisfied with starving himself, Byron sweated off more ounces by exercising while wearing seven coats.

●●●

Electronics inventor Nikola Tesla was a recluse, living his last years at the Waldorf Astoria Hotel on a diet of crackers and warm milk.

●●●

German gourmand Johann Ketzler ate an entire roast ox by himself. Took him forty-two days to do it.

●●●

Someone actually measured the steps away that you could hear someone crunch a good pickle. It's ten steps, according to the National Pickle Packers. Things must have been pretty slow down at the Pickle Packers HQ.

●●●

An eccentric Englishman ate only one food for the last forty years of his life: turnips.

Or perhaps the all-turnip diet lasted only a couple of weeks and it just felt like forty years.

Throughout history, cooking for royalty has been a risky job, with chefs executed in gruesome fashion when their food displeased the king.

That didn't happen to the chef who cooked for the king of Chantilly. But when a supplier failed to deliver the fish in time for a royal feast, the chef killed himself before the king could get to it.

●●●

In 2002 Monsanto announced plans to protect our corn flakes from sogginess by creating a genetically modified crunchy corn flake. How? By injecting a waxy gene into a strain of supercorn.

While they're at it, maybe they could inject a gene that makes dried cereal not stick to the bowl when your kids don't clean up after themselves.

●●●

Sir Tatton Sykes forbade the tenant farmers on his English estate to grow any flowers, commanding: "If you wish to grow flowers, grow cauliflowers."

●●●

Irish writer Jonathan Swift (*Gulliver's Travels*) had an ambulatory dining peculiarity. He took all his meals while pacing around his house, as a way of losing weight while eating.

●●●

While on the campaign trail in Springfield, Illinois, Richard Nixon ate only one bite of a buffalo burger. A Nixon fan scooped up the rest of the burger and kept it as a souvenir.

Think we've got too much government now? During the reign of Queen Elizabeth I in England, the government ordered people to eat fish three days a week because the fishing industry needed the money.

The English also passed a law that prohibited anyone from drinking in taverns late at night—unless they were spies. Must have been rather tricky for thirsty spies to maintain their cover.

•••

We blame the English for English muffins. But they're innocent, at least of this charge. They were American creations, for which we didn't want to take the credit. Let's own up: American muffins, at last the truth can be told.

•••

If Madame Rosa were really psychic, she could make a fortune by opening the Psychic Café. No reservations needed. We knew you were coming, and we have your favorite table ready. No menus either. Here's the food you had in mind, and thanks in advance for such a generous tip.

CHAPTER TWENTY-SIX

Finding Enough Flashlights for the Turtles: The Flamboyant Numskullery of Artists and Writers

Benjamin Haydon was a nineteenth-century British artist. Or so he thought.

But critics scorned him. Collectors ignored him. Art lovers rejected all his efforts at painting. Despondent over his failures to establish himself as an artist, Haydon killed himself.

After his death, Haydon's journal was published as an auto-biography. The book proved to be a hit, popular with critics and readers alike. Haydon wasn't an artist after all; he was a writer—only he never knew it.

This is why the only people who become writers and artists are the people who have to.

The free-spirited American poet Maxwell Bodenheim challenged the eccentric writer Ben Hecht to a formal debate in front of the Dill Pickle Club to determine whether the people who attend literary debates were imbeciles.

Hecht marched to the stage, looked over the audience, and declared, "The affirmative rests."

Bodenheim countered by gazing around the auditorium, then turning to Hecht and declaring, "You win!"

●●●

Artist Robert Rauschenberg once staged a work of performance art in which thirty large turtles were set loose on stage with flashlights strapped to their shells.

Around the turtles, an actor danced with tin cans on his knees. Another actor ripped up a phone book, while three actresses in bridal gowns walked through the audience handing out crackers.

●●●

Louis Stone was an inventive newspaper reporter in the 1890s working for the *Evening Citizen* of Winstead, Connecticut. He turned away from producing the typical boring newspaper story and wrote whoppers instead. But readers liked the stories even when they found out they weren't true.

Instead of being fired by a self-righteous editor, Stone became famous as the Winstead Liar, writing accounts of a cat that could whistle "Yankee Doodle," a tree that grew baked apples, a hen that laid red, white, and blue eggs on the Fourth of July, and a man who painted a spider web on his bald head to keep flies away.

George VI of England didn't know much about art, but then he didn't know much about anything else either.

When the king attended an art exhibit, he commented to a painter who specialized in storm scenes, "Pity you had such bloody awful weather."

●●●

Nobody trashes a writer like another writer. Here's Gore Vidal, on Aleksandr Solzhenitsyn: "He is a bad novelist and a fool. The combination usually makes for great popularity in the U.S."

●●●

You haven't arrived until you're a crop circle artist. Bulgarian artist Daniel Bozhkov turned a Maine hayfield into a crop-circle portrait of TV talk show host Larry King by flattening a field of timothy and milkweed into an artwork entitled *Learn How to Fly Over a Very Large Larry*.

●●●

The half-mad English poet Lord Byron believed the fortune teller who predicted he would die at thirty-seven.

So if you're already a little off and think you won't survive anyway, might you not be tempted to fulfill that prophesy by living wildly toward death? Especially if you were a poet?

Perhaps a more reasoned attempt to survive would have led Byron to a long life. Or maybe not. The poet died at thirty-six. So had his father. So did his daughter Augusta.

Is the cemetery the place where the stupid and the bizarre meet? Poet of the macabre Edgar Allan Poe was buried in a pauper's plot in 1850. Twenty-five years later, fans of his dark verse reburied Poe in an honored grave.

But before they reinterred the poet, they broke off pieces of Poe's rotted coffin and took them home for souvenirs, a debased denouement Poe might have written himself.

● ● ●

In 1989 Colonel Muammar el-Qaddafi, ruler of Libya, informed the world that Shakespeare was not English. He was an Arab.

● ● ●

Painter Marcel Duchamp gave several of his paintings to the artistically revolutionary bata movement. They chopped the paintings to pieces with axes—as artists, not critics.

● ● ●

We all have that picture in our minds of the starving artist in the freezing garret struggling against poverty to produce great, unappreciated art.

Then there's the artist Christo, whose Running Fence, a 1968 installation along the coast of Northern California, was built from 2,050 steel posts, 165,000 yards of cloth, and $2,250,000 in support funding.

● ● ●

British poet Matthew Arnold toured the United States giving a series of readings, including one attended by General Ulysses S. Grant.

But the poet spoke so softly that no one in the audience could hear his poems. When he refused to speak up, people left. Arnold kept whispering his poetry to empty halls.

•••

English playwright George Bernard Shaw was not fond of America, so he was an odd choice to be given the honor of making the first transatlantic phone call. Shaw's historic greeting: "Hello, America, how are all you boobs?"

•••

When George Bernard Shaw toured the United States in 1933, he gave numerous newspaper interviews, during which he advised that the only hope for America was to get rid of the Constitution.

•••

PR flack Harry Reichenbach proved the power of public relations when he hired people to stare in the window of an art gallery at an unknown painting of a nude woman called *September Morn*.

When the publicity led to the arrest of the artist and gallery owner for indecency, the painting became famous and millions of prints were sold.

Three Cases of Stupid Inspiration

1. Writer Hart Crane found poetic inspiration by insulting everyone, getting into fistfights, breaking tables and chairs, then listening to *Bolero* by Ravel.

2. Painter Salvador Dalí grew a long mustache, then waxed it into pointed ends and turned them up, declaring the tips to be inspirational antennas.

   "My mustache is my radar," the artist explained. "It pulls ideas out of space."

3. The nineteenth-century French poet Ferdinand Flocon drew his inspiration from the laws of France. He devoted his life to turning the entire French Civil Code into an epic poem.

The wealthy poet Tristan Tzara and his eccentric friend, the artist Hans Arp, created the absurdist Dada "movement against all movements."

They chose the movement's name blindly out of a French dictionary by stabbing the book with a penknife. The knife landed on the word *dada*, which meant hobbyhorse.

During performances, the Dada artists antagonized people with nonentertainment, and the audience enthusiastically joined in by throwing unusual objects at the performers.

This led one Dadaist to shout at the audience, "You are all idiots," which apparently qualified them to be presidents of the Dadaist movement.

●●●

Dr. Albert Barnes, a millionaire drug manufacturer, owned a vast collection of paintings by Matisse, Renoir, Cézanne, and Picasso. But he refused to let other collectors, art scholars, or art lovers see the paintings.

The only visitors he allowed to view his vast collection of modern art were people who had no interest in it. It was his way of showing the world that the art belonged to him, not to humanity.

●●●

e.e. cummings, the poet who eschewed capital letters, was thrown into prison in France for felony grammar.

French authorities suspected that his eccentric poetry contained some kind of spy code. The poet made good use of the time he spent locked in a prison cell by writing a book, *The Enormous Room*.

English artist Catherine Gregory protested animal abuse by exhibiting mangled animals in an art gallery, including a dog and rabbits cut into pieces, and sixty-three mice flattened and mounted as sculpture.

●●●

The art of mutilated animals was also practiced by Christian Lemmerz, a Danish artist whose 1994 exhibit consisted of six pigs decomposing under glass.

●●●

Sherlock Holmes was the smartest detective in literature. But Sir Arthur Conan Doyle, who wrote the books, had a little trouble with the elementary facts.

In *A Study in Scarlet*, Doyle mentions that Dr. Watson was wounded in the shoulder during the war. But in *The Sign of the Four*, the bullet wound has migrated to Watson's leg.

●●●

What happens when talented writers go Hollywood? They sacrifice their art and make enough money to sit around the pool all day and complain about it.

"I'm a Hollywood writer," playwright Ben Hecht moaned, "so I put on a sports jacket and take off my brain."

●●●

Cartoonist Jules Feiffer nailed the attraction of the artistic life. "Artists can color the sky red because they know it's blue," he explained. "Those of us who aren't artists must color things the way they really are or people might think we're stupid."

"One reason the human race has such a low opinion of itself is that it gets so much of its wisdom from writers," writer Wilfrid Sheed said.

•••

The next time you're visiting a museum and overhear someone pontificating about the meaning of art, remember this bit of wisdom from art lover Edmond de Goncourt: "A painting in a museum hears more ridiculous opinions than anything else in the world."

•••

George S. Kaufman explained that he preferred to write one-liners for comedian Milton Berle instead of Broadway plays because writing jokes "doesn't tire my hair."

•••

Here's the answer writers have been looking for to throw back at editors who criticize the grammatical errors in their work.

The perfect response was offered by nineteenth-century English poet Alfred Austin, who parried an editor's attack with this reasonable defense: "I dare not alter these things. They come to me from above."

Any readers who find typos not to their liking in this book, please see above.

CHAPTER TWENTY-SEVEN

Thirteen-Cent Bail and the Missing Sponge:
The Surprising Numskullery of
Doctors and Lawyers

What's the difference between God and a lawyer? God doesn't think he's a lawyer.

Now, what's the difference between God and a doctor? The doctor doesn't think God's a doctor.

●●●

In North Carolina a surgeon was operating for an aneurysm in 1994 when he stopped in the middle of the procedure to go to lunch. He left the anesthetized patient alone on the operating table while he and the nurses chowed down.

In 1971 a Pennsylvania attorney brought a lawsuit against the devil. But it was thrown out of court because the judge ruled that Satan was not a Pennsylvania resident.

●●●

We've all heard those urban legends about a surgeon who stupidly left a clamp or sponge inside a patient's body, then sutured up the incision.

It's such a wild story—hardly ever happens. Wrong. A 2003 study published in the *New England Journal of Medicine* found that it happens on an average of 1,500 times a year. Hopefully not by the same surgeon.

●●●

In 1979 a man sued the Coors beer company for turning him into an alcoholic. He claimed that Coors beer didn't have a label on the can warning drinkers that it contained alcohol.

●●●

A Pakistani who wasn't a doctor convinced English authorities that he was in 1992 and obtained a medical license. Before he was stopped, he prescribed that patients drink shampoo, take sleeping pills every six hours, or swallow suppositories.

●●●

Nebraska Judge Richard "Deacon" Jones once set bail for a defendant at thirteen cents. Another time he declared bail to be "a zillion pengos," which was hard for the defendant to meet since the judge never told anyone what a pengo was.

But that's to be expected from a judge who sometimes signed court documents as "Snow White."

•••

Doctor, inject thyself. John Hunter, the leading English surgeon of the eighteenth century, injected himself with venereal diseases to study the effect. The effect was that syphilis killed him.

•••

A Dutch doctor, Bart Huges, wanted to experiment with trepanation, the medieval practice of drilling holes in a patient's head to cure various ailments. Huges thought it would help him achieve a permanent and drugless high.

When he couldn't find a doctor to perform the procedure, Huges took an electric drill and bored a hole in his own head in 1965. He survived the operation, which led to a brief flurry of experimentation with self-trepanation, particularly in Great Britain.

•••

In Texas Judge Charles Hearn signed a death warrant by adding a smiley face to his signature. In a 1993 appeal, the defense lawyer argued that it was like the judge saying, "have a nice death."

Eleven Dumb Cures

1. If anyone in the court of Russia's Ivan the Terrible complained about a headache, the czar had his soldiers cure it by pounding nails into the person's head.

    Didn't stop the headaches. Did stop the complaining.

2. As the bubonic plague spread across Europe during the Middle Ages, so did stupid treatments for the disease, including medicines made from pulverized emeralds and melted gold.

    The patient may not have lasted long, but he did feel like a million bucks before he died.

3. A second popular treatment for the plague: spreading lard into the open wounds caused by the disease.

4. In the 1600s doctors came up with an ironic attempt to prevent the plague. They advised patients to smoke tobacco for their health.

5. But that's nothing compared with the cure devised for malaria in the thirteenth century: taking splinters from gallows where the English hung criminals and rubbing the sick person with them.

6. For stomach ailments, doctors in the Middle Ages recommended cleansing the digestive tract with a glass of water and millipedes twice a day.

7. In 2003 a psychic healer became popular in Lithuania by taking toilet paper that was energized by God and wrapping it around sick people to cure their illnesses. Why God would choose to bless toilet paper was not made clear.

8. Europeans once believed that you could cure syphilis by having sex with a virgin.

9. Russians believed that if you hid a piece of pork in the bed of a Jewish person for nine days, then ate it, you could cure your addiction to alcohol.

10. In ancient Greece, people believed you could catch leprosy by drinking beer. On the other hand, they believed that epilepsy could be cured with flute music.

11. In the 1600s people throughout Italy and France were seized by a poison panic, convinced they were slowly being murdered with an invisible poison that had no taste, odor, or color.

    These people thought the only way to protect themselves against the poison was to hold public executions of everyone in their city jails, no matter what their offense, even if they'd not been convicted of anything.

Have you heard the one about the doctor . . . Dana Carvey, the funniest TV comedian to have a generally dull movie career, was put out of commission for several years as he recovered from a botched double-bypass operation in which his doctor cut on the wrong artery.

•••

In 3000 B.C. a Babylonian law decreed that a doctor could have his hands cut off if his patient died—unless his patient was a slave, in which case he merely owed the slave owner another slave.

The unintended side effect of this law was to reduce the number of doctors willing to treat anyone but slaves.

•••

In the early 1900s, Dr. Albert Abrams claimed to have invented a medical tool that could diagnose patients over the telephone. He also claimed he could tell what was wrong with a person by examining his handwriting without ever seeing the patient.

Abrams invented many mysterious medical devices, all of which had the capability to separate gullible patients from their money.

•••

A Pennsylvania judge was tossed off the bench in 1992 for offering to reduce sentences if defendants let him shampoo their hair. Was there no justice for bald criminals?

Eight Great Dumb
Moments in Legal History

All lawyers can't be Perry Mason, but here are some amazingly witless cross-examinations from actual court cases:

1. "Were you alone or by yourself?"

2. "Now doctor, isn't it true that when a person dies in his sleep, he doesn't know about it until the next morning?"

3. "You were there until the time you left, is that true?"

4. "How far apart were the vehicles at the time of the collision?"

5. "How many times have you committed suicide?"

6. Q: "So the date of conception (of the baby) was August 8th?"

   A: "Yes."

   Q: "And what were you doing at that time?"

7. "The youngest son, the twenty-year-old, how old is he?"

8. "Were you present when your picture was taken?"

If you were going to become a medical quack, you should have done it in England during the 1700s. Such remedies as these were popular among the ill (or people who became ill once they took the cures): elk hooves, crab claws (black tips only), live toads, burned coke, live hog lice, skin of a capon's gizzard, pike jaw, newly gathered earthworms, and dried dung (peacock or goose).

●●●

The ancient Greek scholar Pliny developed a fascination with dentistry, although few of his patients shared his interest.

According to Pliny, you could avoid toothaches simply by eating a couple of mice every month.

To get rid of bad breath, he prescribed a combination of toads, frogs, ox, and worms. History does not record how bad the breath was that such a mixture improved.

●●●

In the early 1900s a group of English doctors became convinced that the colon was the cause of numerous diseases. So hundreds of patients had their colons removed as a treatment for diseases that had nothing to do with the colon.

●●●

Russian Premier Vladimir Putin sued the makers of the Harry Potter films for misappropriating his face.

The leader of all Russia felt that Hollywood's SFX guys had digitized his face to create the computer-generated Dobby the house-elf for *Harry Potter and the Chamber of Secrets*. Not only does Putin have a good face for an elf, he's got a great elf name: Putin the house elf.

Dr. Walter Freeman developed a quick method of giving patients lobotomies using an ice pick and a hammer. He toured the country in the 1950s in an operating van he called the Lobotomobile, and convinced doctors and patients to let him perform 20,000 of these crude, on-the-spot operations.

• • •

English doctors in the eighteenth century developed a unique method of extracting diseased teeth. They looped catgut around the offending tooth, tied the other end of the string to a bullet with a hole drilled in it, then fired the bullet (and the tooth) from a revolver.

• • •

A Hungarian doctor, Ignaz Semmelweis, shocked the medical world in the 1850s by suggesting that doctors could protect their patients from infections simply by washing their hands.

This theory was so offensive to the European medical establishment that Semmelweis was forced out of his hospital post.

CHAPTER TWENTY-EIGHT

Hollyweird:
Birdbrains in Tinseltown

You don't have to be a dumbbell to become a Hollywood celebrity. But it certainly can't hurt your chances.

To understand Hollywood, it helps to remember the basic idiotic rule of movies: If you have a movie script with two real ideas in it, what you really have is a hit and a sequel.

•••

When director Cecil B. DeMille made his epic The Crusades, he was having trouble getting the right performance from one of the stars, Loretta Young.

David Niven reported that Young read one of her key lines as, "Richard, you gotta save Christianity." When the director suggested she put more awe into the line reading, she changed it to: "Aw, Richard, you gotta save Christianity."

•••

The dumb Hollywood scorecard: The movie *Dumb and Dumber* was ten times as popular as *Sense and Sensibility* and a thousand times more popular than *The Search for Signs of Intelligent Life in the Universe*.

•••

Movie star Mary Astor claimed that fellow star Joan Crawford was on a movie set on December 7, 1941, when someone rushed into the sound stage to announce that the Japanese had "destroyed Pearl Harbor."

"Oh dear," Joan said, "who was she?"

•••

Party Harvey: At Jimmy Stewart's bachelor party at Chasen's restaurant, the entertainment was provided by midgets dressed in diapers.

•••

Many people who work in showbiz think the Oscars are a joke, despite the pomp and pretense of the annual ceremony.

As actor Vic Morrow put it: "Are we honestly supposed to believe that the Academy Awards are for acting ability when John Wayne has won the Oscar but Richard Burton hasn't?"

Ten Hollywood Insiders
Who Say Other Hollywood Stars Are
Not the Shiniest Coins in the Purse

1. Comedian Totie Fields: "Goldie Hawn is as bright as a dim bulb."

2. French actress Anouk Aimee: "Warren Beatty is like a masculine dumb blonde."

3. Filmmaker Andy Warhol: "Mickey Rourke is just so adorable. Dumb, but with some magic."

4. Pop singer Boy George: "Andy Warhol is an idiot, like a big cheesecake on legs."

5. Movie director Tony Richardson about actress Vanessa Redgrave: "A great actress, not a great thinker. Me, I'm leftist. Her, she's often just plain lunatic."

6. Filmmaker Otto Preminger: "Directing Marilyn Monroe was like directing Lassie. You needed fourteen takes to get one right."

7. Actress Constance Bennett jumping on the Marilyn Monroe bimbo wagon: "There's a broad with her future behind her."

8. Critic John Simon about actress Sandy Dennis: "She balanced her postnasal condition with something like a prefrontal lobotomy, so that when she is not a walking catarrh, she is a blithering imbecile."

9. Director Derek Jarman about actors Melanie Griffith and Don Johnson, who were married to each other at the time: "She couldn't play smart to save her life. Being a dumb blonde must run in that family."

10. And if you think the stars are less than bright, listen to actor John Carradine: "The worst jerks in this business are the directors who think they can write. Directors can't do anything but direct. Otherwise, they wouldn't be directors."

Actor James Coco observed that aging star Don Ameche won an Oscar for "break-dancing in *Cocoon*. Only all his dancing was done by a stunt double. Doesn't the dancer deserve his own junior Oscar?"

●●●

It cost Hollywood $100 million to make the movie *Titanic*. It cost the ship builders $3 million to build the *Titanic*.

●●●

Director Alfred Hitchcock's granddaughter asked for his help writing a school paper analyzing one of his films, *Shadow of a Doubt*. When the girl turned in the paper, they got a C.

●●●

The producers of *All the President's Men*, the movie about the *Washington Post* reporters who exposed Nixon's Watergate scandal, grew obsessive about authenticity. They actually flew trash from the real newspaper out to Hollywood to play the newsroom trash in the movie.

●●●

In Hollywood they just call this normal: Movie star Fattie Arbuckle owned a car with a built-in toilet. To amuse guests, he once staged a fancy wedding between two dogs.

●●●

Here's a rare Hollywood case of reverse ego. "There are not many things that make me laugh," comedian Chevy Chase admitted, "and that includes me."

Movie stars can be just as dumb as regular people. But no one will tell them they don't have a lick of sense because celebrities have what even smart people desire: a license to do whatever they want.

Silent movie star Charlie Chaplin became so big in Hollywood and his own mind that he not only starred in movies, he insisted upon starring at every party he went to.

Chaplin actually negotiated with the hosts for the right to be the first guest to arrive at Tinseltown parties.

●●●

Erich von Stroheim, the eccentric Austrian film maker, set the standard for Hollywood excess in the 1920s by spending a studio fortune on sets and authentic props.

The director explained why he went over budget to outfit a film regiment with real Imperial Guard silk underwear. "The public, of course, will not see the underwear," von Stroheim explained. "But the actors must know they are wearing authentic Prussian undergarments."

●●●

Hollywood makes expensive epics for one reason, and movie producer Joe Levine knew it when he said, "You can fool all the people all the time if the budget is big enough."

●●●

Back in 1952 when deepies (or 3-D movies) first came out, critics predicted no one would go along with wearing special 3-D glasses to see a movie.

But they did. As Paramount exec Bill Thomas pointed out, "They'll wear toilet seats around their necks if you give 'em what they want to see."

Toilet Seats: The Movie—I can see it now.

●●●

In 1988 religious protestors were offended by the film, *The Last Temptation of Christ*. To picket the studio that produced the film, the protestors drove out to Universal Studios, which made $4,500 off them in parking charges.

●●●

Hollywood knows great movies *after* they become hits—but not before.

The entire movie industry loved these two films once they scored big. But the scripts for both movies had gone begging all over Hollywood, with no studios wanting to make the films.

Forrest Gump was turned down for nine years. *One Flew Over the Cuckoo's Nest* was rejected for fifteen years.

Both of them won Oscars for Best Picture.

●●●

Movie stars Errol Flynn and John Barrymore, great friends, were both heavy drinkers. When Barrymore died, his Hollywood cronies stole his body and snuck it into Flynn's house, where they propped the actor up in a chair with a drink in his hand and a cigarette between his lips.

When Flynn entered the room, he was so shocked he took a vow of abstinence on the spot.

Movie studio boss Samuel Goldwyn said the wackiest things, inventing the category of one-liners so dumb, they're smart. Consider:

"I had a monumental idea this morning, but I didn't like it."

"The trouble with directors is they're always biting the hand that lays the golden egg."

"I read part of it all the way through."

"Let's bring it up to date with some snappy nineteenth-century dialogue."

"The publicity for this picture is sweeping the country like wildflowers."

"You've got to take the bull between your teeth."

• • •

You don't have to look far to find stupidity in Hollywood. But it's worth a trip back to the dumb days of the 1950s, when they matched some of the silliest movies ever made with some of the silliest movie promotions.

Here's how they tried to shock audiences with B-movie schlock (and oh, how quaint it all looks now):

High School Hellcats—"The facts about the taboo sororities that give them what they want!"

The Cat Girl—"Screaming terror. To caress me is to tempt death."

Alimony—"Alimony racketeers prey on innocent dupes!"

The Unholy Wife—"Half angel, half devil, she made him half a man."

Blonde Ice—"Beautiful, evil, bedeviling, daring!"

Blonde Bait—"The kind of mistake a man can only make once." (Have you ever seen a mistake a man can only make once? Usually takes him three or four times just to get rolling.)

Teenagers from Outer Space—"Teenage hoodlums from another world on a horrendous ray-gun rampage!"

Teenage Caveman—"Prehistoric rebels against prehistoric monsters."

Youth Runs Wild—"It explodes in your face!"

I Was a Teenage Frankenstein—"Body of a boy, mind of a monster, soul of an unearthly thing!"

Girls in Prison—"The shocking story of one man against a thousand women."

You just can't find movies this ridiculous anymore. That's what television is for.

CHAPTER TWENTY-NINE

On the Home Front:
Faint-Not Jones and the Family That Never Said No

Americans spend eight months of their lives opening junk mail. So is it any surprise that on average Americans are in a bad mood 110 days of the year?

One more statistic from the home front: 80 percent of all the morons in the world are in families like these:

•••

James Vincent Forrestal, secretary of defense after World War II, was the early model for Workaholic of the Future.

He was working in London when he received a phone call from his two sons, who had missed their plane in Paris. Forrestal told the boys to work out the problem themselves and meet him in London.

His sons were ages six and eight at the time.

●●●

Music was an essential part of utilitarianism, the philosophy dreamed up by Jeremy Bentham in the 1700s.

To surround himself with music all the time, he kept a piano in each room of his house (yes, including the bathroom). Then he hired musicians to play all those pianos day and night.

●●●

In 1990 Imelda Marcos threw a birthday party for her husband, the Filipino dictator Ferdinand—who was dead at the time but attended anyway, inside a refrigerated casket.

●●●

In 1990 a man in Clayton County, Georgia, discovered that his wife had committed suicide. But before he called the police, he realized that he shouldn't make a bad situation worse. So he sat down to watch the rest of the Super Bowl, then called.

●●●

In nineteenth-century England, John Fransham ran for Parliament on a platform of outlawing the making of beds more than once a week on the grounds that it was too effeminate.

Three Things Famous People Said That Defy You to Explain Them to Your Kids

1. "We've got to pause and ask ourselves: How much clean air do we need?"

   —Auto manufacturer Lee Iacocca

2. "Hawaii is a unique state. It is a small state. It is a state that is by itself. It is different from the other forty-nine states. Well, all states are different, but it's got a particularly unique situation."

   —Vice President Dan Quayle

3. "Life is very important to Americans."

   —U.S. Senator Bob Dole

Writer Bill Vaughn pointed out the essential stupidity of sub-urban sprawl: "Suburbia is where the developer bulldozes out the trees, then names the streets after them."

•••

In 2003 a father in Scotts Valley, California, was arrested for leaving his toddler alone in an SUV for forty-five minutes in a mall parking lot. What was Dad doing while baby was waiting in the car seat? Sitting in a restaurant taking part in a Bible study group.

Maybe they were studying family values, you think?

•••

Martin Luther, the great religious reformer of the sixteenth century, was determined to liberate people from the abuses of the church. Yet when Luther turned his brilliant, religious mind to the plight of women, he dismissed them by saying, "Let them bear children till they die of it. That is what they are for."

•••

Think people give their kids crazy names today? In the sixteenth century, English Puritans named their children such instructive names as Love-God Smith, Live-Well Johnson, Faint-Not Jones, Accepted Morgan, and Fight-the-Good-Fight Wellington.

•••

Carry Nation led the fight against alcohol and for Prohibition. But she was just as tough on her husband as she was on saloon owners.

Nation's husband was a preacher, but apparently not a good one. So his wife would sit in the front pew and correct him as he preached.

Or she would stand up in the middle of a sermon and lead the congregation out of the church, announcing that he'd said "quite enough for today." Rev. David Nation was left preaching to an empty church because no one wanted to cross his wife.

●●●

John Humphrey Noyes, who graduated from Yale Divinity School, created his own church around ideas that would be advanced in our own time. But Noyes started his free love church in 1835.

His Putney Corporation of Perfectionists owned everything communally and practiced multiple partners. Noyes preached that fidelity in marriage was a "sin of selfishness" and that his congregation had to "love all other members equally," which meant that no one should ever say no to anyone else.

The community thrived for twenty-five years before falling apart from jealous divisions.

Another of Noyes's unusual notions was that parental love was to be discouraged as idolatrous, so that all children were taken from their birth parents and raised by foster parents.

●●●

When Charles II was king of England, he realized there was one greater protection against usurpation than bodyguards—his brother James.

James was so unpopular that Charles told him, "No one is going to assassinate me in order to make you king."

Should divorced fathers pay child support? Consider the Italian court in 2002 that ordered a father to pay $700 a month in child support.

What's wrong with that? The son was thirty years old and made a good living on the stock market. But the court ruled against the father because his son was a *mammoni*, a mama's boy.

•••

Louis XI, king of France, was out riding in a forest when a courtier brought him the news that his baby son had died. The king had the forest burned to the ground.

•••

Novelist John O'Hara was a heavy drinker and a prankster. During Prohibition, he'd dump his empty gin bottles on the porches of neighbors who led the town's anti-liquor campaign.

•••

Before North Carolina became the progressive, liberal state it is today, public libraries required parental permission before children could check out such risqué reading material as the Bible.

•••

Sir Walter Raleigh got into a dispute with his son while both were at a dinner party. The enraged father struck his son, but the young Raleigh was too polite to strike back.

Instead, he turned and hit the man sitting on the other side of him, then told him, "Box about. It will come to my father anon."

The idea of everyone hitting everyone else in line struck the fancy of the British elite as an apt metaphor for the Elizabethan Age, and "box about" became a popular saying.

•••

Lady Hester Stanhope was an eccentric nineteenth-century British aristocrat. She lived her final years in an Arabian monastery, whose rooms she sealed to thwart thieves.

After Lady Hester died, the rooms were opened—to reveal that they contained nothing but rubbish. But at least no one had stolen any of it.

•••

Hollywood is big on excess. When child star Shirley Temple turned eight, she received 135,000 presents.

By the time the kid could play and wear that many gifts, she'd be too old for them. But can you imagine the thank-you notes Shirley's publicist had to write?

•••

In 2002 the Bush administration issued a report that found the silver lining in global warming—it could lower your home fuel bills.

I doubt it. If they make the planet so warm that we could turn down the heat in January, the government would just add on a surcharge for insufficient furnace usage.

On a closing note, here's one from my personal home file: No matter how smart you think you are, your four-year-old knows better.

When my son Teddy was four, he was telling me about his friend Casey, who has five brothers and sisters. "Is Casey the oldest in the family?" I asked him.

"No," Teddy explained, "his dad and mom are the oldest."

CHAPTER THIRTY

Dumb in School:
Vertical Thinking and the Aboriginal IQ Test

"**M**en are born ignorant, not stupid," philosopher Bertrand Russell said. "They are made stupid by education."

Here are the people who got an A for effort:

•••

When Harvard president Charles Eliot was congratulated for helping to make the university a storehouse of knowledge, he said, "I scarcely deserve credit for that. It is simply that the freshmen bring so much and the seniors take away so little."

In 2000 the University of Wisconsin published a brochure to attract students to the college. To show that UW supported diversity, the school digitally added a black student to the cover photo by pasting in his image using a computer program.

●●●

Prime Minister Winston Churchill, who led Britain through the darkest days of World War II, was thought to have "limited intelligence" when he was a boy. Ranked last in his class at twelve, he flunked the entrance exam for the Royal Military College at Sandhurst—twice.

Later, he saved the free world from tyranny and annihilation. Makes you wonder what the people at the head of the class might have done.

●●●

What do you learn at law school? As writer Doris Lessing explained, "In university they don't tell you that the greater part of the law is learning to tolerate fools."

●●●

If you learn the lessons of life, this is the educational path you may follow, as described by politician Harold Macmillan:

"The young fool has first to grow up to be an old fool to realize what a damn fool he was when he was a young fool."

●●●

Were you good at taking tests in school? Consider this view from educator Stanley Garn: "If the Aborigine drafted an IQ test, all of Western civilization would presumably flunk it."

Get Me Rewrite!
Eighteen Dumb Newspaper Headlines

1. Survey Finds Dirtier Subways After Cleaning Jobs Were Cut
   —from the *New York Times*

2. Study Finds Sex, Pregnancy Link
   —from the *Cornell Daily Sun*

3. Low Wages Said Key to Poverty
   —from *Newsday*

4. Malls Try to Attract Shoppers
   —from the *Baltimore Sun*

5. Official: Only Rain Will Cure Drought
   —from the *Westport Herald News*

6. Teenage Girls Often Have Babies Fathered by Men
   —from the *Oregonian*

7. Man Shoots Neighbor with Machete
   —from the *Miami Herald*

8. Tomatoes Come in Big, Little, Medium Sizes
   —from the *Daily Progress*

9. Man Run Over by Freight Train Dies
   —from the *Los Angeles Times*

10. **Free Advice: Bundle Up When Out in the Cold**
    —from the *Lexington Herald-Leader*

11. **Economist Uses Theory to Explain Economy**
    —from the *Collinsville Herald-Journal*

12. **Bible Church's Focus Is the Bible**
    —from the *Saint Augustine Record*

13. **Lack of Brains Hinders Research**
    —from the *Columbus Dispatch*

14. **How We Feel About Ourselves Is the Core of Self-Esteem, Says Author Louise Hart**
    —from the *Sunday Camera* of Boulder, Colorado

15. **Fish Lurk in Streams**
    —from the *Rochester Democrat and Chronicle*

16. **Infertility Unlikely to Be Passed On**
    —from the *Montgomery Advertiser*

17. **Alcohol Ads Promote Drinking**
    —from the *Hartford Courant*

18. **Scientists See Quakes in LA Future**
    —from the *Oregonian*

And here's the syllabus for the graduate course from historian Edward Gibbon:

"Conversation enriches the understanding, but solitude is the school of the genius."

● ● ●

In 1990 the president of American University resigned after he was caught making obscene phone calls from his office. Maybe no one told him the university had a policy against on-campus sexual harassment.

● ● ●

George W. Bush outlined his plan to be the education president: "We're going to have the best-educated American people in the world."

For once, you can't argue with the president—at least until our education system is bought by a Japanese company.

● ● ●

"An educated man knows the right thing to do at the time it has to be done," scientist Charles Kettering said. "You can be sincere and still be stupid."

● ● ●

If you think our busing regulations are tough, in Southampton, England, a preschooler was forced to go to a school thirty minutes away because the city council ruled he didn't live close enough to a school that was located just down the block.

How could the boy be so close and yet so far away? Because he lived on the thirteenth floor of an apartment building. If you added in the vertical distance, he was out of the district.

"I think it's pathetic," his mother said. "I think it's stupid, and I think it's ludicrous." Yes, good points, but remember that's the city council we're talking about.

•••

The scholar William Spooner (whose mixed-up sentences gave us spoonerisms) once asked a student, "Was it you or your brother who was killed in the war?"

•••

To foil the enemy during the dark days of World War II, the Civil Defense authority posted these orders: "Illumination must be extinguished when premises are vacated."

It took President Franklin Roosevelt to convince the officials that high school English teachers were not running the country. He had the signs changed to: "Put the lights out when you leave."

•••

How does education prepare us for life? As writer M. H. Alderson pointed out, "If at first you don't succeed, you're running about average."

CHAPTER THIRTY-ONE

Felonious Hats, Killer Makeup, and Other Fashion Trends

Some people would argue that all fashion is idiotic. Oh, that's right—I am those people.

From shoes that can't be walked in to life-threatening hair, fashion is the perfect obsession for people who are one button short of closure.

•••

In 1797 the English haberdasher John Hetherington invented the top hat. First time he wore his creation on the streets of London, he caused a riot.

He was fined by the police for wearing a "tall structure calculated to frighten timid people." Which is probably why the top hat became so popular.

You'll notice that Hetherington not only created a new fashion, he's also responsible for calling out the fashion police.

● ● ●

Their clothes shocked their parents. Church authorities condemned the fashion as obscene, particularly their tight stockings that revealed in public the intimate contours of their legs and buttocks.

Of course, we're talking about teenagers of the fourteenth century in Venice—and the shocking stockings were worn by boys, not girls.

● ● ●

During the first season, before the TV show *Happy Days* became a monster hit, ABC censors wouldn't allow Fonzie to wear a leather jacket. They didn't want him to project a JD image—even though the Fonz was supposed to be a juvenile delinquent (at least by the standards of 1950s TV).

● ● ●

Georges Clemenceau, premier of France in the early 1900s, insisted he was prepared to handle any crisis that arose at any hour of the day or night.

To maintain a state of total readiness, Clemenceau went to bed in pants, shirt, coat, shoes, and gloves.

Three Whites, One Green:
The One-color People

1. Poet Emily Dickinson wore only white clothes, but few knew it since she seldom left her home. Her fashion was a charming idiosyncrasy in someone so gifted.

2. Then there was Princess Alexandra of Bavaria, another eccentric with an all-white wardrobe. But the princess's charm became questionable when she announced to the court that she had swallowed a grand piano made of glass.

3. Another notorious all-white dresser was Robert Cook, of the seventeenth-century Irish gentry, who had everything from hats to underwear made of white linen. On his farm he only kept white cows and white horses.

4. The Englishman Henry Cope was known as the Green Man in the nineteenth century. He dressed entirely in green, had the furniture and the rooms of his estate painted green, and ate nothing but green food.

Surrealist painter Salvador Dalí had a shoe fetish that began as a child, when he would take his teacher's slipper and wear it as a hat.

• • •

Hetty Green, known as the Witch of Wall Street, came from a wealthy family but was raised in secondhand clothes because they were cheaper.

Hetty increased the Green fortune with astute investments in the 1800s but was even tighter with a dime than the rest of her family.

She kept a considerable part of her fortune stuffed into a petticoat sewn with many hidden pockets, which she washed herself every night and wore again every day.

Even though she made millions in a time when a million dollars meant something, she wore fisherman's boots because they were cheap and long-lasting.

• • •

Ever hear of a shoe diary? Francis Henry Egerton, the eighth Earl of Bridgewater, kept one in the nineteenth century. He wore a different pair of shoes every day, then had the used shoes arranged in chronological order.

His servants were under strict orders never to clean the shoes, so the earl could look back and reflect upon the weather of any particular day by the condition of the shoes he had worn that day.

Lord Salisbury, prime minister of England in the 1800s, dressed so shabbily that he was once booted out of a casino in Monte Carlo because they thought he was a beggar.

His Sunday dress to church was a bit unusual too: Salisbury wore a woolen glove on top of his head instead of a hat.

●●●

Good fashion question from TV reporter Linda Ellerbee: "If men rule the world, why don't they stop wearing neckties?"

●●●

"If you tie your necktie around your knee, instead of around your neck, you are imaginative, but you are imaginative in an imbecile way," said critic John Simon, talking about stupid writers. In fashion, the necktie-around-the-knee look either has been, or will be, somebody's idea of style.

●●●

In the Middle Ages, a strange shoe fad swept Europe: pointed shoes for men called poulaines. As the fashion spread, the pointed toes became longer and longer (up to two feet long among nobles) until men could not walk in them.

This was the shoes' selling point, for it demonstrated that the wearer was so rich he didn't have to work or walk.

Veronica Lake was such a popular movie star during World War II that women across America copied her unusual hair style: straight hair, worn long and falling seductively over one eye.

But many of these stylish women went to work in factories to support the war effort. A series of horrible accidents occurred when Veronica Lake'd women met indifferent machines. Doing her part for the war effort and to protect working women everywhere, Veronica cut her hair.

●●●

Makeup can kill. In ancient Greece, women at the height of fashion applied a white powder to their faces to make themselves more attractive. But the powder contained a heavy dose of lead, which poisoned and killed many of the temporarily attractive women who used it.

●●●

In the Dark Ages, arsenic was a popular ingredient in makeup. Because sudden, mysterious death from innumerable causes was common at that unenlightened time, the women didn't suspect that their own cosmetics were killing them.

●●●

Although women and men have used makeup since ancient times to make themselves seem more desirable, some societies have tried to ban it. In England in the 1700s, a law was passed outlawing makeup; women who wore it could be arrested and tried as witches.

In the late 1800s a fashion for the natural look spread throughout Europe. Women abandoned all their cosmetics.

A French fashion magazine celebrated the new freedom from makeup, declaring: "It hardly seems likely that a time will ever come again in which rouge and lip paint will be employed."

Half of history is the occurrence of that which at one time "hardly seems likely."

●●●

Among the ancient Egyptians, queens and princesses wore such large, elaborate wigs that wig slaves were required to help them walk through the palace.

●●●

While wigs were popular with wealthy Europeans for hundreds of years, the clergy often tried to get people out from under their fake hair. In 692 the Church excommunicated people who wore wigs.

Didn't work. Even bald clergy favored wigs. By the 1600s, the French king employed forty wig makers in his court.

●●●

Buttons of gold and silver became a trend among French royalty in the sixteenth century. King Francis I paraded through court in a velvet outfit adorned with 13,000 gold buttons.

Francis had to be a strong king because that's roughly a hundred pounds of buttons.

During Queen Elizabeth's reign in England, the government passed a law that people must wear hats. Another attempt by the fashion police to legislate style? Not this time. That law was enacted to stimulate business for felt manufacturers, who had fallen on hard times.

•••

Although men have worn hats for centuries, writer and professional opinionator P. J. O'Rourke thinks they have all made a moronic mistake.

"A hat should be taken off when you greet a lady and left off for the rest of your life," he expounded. "Nothing looks more stupid than a hat."

•••

Dumb teenage fads—a thing of the past? Yes, also the present and the future. Back in the 1940s, boys in small American towns wore their car club letter sewn about a foot high across the butt of their jeans.

•••

Actor Cesar Romero believed that to live well you must dress well. And never in the same outfit. His closets held thirty tuxedos, two hundred sports jackets, and five hundred suits.

What in the world does anyone need five hundred suits for? Four hundred, 450 I can see. But five hundred? Absurd!

Three Dumb T-shirt Slogans

1. I Suffer Occasional Delusions of Adequacy

2. (On the back of a passing motorcyclist) If You Can Read This, My Wife Fell Off

3. If at First You Don't Succeed, Skydiving Isn't for You

A Singapore hairdresser started a hot, but brief, fad when he figured out a way to cut hair using a blowtorch.

●●●

In 1988 a Japanese company marketed six-day underwear, which you rotated forty degrees a day for three days, then turned inside out for three more days.

Exactly why was this worth the trouble?

●●●

Louis XIV wasn't crazy about baths. The French king took exactly zero baths in his life. Now you know why the French became experts in making perfumes.

The world's first dry cleaners opened in Paris in 1855. First, the cleaner would completely unstitch your clothes. Then he soaked everything in turpentine and oil. Then sewed all your clothes back together.

Or you could just have the silly thing washed.

•••

In 1999, a tailor in Seoul, South Korea, came up with the idea of manufacturing scented suits for businessmen.

When you pressed a spot on the suit, hidden capsules released the scent of a pine forest. Or peppermint or lavender, if you preferred. To some people, this actually sounded like a good idea.

•••

In the 1800s, a gentleman was expected to know all thirty-two different ways to knot his tie. No wonder people lived at a slower pace. They dedicated all their free time to their ties.

•••

A man in France once left money in his will to buy clothes for snowmen.

•••

In 2002 a Japanese company manufactured underwear that was supposed to reduce fat in your thighs through a mix of seaweed and caffeine rubbed into the fabric.

Must have been tough for Japanese consumers to decide whether they should wear their undershorts or eat them.

When short-short hot pants became a hot fad in the 1960s, Vegas singer Sammy Davis Jr. and his wife showed themselves in public wearing matching hot-pant tuxedos.

●●●

In the fifteenth century, conspicuous excess was considered a privilege of the royal class, and it showed up in their clothes. The Duke of Orléans was a French trendsetter who once had a favorite song embroidered on the sleeve of his cloak, using seven hundred pearls to write the lyrics.

●●●

Whatever French King Louis XI was wearing any time he heard bad news, he never wore those clothes again.

●●●

In Spain during the Middle Ages, ruffs were popular on clothes. But it was against Spanish law for ruffs to be made of anything but white linen, and the pleats had to be no wider than three inches.

●●●

J. Edgar Hoover once fired an FBI agent because he didn't like the man's tie.

CHAPTER THIRTY-TWO

The Business of Idiocy and Vice Versa

Think your boss is mean? All bosses will have to work overtime to catch up to these two trendsetters:

1. Millionaire John D. Rockefeller gave his groundskeepers a Christmas bonus: five dollars each! Then he docked them five dollars each for not working on Christmas Day.
2. John Patterson, founder of National Cash Register, devised odd ways of firing employees who incurred his disfavor. One executive learned he was fired when he arrived at the office and found his desk and chair set ablaze in front of the building.

Welcome to the business world.

Half a million Americans use counterfeit credentials or counterfeit diplomas.

Doesn't it make you wonder how many people with counterfeit diplomas have landed jobs by fooling people with counterfeit credentials?

•••

The phone company promised to send a repairman out the next day to fix a customer's dead phone line, but couldn't be specific about the time. But the company offered to call the customer when the repairman was on the way.

The customer explained that wouldn't do much good since the phone line was dead.

•••

When McDonald's invaded Russia, the American bosses insisted that the Russian counter help give customers the standard Mickey D smile, which kind of looks like an old hamburger curling up at the edges, doesn't it?

Anyway, Russian customers were outraged and insulted because in Russia smiling at strangers means you're making fun of them.

How did Mickey D Russia solve the problem? They hired official Smile Explainers to shout into bullhorns at customers in line (everyone's always in line in Russia): "When you reach the counter, you will be smiled at. This does not mean we are making fun of you."

And that's how Russia became the friendly country it is today.

The basic problem with the free enterprise system is that it often rewards the wrong people with the money. As in, people who are not me.

As economist Walter Bagehot pointed out, "At particular times a great deal of stupid people have a great deal of stupid money."

•••

Some people do everything wrong because it's the only way they can come up winners.

Take Timothy Dexter, an uneducated eighteenth-century Massachusetts farmer who became a merchant when he married into money.

Dexter should have lost everything when he invested all his money in gloves, Bibles, and warming pans—then shipped them all to the West Indies.

He had chosen the absolutely wrong market, since the West Indies was not a Christian country and it was hot there—a place where no one had ever worn mittens or needed warming pans.

But just as Dexter's ship arrived, a religious fervor swept the country, and all his Bibles were purchased at high prices. The gloves were sold to Russian merchants, whose ships happened to be in port at the same time as Dexter's.

But no one wanted the warming pans, so they were dumped in a warehouse. Then a local farmer discovered that if he threw out the lid, the pan made an ideal ladle for processing molasses. As the island's molasses production grew, Dexter had the only molasses ladles available. So he made another killing he didn't deserve.

Eleven Dumb Product Warning Labels

1. "Do not allow children to play in the dishwasher."

2. On a carpenter's electric router: "This product not intended for use as a dental drill."

3. On a public toilet: "Recycled flush water unsafe for drinking."

4. On a baby stroller: "Remove child before folding."

5. On a handheld massager: "Do not use while sleeping or unconscious."

6. On a cartridge for a laser printer: "Do not eat toner."

7. On a household iron: "Never iron clothes while they are being worn."

8. On a dashboard sunshield: "Do not drive with sunshield in place."

9. On a can of self-defense pepper spray: "May irritate eyes."

10. On a pair of shin guards for bicyclists: "Shin pads cannot protect any part of the body they do not cover."

11. On a fireplace log: "Caution, risk of fire."

But wait, that's not all. Our fabulously inept businessman Timothy Dexter was fooled into loading a ship with coal from Virginia and sending it to England, to the town of Newcastle.

Yes, coals to Newcastle, the coal-mining capital of Great Britain.

But Dexter's phenomenal luck held: As his ship arrived, the coal miners went out on strike, and Dexter sold his entire load at a high profit.

● ● ●

Will the real dummy please stand up? AT&T fired its president, John Walter, after nine months on the job, saying he lacked intellectual leadership.

Walter received a $26 million severance package. If that's not intellectual leadership, then the world can get along without it.

● ● ●

Does it take brains to succeed in business? Or do they just get in the way?

"The brain is a wonderful organ," poet Robert Frost pointed out. "It starts the moment you get up in the morning and does not stop until you get to the office."

● ● ●

A Boston man was considered a fool in 1903 when he was fired from a railroad after taking a train for a joyride. When he went to work as a stable hand, he was fired for not taking care of the horses. Then he tried his hand as a deliveryman, but lost that job for losing packages.

But that fool, Alfred Fuller, became a millionaire by going to work for himself, selling household products door-to-door as the Fuller Brush Man.

●●●

Ford Motor Company invested heavily in launching its new car, the Edsel, back in 1958. The only thing Ford didn't do was find out first that the Edsel was exactly the kind of car no one wanted.

The company lost a quarter billion before they gave it up. For the few people who did buy Edsels, there was a silver lining to the fiasco: There was only a single report of anyone stealing an Edsel.

Ford had managed to design a car that even thieves didn't want.

●●●

When showman P. T. Barnum opened his museum of oddities, he did such a good job that people didn't want to leave. They hung around gawking at his exhibits so long that he couldn't get enough new customers in the door.

Barnum finally ran into the main room and banged open the exit door, shouting, "This way to the egress. Folks, see the greatest egress in the world."

When people rushed out, thinking they were going to see a new marvel, Barnum slammed the door behind them. He left them all in the alley, without a dictionary to look up the word egress, as he went around front to sell more tickets.

Victoria Woodhull was the first woman to run for president of the United States, which she did in 1870, long before women were allowed to vote.

Before Woodhull turned to politics, she was a spiritualist, conducting séances for wealthy clients and preaching free love. When that failed to produce enough income, she opened up a stock brokerage and served the same wealthy clientele, this time becoming rich—although her stock advice was no more successful than her spiritual advice.

●●●

In Tacoma, Washington, a woman went into a drugstore to get her prescription refilled for painkillers for her brain tumor.

The pharmacist thought it was a fake prescription, so he called the cops and had her arrested.

The woman tried to explain that she got the same refill at the same store every month. But no one would listen. She asked them to call her doctor. But they hauled her off to jail instead. Can you see the lawsuit coming?

●●●

Phone company AT&T has a division that provides cable TV for parts of California. When a customer called the cable office to inquire about programming changes, a clerk told him he'd have to get the information by going down to the company's office.

When the man explained that he simply wanted their phone number, the clerk said, "You have to go there, they don't accept phone calls."

"Excuse me. AT&T doesn't accept phone calls?"

In the 1960s, marketers tried to sell Americans on the idea that what they really needed to make their lives easier was a tooth-brush with an aerosol tube embedded in the handle to speed up the toothpaste-loading procedure.

When time management and productivity consciousness come to your toothbrush, your life is already under far too much control.

●●●

If you think protest marches were invented by a consortium of hippies and the promoters of the Vietnam War, consider that in 1946 Philadelphia children took to the streets in passionate pro-test marches.

Their cause? Stores had doubled the price of bubble gum, from one penny to two.

Five Things That Didn't Click
Even Though They Aren't That Much
Dumber Than Things That Did

1. Paper dresses

2. GTO muscle shoes

3. Dear Ear ear makeup

4. Knee Glo knee makeup

5. Refrigerator racing

If you want to be successful in business, remember never to let the facts get in your way. Truth is only one option.

In 1913 a factory worker from Illinois named Marshall Gardner published a book that advanced the theory that the earth was hollow. A small interior sun provided light and energy, Gardner claimed, and you could enter this inner world through huge holes at the north and south poles.

Although he had no facts to support his views (which weren't even original), Gardner's book was a big hit. He then became popular on the lecture tour and never went back to factory work again.

Like many American newspaper publishers, William Randolph Hearst never let the facts get in the way of selling more papers.

In 1913 Hearst ran front-page photos of Mexican children standing in a river with their hands raised. The story explained that the kids were surrendering to Mexican federales, who then shot them dead.

The photo and shocking report sold papers, even though the photographer took the shot in Honduras (not Mexico) and the children weren't killed. The reason they had their hands raised was because he asked them to wave for the camera.

• • •

William Randolph Hearst also ran phony photos of Russian peasants starving on the streets. The photos turned out to be of famine victims taken years before and not even in Russia.

• • •

Hearst wasn't the only newspaperman who resorted to fake news to sell papers. In 1835 editor Richard Locke pumped up sales of the *New York Sun* with a phony series about a scientist whose advanced telescope had spotted life on the moon, creatures that were half man, half bat.

Scientists didn't believe the *Sun*'s stories because their telescopes weren't powerful enough even to scan the surface of the moon, much less find creatures on it. But the public bought the hoax, making the *Sun* the most popular paper in the city.

Locke's greatest trick: getting other newspapers to buy into the phony story and print their own reports of moon people who never existed.

"Quite a few people are already working four-day weeks," newspaper columnist Earl Wilson pointed out. "Trouble is, it takes them five or six days to do it."

•••

The English minister Reverend John "Mad Jack" Alington was kicked off his pulpit for preaching free love in the nineteenth century. So he simply started his own church, drawing a congregation by providing free brandy and beer.

During services, Mad Jack would dress in leopard skins and have servants pull him up and down the aisles while he preached astride a wooden hobbyhorse.

•••

When Domino's Pizza ran a promotion in 1988 promising customers they would deliver pizza within thirty minutes, eighteen hustling delivery drivers died in car crashes.

•••

During the winter of 1979, the Allied Roofing Company of Grand Rapids, Michigan, developed a lucrative sideline clearing store roofs of snow to prevent the heavy snowfall from collapsing the roofs.

But one Grand Rapids business did have its roof collapse from snow buildup. That's right, the Allied Roofing Company roof.

•••

Book publishers are in the business of knowing which manuscripts are good enough to publish, right? Well, every now and then. But they also reject plenty of books that go on to become best-sellers for someone else.

Hans Christian Andersen's *Fairy Tales*, now considered a classic, was rejected by every publisher he could find. So the author had to publish the collection at his own expense.

Same story for Daniel Defoe's *Robinson Crusoe*.

Pearl Buck's *The Good Earth* was turned down by twelve publishers.

J. P. Donleavy's *The Ginger Man* was sent back thirty-six times before it was finally published to great success.

●●●

French tailor Barthelemy Thimmonier invented one of the first sewing machines in 1830. He was run out of town, and all his machines were destroyed by a mob of angry tailors, who thought his sewing machines would put them all out of work.

●●●

About the same time, an American inventor named Walter Hunt developed a sewing machine, but he never pursued the idea because he was afraid it would put tailors out of work.

Hunt also invented the safety pin and sold the rights to it for four hundred dollars.

●●●

In the eighteenth century the Luddites of England destroyed new weaving machines when manufacturers installed them. The Luddites thought they could preserve their old ways of life if they could only get rid of the replacement machines. They were wrong, and Luddite-minded people have been wrong ever since.

When toilet paper was invented in 1857, no one in America bought it. People were happy using newspaper and store catalogs instead.

•••

Bankers are highly trained professionals—no, really. An Australian bank gave a woman a thirty-year loan to buy her first home. The woman was ninety-two years old at the time, so she won't have to pay off the loan until she's 122. Now where can we get hold of that banker?

•••

Why is the ducktail big in Bulgaria? A bankrupt Bulgarian company paid off employees' salaries with hundreds of cheap plastic combs because that's all they had left after the money ran out.

"I can throw a comb away every time I comb my hair, and I've still got enough for the rest of my life," one worker said.

•••

As Hitler rose to power in Germany, the United States grew concerned that if American companies sold helium for German zeppelins, the Nazis might use the fuel for military advantage.

So the American supplier—the only source of helium in the world—priced the gas too high for the German company that ran the *Hindenburg*.

Making one of history's dumbest business decisions, the *Hindenburg*'s operators filled the huge blimp with hydrogen instead.

Hydrogen is the perfect gas to use if you want to start a really big fire. Which is exactly what happened after the *Hindenburg* crossed the Atlantic and was trying to dock in New Jersey.

A stray spark ignited the hydrogen, and the blimp burst into flame, burning to its shell in less than a minute, costing thirty-five lives and putting an end to the zeppelin business.

●●●

To promote a B-movie called *His Kind of Woman*, producer Howard Hughes built a special billboard on Sunset Boulevard. To show fans just how hot the movie would be, hidden jets shot out gas flames from the bodies of the stars.

The billboard worked once, then Hughes shut it down. The movie wasn't so hot either.

●●●

The first pilots' licenses were issued in France in 1909 to sixteen pilots. Not one of them was required to take a test or prove that he could actually fly a plane, safely or otherwise. You may think you've flown with some of those pilots.

●●●

In 2003, two airline pilots, who may have been descendants of those first French airmen, were fired for flying naked—even though they explained they were just playing a joke on the stews.

●●●

To keep teenage boys from hanging around out front, in 1990 7-Elevens began to pipe elevator music into their parking lots.

That got rid of the skateboarders and slouch champions. But all of a sudden convenience-store parking lots were filled with junior executives and support staff wandering around aimlessly, asking someone to push the button for twenty-seven. Or not.

History's first advertisement appeared on walls in Egypt about three thousand years ago: a notice offering a reward for the return of a runaway slave. Advertising has attempted to enslave people psychologically ever since.

•••

According to the United Nations, the ten richest men in the world have more money than five countries apiece. The top 447 millionaires are richer than half of everyone else.

•••

In 1988, when he was still kicking up a rock 'n' roll storm, an Austrian company tried to acquire future rights to Mick Jagger's body.

The company planned to cremate Jagger and pack the ashes into hourglasses to sell to Rolling Stones fans.

•••

In 2002 an Australian bank called the Bank of New Zealand switched from paying lousy interest on savings accounts to giving account owners lottery tickets instead.

You're probably not going to make money either way. But with lottery tickets at least you can enjoy a remote chance of getting rich.

Just asking, but shouldn't the Bank of New Zealand be a New Zealand bank?

Three Reasons Advertising Is More Effective If You're Selling to Idiots

1. Showman P. T. Barnum didn't invent the sideshow of freaks, but he did invent the way to make a fortune from it—through advertising, which he defined as "selling the public on the idea of throwing away the things they need and buying the things they don't need. So far it's made me a rich man."

2. Writer Stephen Leacock nailed advertising as "the science of arresting the human intelligence long enough to get money from it."

3. Writer George Orwell took the glamor right out of the ad biz when he said, "Advertising is the rattling of a stick inside a swill bucket."

A Thai company called Anything You Can Think Of provided unusual services for its clients, including engaging in arguments, slapping your enemies, or providing professional mourners to cry at your funeral.

If you wanted Anything agents to argue with your enemies while slapping amateur mourners, that was extra.

•••

Opera singer Giovanni Martinelli once appeared in a cigarette advertisement, even though he was a nonsmoker. The ad promised smokers that their brand did not irritate the throat.

"How could it irritate my throat?" Martinelli explained. "I have never smoked."

CHAPTER THIRTY-THREE

Dumb Crooks:
Quick, Let's Hop on the Motorized
Bar Stool and Make Our Getaway

Dumb crooks are good for the economy. If it weren't for the stupid criminals, we'd need twice as many cops to catch the smart ones.

So let's all give a round of applause to those crooks putting out that extra effort to get into prison.

●●●

A robbery suspect in an LA lineup got incensed when cops asked the other men in the lineup to say, "Give me all your money or I'll shoot."

"That's not what I said!" the suspect corrected them.

Okay, the rest of you guys in line can go home now.

A Swedish woman got out of a tax fraud charge when she convinced the court that rats in her attic ate all her financial records. But the rat got five to ten.

•••

England in the nineteenth century was a rough place to be a criminal, or even suspected as a criminal. Among the reasons judges condemned people to be hung: cutting down a tree, damaging a pond, associating with gypsies, writing on a bridge, and walking in public with a dirty face.

•••

When a pharmacist in Santa Cruz, California, opened up shop one morning, he saw a pair of legs dangling from the ceiling inside the store. He found a burglar stuck in the ceiling vent.

The man told police he was walking his dog on the roof of the pharmacy and had accidentally fallen through. Police arrested him anyway—just another case of cops harassing a guilty man.

•••

In 2003, a Pennsylvania couple dressed their seven-year-old son in a Cub Scout uniform and went door to door through their town raising money for his scout troop.

Doesn't sound like a crime? The boy wasn't a Cub Scout, and there was no such troop.

They conned 150 neighbors out of $667 before they got caught. How? They knocked on the door of an Eagle Scout, who saw right away that the parents had knotted the boy's tie. Cub Scouts use scout slides on their ties, not knots. Hey, it's all right there in the manual.

If you owe the bill collectors and they don't believe you when you said the check was in the mail (and they won't buy the one about your dog eating the bill), not to worry. The post office is here to help with a great excuse.

In 1989, mail inspectors in Boulder, Colorado, found that one of their carriers had buried 6,500 pounds of mail in his backyard instead of delivering it. Oddly enough, he wasn't awarded a medal.

●●●

In Port Royal, Virginia, in 2003, a bank robber set a record for botching the job, sprint division. He robbed a bank, then left a trail of dropped $100 bills all the way out to his car.

When he got to the car, he couldn't make his getaway because he had locked the keys inside. He tried to break a window but wasn't strong enough to smash the glass.

When he saw people from the bank coming after him, the bank robber fled on foot. When they caught up with him, he turned his gun on them . . . and shot himself in the leg. Finally, the cops came to give him a break and take him to jail.

●●●

In 2001, a man in North Carolina called police to complain that a thief had stolen his marijuana plants. When the police showed up, the victim led them into his garden, where the thief had ripped out the illegal pot plants.

Wait! It gets dumber, because the thief hadn't ripped out all the plants. Growing in the garden were another twenty-two pot plants worth millions. The police led the man off to jail when they were able to stop giggling.

Two Michigan store owners started a fire to burn up their inventory, which wasn't selling, and collect on the insurance. But the fire got out of control and burned the store next door.

The men who set the fire then sued the insurance company, arguing that the second fire was an accident and should be covered by their policy. They lost the suit.

•••

In 2003, an inventive if dim-witted crook robbed a Wiener-schnitzel fast food restaurant in Long Beach, California. To disguise himself, he smeared chocolate pudding all over his face.

Maybe if he'd used mustard, the robber would have blended in with the scene of the crime and gotten away with it.

•••

A man in New Zealand was arrested for setting his underwear on fire and riding through town on a motorized bar stool. The charge? Driving without a license.

•••

In Illinois a man kidnapped a driver at gunpoint and forced him to drive to two automated teller machines. But the gunman didn't steal any of the driver's money. Instead, the almost-not-a-crook withdrew money from his own bank accounts.

When caught, the man couldn't be charged with robbery since he hadn't taken anyone else's money. Unfortunately, he was charged with kidnapping.

A robber wasn't satisfied with the take from a holdup at a Topeka convenience store. So he gagged the clerk and worked the front register himself for three hours.

Then just as he made enough money for one night's work, the cops showed up at the store and busted him.

This is one of those rare crimes where the thief actually made money for the victim.

● ● ●

Some dumb crimes are notable for the stupidity not of the crooks but of their victims.

In 1906, a poor German shoemaker named William Voight pulled off one of the most daring stunts in history. First, he spent all the money he had left on a used army captain's uniform. Then he took a train to a small town and ordered the soldiers on duty there to arrest the town officials for fraud. Finally, he collected all the money from the town treasury for evidence.

Such was Voight's air of authority that everyone obeyed his orders. Although he only walked off with a few hundred dollars, his daring crime made him famous. After serving a short jail sentence, he made a small fortune on the vaudeville stage reenacting his audacious fraud.

● ● ●

Police in Oakland, California, surrounded a house where a gunman had barricaded himself inside. When they couldn't talk him out, the cops shot tear gas canisters through the windows.

But nothing happened until the police found that the gunman was standing outside right next to them, calling toward the house, "Please come out and give yourself up."

A snatch-and-grab thief in Chicago decided to see how much he could scoop up from the display window of a jewelry store. But first he needed to break the window.

No problem. He pried a manhole cover out of the street and smashed it through the window. He grabbed jewelry and took off running. And he might have gotten away with his crime if he hadn't fallen down the open manhole.

•••

A German blackmailer came up with an original scheme to extort money from the Nestlē Company. He ordered company executives to place diamonds in tiny bags, then tie them around the necks of homing pigeons.

He was captured when the police simply followed the pigeons to their destination.

•••

You don't have to be a politician to spin history. Here's Abu Abbas explaining away the murder of an American hostage in a wheelchair when Palestinian terrorists hijacked a cruise ship in 1985: "The media didn't tell the world that Abu Abbas saved the lives of six hundred passengers, only that a disabled man was killed."

He didn't specify what the appropriate ratio of people you don't kill to people you do kill should be to merit the world's thanks.

Wonder why jails are overcrowded? Because people like this insist on filling them.

In 2002, a Michigan shoplifter dropped her handbag as she was chased from a store. She later called the police to see if anyone had turned in her purse.

"You're in luck," an officer told her. When she showed up at the station to get her purse, the cops busted her.

●●●

Introduction to Robbery 101: Two crooks in Italy stole a car at gunpoint from a woman who was waiting in line at a gas station.

The cops caught them a couple miles down the road. Why? The crooks forgot the first rule of getaways: Don't steal the car *before* the driver fills it up with gas.

●●●

Perhaps the third time's the charm. A Colorado bandit robbed the same convenience store twice in the same day, then told the clerk he'd be back after she made more money.

The robber actually did return and was arrested by the cops, who were still questioning the clerk about the first two robberies.

●●●

In 1978, a Baltimore robber found a unique way to get himself arrested. When the woman he was robbing didn't have much cash on her, he suggested she write him a check.

She did, and the police simply traced the cashed check back to the robber.

In Massachusetts police had an easy time arresting a bank robber who got so nervous during the holdup that he fainted.

●●●

In 1983, two Arizona men were having car trouble on the side of the highway. Yes, they had been drinking. No, no one driving by stopped to help them.

So they figured out a great way to get people to stop: They took out their guns and shot at passing cars. And someone did stop—the cops.

●●●

The irony is more than we asked for. The founder of a group that helps people with drinking problems pleaded guilty in 2000 to vehicular homicide after hitting two people while driving drunk. Her group, Moderation Management, claims that moderate drinking can work for some drunks.

●●●

In 1988 John Zaccaro Jr. was given a four-month sentence for selling cocaine. He spent three months of that detention living in a luxury condo in Burlington, Vermont. But as his mother pointed out: "He didn't have a maid."

Remember his mom? Geraldine Ferraro, who ran for vice president on the Democratic ticket with Walter Mondale.

●●●

In California last year the San Bernardino County sheriff's department sent offers to people wanted on felony warrants for free hiking boots made by "Stockdum Scelestus."

What none of the felons who showed up figured out was that the manufacturer's name was a mix of German and Latin that meant "utterly stupid criminal."

That's what the felons must have felt like when instead of being given free boots, they were busted.

●●●

The nineteenth-century British aristocrat John Mytton carried too much money with him for someone who drank so heavily in taverns. He was known as an easy mark for robbers.

But nineteenth-century highwaymen weren't necessarily any smarter than rich drunks. As Mytton left a tavern, he was grabbed by rival gangs at the same time and became the rope in a larcenous tug of war.

Neither side would let go of their quarry, so Mytton, in his drunken strength, knocked them all down and held several of them until the police arrived.

●●●

Big Brother is also watching Big Brother. In 2002, cameras used to catch speeders in Holland were destroyed by angry drivers. So the police tried to catch the vandals by installing new sets of cameras to watch the other cameras.

●●●

Neighbors in the town of Offenbach, Germany, thought a horrible crime must be happening when they heard the screams from next door. So they called the police.

When the cops got inside the home, they found a seventy-six-year-old woman practicing her yodeling.

"The officers weren't able to judge whether the neighbors were unfamiliar with Bavarian folk music," the police report concluded, "or whether the lady still requires a lot of practice."

●●●

Even when they do go to prison, corporate big shots still live better than most people do outside prison.

That's why *Forbes* magazine reviewed the best prisons in America, the minimum-security jails for white-collar criminals, evaluating them on their accommodations, food, and such amenities as recreational and athletic facilities.

CHAPTER THIRTY-FOUR

Dumb Ways to Die:
Buried Alive but Not for Long

Most of us manage to die without the help of harmonicas and lions. We don't tempt fate with our bathing suits. We feel no need to exert our mental powers on speeding trains.

But if there weren't plenty of people who volunteered to run the gamut to dumb deaths, these pages would be blank.

•••

In 1937, the Reverend Harold Davidson went on a hunger strike after the Church of England defrocked him for consorting with prostitutes. He was then arrested for attempted suicide, a crime in England.

As the trial began, he had himself hauled into court locked in a cage with a lion. This was Davidson's idea of a publicity stunt that was supposed to gain him popular sympathy.

Before Davidson could take the stand to prove his innocence, the lion killed him.

•••

In the eighteenth century, an Italian duke named Antonio Fernando was told by a fortune teller that alcohol would be the death of him. So he stopped drinking.

One night Fernando used an alcohol rub to soothe his aching muscles. The alcohol caught fire and he burned to death.

•••

In the 1800s, European doctors recommended that patients take to the waters at the seashore, lakes, and springs for their health. Modesty demanded that women wear bathing suits with under-layers made of flannel, topped by skirts, bloomers, and shoes.

While seeking their health in the water, many women drowned under the weight of their heavy bathing outfits.

•••

The Indian mystic Khadeshwari Baba had his followers bury him alive in 1980 to demonstrate his remarkable control over body and spirit. When he was dug up ten days later, he was demonstrating his powers on some other plane of existence. On this plane, he was dead.

The evidence may have been circumstantial, but what jury could resist so many coincidences? In 1911, three men were convicted of murdering Sir Edmund Berry at Greenberry Hill.

The killers were hanged for their crime. Their names weirdly enough: Green, Berry, and Hill.

●●●

Here's a dumb way to be forced to die. Lawyers for a death row inmate in Arkansas appealed to federal court in 2003 that their client should not be executed because he was insane and a Supreme Court decision prohibits execution of the insane.

But the appeals court ruled that the prisoner should be given antipsychotic drugs involuntarily so that he would return to sanity and could then be legally executed.

As the judge wrote, explaining the court's decision: "Eligibility for execution is the only unwanted consequence of the medication."

Can't you see the prescription warning label: "Side effects may include nausea, dizziness, anxiety, impotence, and eligibility for execution."

●●●

A psychic healer in Russia, known as E. Frenkel, wanted to demonstrate his ability to stop a train using only the power of his remarkable mind. So in 1998, he stepped in front of a freight train.

Brakes eventually stopped the train, but long after Frenkel had learned the bumpy limitations of his psychic powers.

Musicians often add novelty items to their acts to draw audience attention. Ramon Barrero, a Mexican musician, had a clever gimmick: playing a tiny harmonica so small you could barely see it when he played it.

Unfortunately, in 1994 the harmonica slipped from his fingers as Barrero inhaled and he choked to death on stage.

●●●

In 1902, the scorekeeper at a baseball game in Morristown, Ohio, was sharpening his pencil with a knife when a foul ball was lined back into the stands. As unlikely as it sounds, the ball slammed into the scorekeeper's hand, hammered the knife into his chest, and killed him.

●●●

An Illinois woman died in 1996 when she was smothered in the trash. But she didn't die in a tragic garbage can accident or down at the dump.

The woman was an obsessive collector of trash, piling it up inside her house. One day the trash piles collapsed on top of her.

●●●

Matthew Webb was the first person to swim across the English Channel and live. It took him nearly twenty-two hours to make the arduous crossing in 1875. His achievement was hailed internationally.

Eight years later he got the bright idea of swimming across the waters above Niagara Falls. He died when he was swept over the falls. Wouldn't have become incrementally more famous if he had succeeded.

In 1989, not one but two people got so angry at unfulfilling vending machines that they grabbed the offending machines and shook them to get out their purchases. The machines toppled over and killed them—two rare cases of death by vending machine.

● ● ●

One tastes like chickpeas, the other bubbles. An Israeli man died at ninety-one when his nurse spread dishwashing detergent on his bread instead of the chickpea spread hummus.

The nurse told police he couldn't read the Hebrew writing on the detergent container.

● ● ●

But did he reach level five? A game-loving Korean man played computer games for eighty-six hours without stopping to eat or sleep. Then he died, having gamed himself to death.

● ● ●

In 1705, the people of West Hartlepool, England, thought they had captured a French spy, so they hung him. The "spy" was an ape. Not a big dumb guy—a real ape.

Two Tough Ways to Almost Die

1. In 1906, a man named Alfredo Bindi tried to commit suicide by eating his suspenders. He failed.

2. In 2000, an Italian man tried to drown himself in a river, but was swept away into the Milan sewer system instead. He floated in the "stinking, filthy water" for six hours before rescuers pulled him out through a manhole.

George II of England died after falling off his throne. But it wasn't so noble. The throne he fell off of was his toilet.

●●●

A Zimbabwe spiritual leader drowned during a tribal rite in 1990. His followers didn't pull him out of the water because they thought his magical powers were protecting him, enabling him to breathe underwater, where he lay for two days.

●●●

In 1990 a hunter wounded a deer, but the deer wouldn't quit. So the man clubbed it with his shotgun, which fired by accident, killing the hunter.

In Virginia in 2003, a man was bit by a dog. He went after the mutt with a rifle, determined to beat the dog to death with the butt of the gun.

You can see this one coming, can't you? While the man was thumping the dog, the rifle went off and the man shot himself to death. The dog recovered nicely.

••••

In 1989, a man in Connecticut called his wife a "fat ox," but shouldn't have. Upset, she stumbled, fell, and landed on top of him. Before she managed to get off, he was crushed to death. She weighed 500 pounds.

••••

In 1899, an Englishman was taken by a car salesman on the first demo ride in British history. The salesman crashed the car, killing them both. It was the first car collision in history in which someone other than the driver died.

••••

In the sixteenth century, Sir Richard Grenville, captain of the English ship *Revenge*, took on twenty Spanish galleons and refused to surrender, even when his ship had been riddled by eight hundred cannonballs and all his men were dead or wounded.

Instead, Grenville smashed a wine glass, then ate the glass and bled to death.

Millions of peasants in the Soviet Union were starved to death in the famine years of 1932 to 1934 even though they would have survived if they had been allowed to eat the food they grew.

They died not because there wasn't enough food but because it was politically expedient. Soviet dictator Josef Stalin wanted to demonstrate the success of his collective farms by exporting the grain harvest around the world. Incidentally, he denied his own people the food that would have kept them alive.

● ● ●

If you were a good athlete in Central America in ancient times, you probably played *tlachtli*, especially if you were a slave athlete.

The game pitted two teams that hit a ball without using hands or feet—tricky business. But you wanted to be skillful at it since the losing team was slaughtered after the game.

That's why team owners used slaves. Can't you see wheels spinning at the NFL?

CHAPTER THIRTY-FIVE

Oofty Goofty, Screaming Meemies, and Other Amazing Acts of Popped Culture

Composer John Cage wrote a song called "As Slow as Possible." Cage's idea: the song would take 629 years to play.

And they say pop culture has no lasting value.

•••

Most kids think their fathers are idiots at one time or another. But most dads don't give their kids proof.

Then there's Hollywood. As movie director Billy Wilder pointed out, "A bad play folds and is forgotten, but in pictures we don't bury our dead. When you think it's out of your system, your daughter sees it on television and says, 'My father is an idiot.'"

Among the stranger acts in the history of show business was the display of pain tolerance by a nineteenth-century San Francisco street performer known as Oofty Goofty. For his act, Oofty charged people to punch, kick, and beat him with a bat.

Boxing champ John L. Sullivan took Oofty Goofty up on the offer to hit him with a pool cue for fifty cents. Sullivan broke Goofty's back, and that was the end of his showbiz career.

●●●

Two days after the United States invaded Panama to depose the country's ruler, Mañuel Noriega, a computer company released a war game called Find Noriega.

●●●

To ring in the new year, a Florida radio station played "Stairway to Heaven" 181 times in a row on December 31, 1989. Dumb enough. But nothing is so dumb that it can't be trumped.

The DJ who played 181 "Stairways" was trumped by the person who listened to them all and kept count, making sure no one was trying to short fans a "Heaven" or two.

●●●

Back in the 1950s, Fess Parker's TV show made everything Davy Crockett a hit. Not only did they sell more coonskin hats than anyone ever wore in wild frontier times. But one sporting goods store owner figured out how to sell his stock of 200,000 pup tents.

He simply wrote the name Davy Crockett on the tents and sold them all in two days.

In the 1950s, college students got into a fad that would be all but impossible today: stuffing themselves into phone booths. The record: thirty-four students crammed into a single booth.

Remember phone booths? Think of them as large, clunky cell phones.

●●●

Disco fever? Hip-hop frenzy? Nothing compared to the frenetic dance madness that swept through Europe in the Middle Ages.

Today you'd have to pay a crazy fortune for concert tickets and the privilege of dancing yourself into a mind-altering state with hundreds of strangers.

Back then people would suddenly break into wild, convulsive dancing in the streets. Didn't cost them a thing, other than possible imprisonment as witches and such injuries as cobblestone heel.

Think you've danced till the sun comes up? The medieval dance craze lasted for two hundred years, into the sixteenth century.

To cure dance fever, cities banished the color red from buildings and clothes. It was thought that anything red drove the dancers wild.

Three Tries to
Trash the Rock

1. Talent helps if you're trying to make it in rock 'n' roll, but brains will usually trip you up. As Frank Zappa of the Mothers of Invention pointed out, "The typical rock fan isn't smart enough to know when he's being dumped on."

2. Even though he recorded several rock 'n' roll songs, singer Frank Sinatra didn't care for the music, declaring rock to be "phony and false, sung, written, and played for the most part by cretinous goons."

3. The Guess Who had a hit in 1970 with "Share the Land." But the song was banned across the South because politicians thought it was promoting communism.

    As the band later explained, the song was about heaven. Wouldn't those red-baiting politicians have served the country better by investigating the subversive lyrics in "Louie, Louie"? Oh that's right, they had the FBI handle that investigation.

You've heard of songs that are number one with a bullet? Here's a tune that was number one with a goose.

In 1974, a man in England was listening to a record of Frankie Lane singing "Cry of the Wild Goose" when he heard something crash in his bedroom. He ran into the room and found that a wild goose had flown through the window. Two more geese crashed into the window and bounced off outside. Now that's singing.

●●●

Here's a new way to think of the amnesia-inducing empty-headedness of TV: Cellist Gregor Piatigorsky agreed to make his first TV appearance when a friend explained that it would "take over one hundred years for that many people to hear me in concert," the cellist recalled.

"He failed to tell me how many seconds it would take them to forget."

●●●

During the Vietnam War, the South Vietnamese government didn't have much luck fighting the Viet Cong. They had more success in the battle against American pop culture, banning the twist because the dance was "not compatible with the anticommunist struggle."

●●●

Who would have guessed that at their opening night party, the original cast of *West Side Story* danced to the music from *My Fair Lady*? Oh, those teenage rebels of the fifties.

Don't know how many people listen to music each day, but we do know that every day 80 million people around the world hear Muzak.

•••

When a teenage Bob Dylan and his first rock 'n' roll band played for a dance at his Minnesota high school, the school principal pulled the plug on the singer's microphone.

•••

Composer George Antheil, known as the "bad boy of music," gave avant garde concerts in which a player piano made all the music. Antheil sat at the piano and pretended to play, moving around so aggressively and with so many contortions that he drove himself to the point of total collapse—without actually making any music.

These shows made him the toast of Paris in the 1920s.

•••

John Barrymore was the first American actor to play Hamlet on the London stage. At the premier, he made his entrance drunk out of his mind.

Throughout the play, he had to lean on other actors to keep from falling, and he rushed offstage several times to throw up. To deliver Hamlet's famous "To be, or not to be" speech, Barrymore staggered to a chair and sat down so he wouldn't fall down.

The English critics raved—not at Barrymore, for him. They thought his drunken maneuvers created a masterful interpretation of Hamlet, especially his daring, seated presentation of the "to be or not to be" speech.

In the eighteenth century, Robert Coates was considered by critics and audiences to be the worst Shakespearean actor anyone had ever seen. When he played Romeo, the London audience responded with a barrage of garbage. The star had to crawl off-stage to escape.

But Coates had his revenge. His performance was so ludicrous that six people in the audience laughed themselves sick and had to be hospitalized. That may have been the first and only time *Romeo and Juliet* was interpreted as a comedy.

● ● ●

During the Great Depression, flagpole sitting became an unusual and incredibly foolish fad, sponsored by businesses trying to draw crowds.

Shipwreck Kelly became the most famous flagpole sitter in the United States, setting the world record by swaying atop a pole for forty-nine days and nights. His nickname: The Luckiest Man Alive.

Kelly's record stood for fifty years, primarily because few people were dumb enough to want to break it. Then in 1976, Frank Perkins smashed the record by sitting atop a flagpole at a used car lot for an entire year.

● ● ●

What is it with teenage girls and the need to squeal at high decibels? It's not a rock 'n' roll phenomenon. It goes back at least to the 1940s when girls gathered in cities across the nation to squeal at Frank Sinatra's performances. They were known then as "screaming meemies."

Only after Sinatra's fame was secured was it revealed that his PR guy paid girls to squeal, swoon, and faint at those first shows.

During the reign of King Louis XIII, the place to be seen was the court ballet, where the trendsetters of France strutted about in their most elaborate fashions.

Eventually, so many pretenders spilled onto the stage that there was no room left for the dancers, and performances were canceled. People who went to the ballet never actually saw the ballet. But perhaps it was better that way.

•••

The world's first ballet was performed for the king of France in 1581. It was such an expensive staging (costing over three million gold francs) and lasted so long (five and a half hours) that it was only danced once. Fans have been grateful ever since.

•••

Fiddler on the Roof was banned in Chile for sixteen years. But in 1990, the ban was lifted and Chileans were finally allowed to see the daring musical about Russian Jews, which must have caused a large portion of the Chilean population to go: Huh? We waited sixteen years for that?

•••

Can we open that window for you, Mr. Richards? The Hyatt Hotel in West Hollywood was known as the Riot Hotel in the 1970s because of rockers like Keith Richards, who tossed furniture out the window; Led Zeppelin, who rode their motorcycles up to their rooms; and Jim Morrison, who tempted fate by hanging from balcony railings.

The Best of Click and Clack, heard on the *Car Talk* radio show: "Now for another short break. In other words, it's time for you to scan the dial and see if there's anything less moronic on."

•••

A parting shot from critic Ian Shoales: "When I saw *Annie* I had to hit myself on the head afterward with a small hammer to get that stupid 'Tomorrow' song out of my head."

•••

And yet another parting shot from baseball great Yogi Berra: "It was pretty good. Even the music was nice." Yogi was talking about his first trip to the opera.

CHAPTER THIRTY-SIX

Anthro-dimology:
The Study of How Stupid Ancient People Were
Before They Became Us

The great thing about the past is that we can look back and laugh at them, and they can't laugh back. Time makes us smarter by cutting off the argument in our favor.

•••

Back before we had scientists to explain everything to the rest of us, there were still plenty of know-it-alls who thought they knew how things worked.

Here are some popular beliefs that now look idiotic to our enlightened selves. But I wonder which of our current beliefs will be proven just as dumb when we do the year 3004 edition of this book.

Beekeepers could create new bees by letting veal rot (seventh century).

To have a boy baby, a wife should grind up the male sexual organs of hares and drink them mixed with wine (eleventh century).

Baby bears were blobs at birth and did not become bear-shaped until they were formed into bearlets by their mothers (twelfth century).

Lion cubs remained lifeless after they were born until a male lion breathed on them (thirteenth century).

You could soften diamonds by soaking them in goat blood (seventeenth century). Why you would want a soft diamond in the 1600s was never made entirely clear.

A doctor treating the victim of a sword wound should apply his medicines to the sword instead of the wound (seventeenth century).

Ketchup and mustard led people to uncontrollable lust (nineteenth century). Well, have you been to a Jack-in-the-Box lately?

• • •

In Victorian times, pianos were considered risqué. So in proper English households, skirts were put around pianos to shield their legs.

In England during the Middle Ages, it was considered unmanly to sleep on a mattress or any other soft surface. Real men slept on the floor in their clothes because they thought it made them better fighters.

But real men had trouble explaining why the tough-sleeping English lost several wars to the soft-sleeping French.

● ● ●

In Italy during the 1500s, men were considered effeminate for eating their food with a fork. So boys, next time your mom scolds you for picking up your food with your hands, just tell her you're a man.

● ● ●

Even before Emily Post, there were proper manners. But in the Dark Ages in Europe, manners were a little different than they are in today's polite society. Back then if you were a lady or a gentleman, you were expected to adhere to the following rules:

Don't pick your teeth with your knife.

Don't chew on a bone, then put it back in the common dish.

Don't blow your nose on the tablecloth.

Don't spit across the table.

In ancient Europe, people thought that to build a bridge was to tempt fate. So to appease the gods and keep the bridge from collapsing, children were sacrificed, buried alive inside the bridge's foundation.

•••

We throw rice at the bride, as they did at weddings centuries ago. They also threw wheat to wish the new bride many children.

Oh, and they threw one more thing at weddings. For fertility insurance, well-wishers tossed old shoes at the bride. That's how we get the shoes tied to the rear of cars, a modern relief for shoe-ducking brides everywhere.

•••

We celebrate Christmas Day as the birth of Christ. But in the third century, the Catholic Church considered it a sin to celebrate Jesus's birth.

Even the attempt to figure out exactly when Jesus was born was labeled sacrilegious.

•••

During the Dark Ages, kings were the only people who had birthday celebrations. Ordinary people celebrated only the day of their deaths because it marked their escape from this world of woe into a better life in heaven.

In ancient times, the dead were buried in coffins not out of respect but because people feared the deceased would come back and haunt them. That's why coffins were nailed shut.

A large stone was placed on top of the coffin, not as a commemorative tombstone, but to keep the dead from escaping.

●●●

Every culture comes up with its own story to explain the creation of the world. All creation stories have, what they call in Hollywood, holes in the plot. But some are more creative than others.

In the South Pacific, people believed that the human race was created from sugar cane, with one bud of the stalk turning into the first man and another bud into the first woman.

This explains why women are so sweet—and why men are so . . . sweet also. No, that doesn't hold. Maybe this story explains why sugar is bad for you.

●●●

In the early 1800s, the stylish young upper-class Englishman was known as a dandy, buck, or beau. To be a proper English dandy, you had to throw away all your family money on gambling and elaborate dinner parties.

If you did it right, you went deeply into debt, then fled the country for France when you couldn't pay your bills.

But the one thing you never did, no matter how dire the circumstances, was go to work to pay off your debts. It simply wasn't done in polite society.

If you were traveling back in time to the Middle Ages and could take along only one thing, what would you take?

You probably didn't say a clothespin. But it would come in useful clipped firmly around your nose, because Europe in the Middle Ages was the stinkiest age the human race has yet contrived.

Especially in cities like Paris and London, where people dumped their refuse into the gutters—or on the sidewalks if they had a weak slop pot arm and couldn't reach the gutters.

Most people never bathed; it was considered sinful and unhealthy. They rarely washed their clothes.

If all that wasn't smelly enough, they invented a clever strategy to combat the mice and bugs that shared their straw bedding: They stuffed garlic in with the straw before going to sleep.

● ● ●

Sometimes those old fairy tales we read to our children are too gruesome for the little ones. If only the kids knew that most of them were actually toned down from the original, centuries-old stories.

> In the first version of *Snow White and the Seven Dwarfs*, the wicked queen is punished by being forced into iron shoes. The shoes are then set in a fire until the queen burns up dancing to death.

> In the original *Cinderella* tale, the put-upon girl murders her evil stepmother. But her father then marries an even more evil woman.

In another early version, when one of Cinderella's gross stepsisters can't fit her fat foot into the glass slipper, her mother simply hacks off part of her foot—and the shoe fits!

Little Red Riding Hood gets eaten by the wolf (as does her grandmother) in the original tale.

As for Sleeping Beauty, the prince rapes her while she sleeps and she gives birth to twins while still in a coma.

But parents can be relieved because kids don't always pick up on the gruesome nature of these fairy tales. Instead, they may get this interesting message from a lot of fables: Even though adults are in charge of the world, they're dumb and can easily be fooled.

• • •

In the fifteenth century, an English bishop named Reginald Pecock tried to purify the English language by getting rid of words of Latin origin.

His idea ran out of popular steam when he recommended such changes as "inconceivable" to "nottobethoughtable."

• • •

You think our nonsmoking rules are too strict? Or not strict enough?

Consider what happened to the first cigarette smoker in Europe. A sailor in Christopher Columbus's crew, Rodrigo de Jerez, brought cigarettes back to Europe from his explorations of Cuba.

He also became the new era's first cigarette addict, and the Inquisition threw him into prison for the "devilish habit" of smoking.

•••

Around 1400, the French University of Toulouse wasn't bringing in enough money through student tuition. How did they raise the cash? Not from alumnae. But by opening the Abbaye, a university-sponsored brothel.

•••

Capturing Africans and selling them into slavery was not a barbarism invented by greedy Europeans or American plantation owners. The Islamic world had been enslaving Africans for a thousand years before European capitalists moved in on the slave trade.

•••

We look at ancient Greece for the shining light of freedom and democracy. Yet all the great achievements of that enlightened culture were built on the backs of slave labor. Not only did the Greeks originate the concept of freedom but also the abuse of freedom.

•••

In the Dark Ages, when the poor people of Paris died (often of plagues), they were dumped in unmarked graves in the Cemetery of the Innocents.

In the thirteenth century, that cemetery became a Parisian promenade, where the fashionable shopped and strolled of an evening, past mounds of human bones.

●●●

In medieval times the French and the English held low opinions of each other. One popular belief in France was that Englishmen were born with tails.

CHAPTER THIRTY-SEVEN

Riding the Bull, Mourning the Cowwws: The Wonderful World of Stupid Eccentricities

Can you be a knucklehead and eccentric at the same time? Sure, if you're willing to put in the extra effort.

Like John Mytton, a nineteenth-century British aristocrat who felt guilty about his inherited wealth. When that happens to the relatively normal rich, they give away some of their money to a worthy cause and usually feel better enough to fly off to the Riviera guilt-free.

Not Mytton. His guilt led him to the odd habit of hunting ducks naked in the snow. One other manifestation of his loose-brained eccentricity—his nickname: Mango, the King of Pickles. No, really.

But Mango was in good company:

Writer Louisa May Alcott's father, Amos, believed in the nonviolent and ethical treatment of bugs.

But that didn't make him a good neighbor. When Amos found potato bugs in his garden, he carefully picked them off, but didn't kill them. Instead, he dropped the plant eaters over the fence into his neighbor's garden.

●●●

To demonstrate how he earned the nickname the Mouth, Jim Purol smoked 140 cigarettes at the same time in 1983.

For some reason, Purol's attempt to apply economy of scale to the strategy of suicide by cigarette was not recognized by American industry.

●●●

Cambridge scholar Charles Ogden disliked being disturbed during his studies, particularly by noise from the street outside his home. To drown the outside noise, he filled his rooms with loud chiming clocks and radios playing at full volume. Then he'd work through the night on his research. He'd have dinner at dawn.

●●●

The Christian Apostolic Church was a repressive sect in Zion, Illinois, led by the preacher and General Overseer Wilbur Voliva in the 1880s.

Among his strange personal habits that became the group's commandments: no bacon, no oysters, no humming, no whistling. Everyone had to be indoors by ten p.m., and all of his followers had to agree that the earth was flat.

Actress Sarah Bernhardt always kept a bizarre good luck charm with her when she went on tour: a coffin.

●●●

Queen Elizabeth I of England was a charmer in some ways, but for the last ten years of her life she refused to wash her face.

●●●

Hermit and artist Edward Leedskalnin spent twenty years creating a coral castle and vast garden of coral sculpture in a remote part of Florida, where few people ever saw his creations.

Although he had no family, Leedskalnin wrote and published a family advice book instructing parents to stop their kids from smiling because it caused wrinkles.

●●●

William Hervey, a seventeenth-century doctor to English kings, had an unusual writing habit: He added more letters to the end of words than were needed, so that *cow* became *cowww* and *man* became *mannn*.

●●●

Martin van Butchell, a prominent London doctor of the eighteenth century, painted his white horses with purple spots when he rode around town.

Another English eccentric, Sir Tatton Sykes, was obsessed with maintaining body warmth. He would walk through the countryside wearing layers of overcoats, which he simply discarded along the road as the day got warmer.

Village boys made good money following him on his walks, then returning the coats for a shilling apiece, over and over again.

● ● ●

The Archduke Franz Ferdinand of World War I fame despised wrinkles and creases in his clothes. So he had servants sew him into his suits before he appeared in public.

The obsession backfired when Ferdinand was shot by Sarajevo assassins. His people couldn't cut his clothes off quickly enough to stop the bleeding. World War I might have been averted by better buttons.

● ● ●

Matthew Robinson was an eighteenth-century English lord, so he got away with his odd behavior, which was mostly of the watery variety.

A semi-hermit, Robinson spent his days in the ocean—the entire day. During the winter, he bathed the day away in an outdoor tub, having servants bring his meals there and conducting all the business of his estate while submerged to the neck in water.

● ● ●

Beatnik poet Joe Gould spent cold nights sleeping out in Greenwich Village, stuffing newspapers inside his suit for warmth. But Gould, a true bohemian, refused to use any paper for insulation but the *New York Times*, proclaiming himself to be a "snob at heart."

English eccentric Charles Waterton turned his estate into a bird sanctuary, but not for the kinds of birds most people keep as pets. Instead, he gave over the preserve to buzzards, carrion crows, and magpies, claiming they were the victims of discrimination.

Waterton slept on the floor of an empty room in his mansion, using a block of wood for his pillow.

He also had the odd habit of hiding from his houseguests, then jumping out to bite their ankles.

● ● ●

John Henry Patterson, the wealthy founder of National Cash Register, took four baths every day. He had his underwear made of the same felt they use for pool tables.

● ● ●

Jemmy Hirst was a great practitioner of the proper British hunt in the mid-1800s. Well, not quite proper. When Hirst went hunting, he eschewed the horse and hounds that other English gentlemen used. Instead, he rode upon a bull and used trained pigs to lead the chase.

● ● ●

Edward VII, king of England, had one of those hobbies it's best to be king if you're going to have. He had servants record in ledgers the weight of every visitor to his castle.

Jonathan Swift, who wrote *Gulliver's Travels*, developed his own odd way of traveling: He counted every footstep. That way, Swift knew how many steps his daily walks through the countryside would require.

•••

Saints often test themselves to prove their devotion to their mystical vision. Saint Francesca came up with the kind of test only someone on the saint track would not get rubber-roomed for—burning herself with hot bacon.

•••

When he was in the thick of his research, the English physicist Oliver Heaviside would live on nothing but bowls of milk. He kept warm while he worked in his drafty lab by bundling up in layers of blankets and wearing a tea cozy on his head instead of a hat.

•••

In Liechtenstein farmers publish obituaries in the local paper when their cows die.

•••

The nineteenth-century earl of Aldborough, Benjamin Stratford, threw away his family fortune trying to build the world's largest balloon. His attempts burned up when his hangar caught fire.

The earl spent the last years of his life as a hotel recluse, having all meals sent to his room but refusing to allow maids to remove the trays afterward.

When he died, his room was piled from floor to ceiling with dirty dishes.

•••

Oxford professor Richard Porson was such a heavy drinker that he ruined his nose, the busted veins leading to ugly disfigurement. The professor cared nothing for appearances and could be seen walking around campus wearing a coat covered with cobwebs and a cone of paper pasted to his nose.

•••

John Bigg was a scholar and respected member of the judiciary during the reign of Charles I of England. Bigg had one quirk that set him apart from the rest of England's elite: sewing odd pieces of leather all over his clothes.

CHAPTER THIRTY-EIGHT

Fools for Love:
Tom Cruise Mows the Lawn;
Ivan the Terrible Solves Virginity

Do I believe in love at first sight? Almost exclusively. Second sight tends to make Hamlets of us all. Or Houdinis.

So who plays the fool for love? The volunteers, baby.

● ● ●

When Edgar Allan Poe, the poet of gloom, was a boy, he showed his affection for the girls in his town by hiding in the bushes and throwing live snakes at them.

An Iranian man who married 168 women attributed his romantic allure to his diet: two pounds of onions a day.

•••

A survey found that 52 percent of American women would give up a year of their lives to have their ideal body.

The problem with such surveys is they don't ask: Which year of your life? People might give up their eighty-second year for a great body. But would they give up their twenty-eighth year?

•••

Reason number 157 why you should never marry anyone from Hollywood: A society girl named Doris Lilly married movie director John Huston in a Mexican ceremony. Then she caught him cheating on her. She was even more surprised when he announced that he couldn't be cheating because they were never married.

Huston had talked one of the actors from his movie *Treasure of the Sierra Madre* into playing the minister at a fake wedding ceremony.

•••

There are over one hundred romance novels published each month. That's more than the actual number of true romances.

•••

A Bible printed in London in 1631 included an embarrassing typo. Instead of "Thou shalt not . . ." it read, "Thou shalt commit adultery."

There's one commandment that could be followed by people who couldn't follow the other nine.

•••

Czar Ivan the Terrible announced that he would choose his bride from a lineup of one thousand virgins gathered from all over Russia. The decree proved surprisingly popular with the young men of Russia.

An unusual number of young women quickly gave their virginity to almost anyone else, in order to disqualify themselves before they could be summoned to the Kremlin for inspection.

•••

Writer Charles Dickens had an endearing nickname for his wife: Dearest Darling Pig. She later divorced him.

•••

The Indian potentate Gaikwar of Baroda was so romantically inclined that he spent $2 million on weddings. Not his own, not his kids', not his court's—he spent that much money on lavish weddings for his pets.

•••

Can international relations actually be more romantic than romance itself? Few love notes compare to the one sent by Idi Amin, president of Uganda, to Julius Nyerere, president of Tanzania (a country Amin was planning to invade).

"I love you so much," Amin wrote, "that if you were a woman I would consider marrying you."

The invasion failed too.

You've got to have heart. Peter the Great, czar of Russia, kept the head of his favorite mistress in a jar by his bed.

But Peter the Great was not just nostalgic. He was also a jealous lover. When he suspected that his wife had a lover, he removed the paramour's head and forced his wife to keep it in a jar by *her* bed.

●●●

Poets take a slightly different approach to love. When the poet Percy Bysshe Shelley died young, his romantic wife Mary wanted to keep his heart with her always, wrapped in a piece of silk. But they were poets, not anatomists, and Mary ended up with Percy's liver.

But who's to say the liver can't be as romantic as the heart?

●●●

Not nearly so romantic was the German wife who divorced her husband on the grounds that he ate too much celery in bed and the constant crunching kept her awake.

●●●

In 1946, an Ohio flag pole sitter and his fiancée got married while perched on top of a 176-foot pole. Like many marriages, it was a long way down from there.

●●●

In nineteenth-century England, a visionary named Thomas Harris formed a religion called the Brotherhood of the New Life, under the theory that God was bisexual. To get close to God, followers had to get close to Father Harris, who particularly wanted to get close to young women.

Father Harris didn't do this for his own gratification, but because his bisexual counterpart in heaven was a spirit called the Lily Queen. She wanted to comfort followers of her own sex, which she could only do on Earth through the body of Father Harris.

"By getting into his arms," women adherents were told, "we get into her arms."

Enough people actually bought this line to keep Father Harris from getting lonely at night.

●●●

On his wedding night, Charles Joffe took his new bride to a performance by stand-up comedian Woody Allen. Joffe was Allen's manager at the time. Joffe's bride was dragged into the nightclub in her wedding gown.

●●●

When he was a Broadway producer, George M. Cohan fired a young actor from one of his shows because he had no romantic appeal. The dumped actor? Clark Gable.

●●●

Johnny Depp, in love with Winona Ryder, ordered up a "Winona Forever" tattoo. After they split, he had it changed to "Wino Forever."

Four Foolish Skirmishes
in the Battle of the Sexes

1. "Love is the triumph of imagination over intelligence," said the unhappy-in-love author H. L. Mencken.

2. Writer Pearl Buck cautioned her daughters about the realities of married life with this estimation of men:

   "The bitterest creature under heaven is the wife who discovers that her husband's bravery is only bravado, that his strength is only a uniform, that his power is but a gun in the hands of a fool."

3. Anthropologist Margaret Mead may have been answering Pearl Buck when she said: "Women want mediocre men, and men are working hard to be as mediocre as possible."

4. "Girls have an unfair advantage over men," actor Yul Brynner countered. "If they can't get what they want by being smart, they can get it by being dumb."

In 1989, a boy asked a girl to their high school prom. Then on the big night, he stood her up.

The girl's mother sued the boy. What did she want in damages? $49.53. How high did that leave her daughter's self-esteem? First, she gets dumped. Then her own mother thinks she's not even worth an even fifty dollars.

•••

President Grover Cleveland waited until 1905 when he was out of the White House to embarrass himself with this remark: "Sensible and responsible women do not want to vote. The relative positions to be assumed by man and woman in the working out of our civilization were assigned long ago by a higher intelligence than ours."

Apparently, that higher intelligence found it necessary to work through such a lesser intelligence as Cleveland.

•••

Peek-a-boo-boo? In the early 1900s, upper-class English gentlemen hoarded naughty pictures of harem women from the Ottoman Empire, posed peeking out from behind their veils.

But since women in Turkey weren't allowed to pose for photos, many of these pictures were of men posing as women.

•••

What says love better than a fourteen-karat gold birthday present? That's what filmmaker Carlo Ponti gave his wife, the actress Sophia Loren, on her fortieth birthday. Romantic? Well, maybe. He gave her a solid gold toilet seat.

Just because you can do something to get into the Guinness Book of World Records doesn't mean you should.

Take Jack Moran, who was married forty times. So was Edna Moran. The Seattle couple married each other forty times starting in 1937, enacting repeat wedding ceremonies all over the world.

● ● ●

When the artist Marcel Duchamp was married, he ignored his bride on their honeymoon and instead played chess. She countered by gluing the chess pieces to the board. He countered by divorcing her three weeks later.

● ● ●

"You don't choose your best friend because they have a cute nose," writer Fran Lebowitz said. "But that's all you're doing when you get married."

● ● ●

"I've never been an in-between type woman in romance," TV talk show host Kathie Lee Gifford said. "If I'm in love I want to get married. That's how stupid I am."

● ● ●

When comic actor Poodles Hanneford got married, he wouldn't carry his bride across the threshold. Even though the practice is antiquated, she expected him to do his part. But Poodles explained, "I am an actor, not a porter."

The English writer Thomas Hardy loved his wife, Emma, so much that he requested to be buried next to her.

But Hardy, who wrote *Tess of the d'Urbervilles* and *Far from the Madding Crowd*, was considered a national treasure. So after he died on January 11, 1928, his body was interred in the Poet's Corner of Westminster Abbey.

But before the ceremony, his heart was removed, to be buried in Emma's grave. A touching gesture. However, before that could happen, Hardy's housekeeper placed his heart on a kitchen table and the cat ate it.

●●●

An unusual way of coming out. Here's how comedian Rosie O'Donnell let everyone know she is gay: "I never once said I want [Tom Cruise] naked in the bed doing the nasty. I want him to mow my lawn and get me a lemonade."

●●●

In Paris in the fifteenth century, a romantic-minded young man would take the girl of his heart for a dinner picnic at the public execution grounds. Which shows you the lengths people would go to for a date before they had movie theaters.

●●●

J. Edgar Hoover once fired an FBI agent because he married a woman of Arab heritage, which the head of the FBI declared to be an un-American romance.

In 1998, *People* magazine named actor Harrison Ford the "sexiest man alive." Ford was fifty-six at the time.

Apparently, all the editors at *People* were fifty-six, too. They assumed that in our youth-maniacal culture what most young women really want is to make love to an old man. Say, a fifty-six-year-old movie actor. Or if he's busy, a fifty-six-year-old magazine editor.

Unless, of course, *People* magazine meant sexy in the sense of let's run his picture on our cover and see if anyone will still buy it.

●●●

In seventh-century England, a man could legally divorce his wife for a wide range of misbehaviors, including being too friendly, too unfriendly, too hungry, too amorous, or too silly.

Who made the call? The husband, of course. His accusation was the divorce. It was that kind of world.

●●●

In eighteenth-century England, poor men who could not afford an expensive government divorce might choose to auction off a wife who proved unsatisfactory.

If he was a country man, he would put a halter around his wife and lead her to the auction block like cattle, then sell her to the highest bidder. It was still that kind of world.

CHAPTER THIRTY-NINE

Rich but Stupid:
The Barefoot Explorer and the Witch of Wall Street

If you believe that rich people must be smart or they wouldn't have so much money, then you haven't met these wealthy ding-dongs.

•••

Russell Sage was one of the richest men in America in the 1800s. But when he saw his wife feeding peanuts to squirrels, he reprimanded her, insisting she feed them stale bread instead because it cost less.

Sage made millions—but never spent it. He lived in cheap lodgings and wore the cheapest of clothes. After he died, his widow spent the rest of her life giving his money to good causes. Ah, sweet charity revenge.

●●●

Billionaire Howard Hughes, during one of his more eccentric phases, lived for years on nothing but ice cream. Some of that ice cream he ate while in his private movie theater watching the film *Ice Station Zebra* more than one hundred times in a row.

People who didn't have a tenth of a tenth of his money couldn't make it through that movie once.

●●●

Enrico Caruso made a fortune singing opera all over the world. Yet his early poverty made him obsessive about spending any of his wealth. He wrote down every single expense, including food, clothes, and the smallest of tips in little black books, while stashing millions of dollars in the bank.

When Caruso died, he left behind hundreds of these account books, full of meaningless figures.

●●●

Millionaire Hetty Green, known as the Witch of Wall Street in the 1800s, was so cheap and senseless that when her son injured his leg, she refused to pay for medical care.

She told the boy there was no point in paying a doctor because he'd recover anyway. Her son's leg became infected with gangrene because the wound wasn't treated, and had to be amputated.

When you're poor, you have buddies. When you're rich, you have an entourage, and they can be so much fussier.

Movie star Jennifer Lopez took her entourage to London and put them up at a fancy hotel. One night they decided to go to another hotel for dinner.

It took six limousines and half an hour of sorting out who rode in which car before they could make the drive from the first hotel to the second—which was located one hundred yards down the street.

•••

The nineteenth-century Wendels were eccentric millionaires whose motto was "Buy, but never sell New York real estate."

In 1856, the family owned a five-story mansion on Fifth Avenue. They kept the grand entranceway boarded up, so everyone had to enter through the rear door.

Although they became one of the richest families in New York history, they didn't believe in electricity or automobiles. In the 1930s they still rode through New York in a horse-drawn carriage.

•••

John Wendel, the patriarch of the rich but cheap New York family, insisted that no business property he owned ever have signs on the buildings in case the signs "fall down and hurt someone."

He had an even odder reason for prohibiting wires connected to any of his buildings: "They might hurt a bird in flight."

The seven Wendel sisters refused to marry so no gold-digging men could steal their fortune.

Josephine Wendel lived in a country house where she entertained no visitors. Yet servants set places for six at the table every night. Josephine would move from seat to seat and conduct conversations for all her imaginary guests.

Another sister, Ella Wendel, had a French poodle named Tobey as her only companion. Tobey slept in a four-poster bed that was a precise replica of Ella's own bed, and he ate at a table covered with velvet cloths.

●●●

Celestina Collins was a wealthy Englishwoman in the nineteenth century who had the odd habit of sharing her bed with three dozen hens, ducks, and other fowl. You can imagine how foul that practice became.

●●●

A wealthy eighteenth-century Englishwoman, Lady Lewson, refused to bathe, thinking immersion led to illness. Instead, to preserve herself she coated her body daily with hog's lard. She lived for ninety years that way.

●●●

Business magnate Andrew Carnegie spent $250,000 to establish the Simplified Spelling Board, which tried to convince everyone to change "tough" to "tuf," "trouble" to "troble" and "philosophy" to "filosofy."

Sir Harvey Elwes, a wealthy Englishman of the 1800s, was a miserly millionaire. He dined only on partridges, since he could shoot them for nothing on his vast estate.

During the cold English winter, Sir Harvey forbade a fire in his mansion. Instead, he walked endlessly up and down the halls to keep warm.

• • •

Sir Harvey's nephew, John Elwes, equally as rich, was equally as cheap. He walked everywhere through the London rain to save the price of a coach. He wore a wig a beggar had thrown away and kept wet clothes on all day, rather than spend money on a fire to dry them out.

Oddly enough, although Elwes refused to spend money on his own basic needs, he threw away fortunes gambling.

• • •

The Elweses were rivaled for stinginess among the English rich by Daniel Dancer, who would pick up stray dung off the road to use as fertilizer for his estate.

Dancer's dog was his favorite companion. But he broke the dog's teeth so he couldn't bite sheep because Dancer didn't want to pay local farmers compensation for any sheep the dog might injure.

Instead, Dancer spent his days searching the fields for old animal bones, which he broke into pieces so the half-toothed dog could eat them.

When money goes with fame, you can indulge childhood fantasies. Comedian Billy Crystal did, spending $400,000 to buy one of Mickey Mantle's used baseball gloves.

Other people may see the glove as a piece of old leather too worn to play ball with. But Crystal looked upon it as a $400,000 work of art.

•••

In the eighteenth century, British Colonel George Hanger arranged for a strange ten-mile race between twenty turkeys and twenty geese. Although the colonel set the course and trained all the birds himself, he bet on the turkeys, which were trounced.

Colonel Hanger eventually lost all his money gambling and died in debt.

•••

Abdul Hamid II, sultan of Turkey in the nineteenth century, was obsessed with defending himself against assassination attempts.

The sultan hired twelve architects to design different portions of his palace so none of them would know the complete floor plan. He filled the place with thousands of bodyguards and hundreds of trained parrots, which were to sound the alarm if anyone attacked.

To prevent assassins from poisoning his milk, the sultan placed a round-the-clock bodyguard on his cows. When forced to travel outside his fortress, he rode in an armored carriage and always kept one of his children on his lap to use as a shield.

Charles Waterton was born to a wealthy English family in the 1780s, but gave up his position in society to become an explorer and naturalist in South America. He explored the rainforest barefoot because that was the best way to climb trees.

In his eighties Waterton would amuse his friends by climbing high walls, then hopping along the top of the wall on one foot.

When Waterton wanted to study the vampire bat, he tried to lure them from their cave by sleeping barefoot in a hammock after bathing his toes in animal blood.

●●●

Wealthy eighteenth-century Englishwoman Hannah Beswick was afraid she'd be buried before she was actually dead. So she left her doctor a small fortune if he would keep her body until he was positive she was dead.

The doctor kept her body, embalmed and stuffed inside his grandfather clock, for the rest of his life.

CHAPTER FORTY

Government by the Idiots:
How to Get Elected to Anything

Should politicians have to pass an intelligence test before they can hold public office? Could they?

College professor Bergen Evans offered this view on the people who run our government: "Legislators who are of even average intelligence stand out among their colleagues. . . . For the most part our leaders are merely following out in front."

•••

Hi ho, Frankerino. In 1945, two popular show business figures were denounced in Congress for turning American youth into juvenile delinquents: Frank Sinatra and the Lone Ranger.

People say that if you don't like the way our government is run, why don't you do something about it?

Hey, complaining is doing something.

Then there's Canadian fisherman Russell Arundel, who declared a small island off the coast of Nova Scotia an independent country in 1949.

Arundel named himself Prince of Princes of the Principality of Outer Baldonia.

He wrote a bill of rights that applied only to fishermen, including the right "to lie and be believed" and freedom from "nagging and interruptions." The man had created a veritable utopia.

So all hail Outer Baldonia, the only nation in the world where lying is protected by a bill of rights.

In all other countries, lying is protected by the people in power.

●●●

But Arundel isn't the only visionary to create his own country when he didn't like the one he was stuck in.

An Australian farmer named Leonard Casley got so mad at the government that in 1970 he seceded, declaring his farm a separate nation, the Province of Hutt River.

Casley found to his surprise that he made more money from selling T-shirts and Hutt River souvenirs than he did from farming. Come to think of it, maybe that doesn't come as a surprise to a farmer.

Twelve Stupid Things
the Federal Government
Spent Our Tax Money On

1. The Department of Agriculture decided that Americans needed to know how long it takes people to cook breakfast. So department officials funded a study for only $46,000 to find out what anyone who's ever cooked breakfast could have told them for $7.98 plus postage.

2. The National Institute on Alcohol Abuse spent a million dollars in the 1970s to discover If drunk fish are more aggressive than sober fish. Turns out they are, which is why you never want to go fishing after the fish have been drinking heavily.

3. You ever drive down a highway with a huge semi on your tail? The Federal Highway Administration wanted to find out how people felt about that. So the agency spent $222,000 to study "Motorist Attitudes Toward Large Trucks."

4. The National Science Foundation spent $84,000 on a study to find out why people fall in love. For $1.98 the Beatles could have told them that money can't buy you love.

5. Considering the typical expense of military testing, we should probably be thankful that it only cost the Air Force three thousand dollars to run a six-month system test back in 1979. What was the Air Force testing? How soldiers used umbrellas while in uniform.

6. In 1985, the Department of the Navy managed to snag a ten-foot doormat for only $792.

7. Your kids ever need braces? Fun, huh, and cheap? But you'll be happy to know that the money was well spent, which the National Institute of Dental Research proved in 1984 by funding a five-year study to determine the "effects of orthodontia on psychosocial functioning." Smile, it only cost half a million of your tax money.

8. In 1977, the Smithsonian Institution bankrolled development of a dictionary of Tzotzil, a language spoken by only 120,000 poor farmers in Southern Mexico, nearly none of whom could read or write— and, therefore, didn't have much use for a dictionary.

    If the government had simply given the farmers the $89,000 it spent on the dictionary they didn't need, they wouldn't have been so poor.

9. Next time you go on family vacation, you'll want to visit the famous Trenton, New Jersey, sewer that the Environmental Protection Agency preserved as a historical monument for only $1 million.

10. Why should Americans have to put up with the inconvenience of traveling all the way to the other side of the world to see the Great Wall of China simply because the ancient Chinese lacked the foresight to build the wall in a more convenient location?

    So in 1981, the Department of Commerce spent $200,000 to erect an 800-foot limestone replica of the Great Wall of China in Indiana, right where the Chinese should have built it all along.

11. In 1985, the National Institute of Neurological and Communicative Disorders invested $160,000 of the taxpayers' money on a study to find out whether you can jinx rivals by drawing X's on their chests. Somehow they missed out on the all-important XX and XXX jinx studies.

12. The federally funded National Endowment for the Humanities once spent $2,500 on a study to learn why people act rudely when they play tennis. They could have borrowed a racket, gone out to a tennis court in a public park, played a couple of sets for free, and found out for themselves.

Janet Napolitano won a close race to become governor of Arizona in 2002. Or did she?

A year after her election, the new Arizona phone book was published, listing her defeated opponent Matt Salmon as the new governor. What did the phone book company know that the voters didn't?

●●●

In 2002 North Carolina Congressman Cass Ballenger came up with an original way to prove to critics that he wasn't a bigot: He had the lawn jockey in his front yard painted white.

●●●

Tired of the same old Democrats and Republicans when you hit the voting booth on election day? You should have been around in 1952 when the Reverend Homer Tomlinson ran for the presidency on the Theocratic ticket, promising to substitute tithing for taxes and create a cabinet post of Secretary of Righteousness.

Tomlinson wasn't upset when he lost the election. He simply declared himself King of the World.

●●●

English politicians are a bit different, which is how Screaming Lord Sutch came to run for Parliament from the Monster Raving Loony Party, on a campaign of improving Britain's climate by towing the entire island into the Mediterranean.

Three Politicians Who
Could Have Been Comedians

1. President Ronald Reagan: "Now we are trying to get unemployment to go up, and I think we have succeeded."

2. Virginia Governor Douglas Wilder: "The first black president will be a politician who is black."

3. Vice President Dan Quayle: "Republicans understand the importance of bondage between parent and child."

Time and *Newsweek* have always been tough competitors, but sometimes you'd think the two news weeklies were put out by the same editorial staff.

On November 19, 1962, after Richard Nixon lost the race for governor of California, both magazines went on record as predicting the end of Nixon's political career.

Newsweek called Nixon a "political has-been." *Time* said that "barring a miracle" his political career was over.

Oops. Six years later, Nixon the "has-been" got his "miracle" and was elected president.

Here's how they get things done in Washington: The Dirksen Building was built in 1958 for senatorial offices. When the building was finished, they discovered that the floor was too slippery. So they covered it with carpet.

But the carpet was too thick, so the doors wouldn't close. So they took off all the doors and planed them down to fit the carpets they wouldn't have needed if they had put down the right floor in the first place.

•••

Days before the 1936 election, a national poll predicted that the Republican candidate would swamp Franklin Roosevelt and take the White House.

Voters were rude enough to prove the poll wrong. FDR won the electoral vote 523 to 8.

How had the poll been so incredibly wrong? They took the poll by phone. Back in 1936, well-off Republicans owned phones; poorer Democrats did not.

•••

So you say you want a government job? Do you have the imagination required for such demanding work? Take the Louis Nel test.

Nel was the deputy minister of information in the old South Africa. When called upon to defend the government against charges of censorship, Nel set a high standard for other government officials with this beaut: "We do not have censorship. What we have is a limitation on what newspapers can report."

In the old Soviet Union, it was illegal to play the game of Monopoly.

Scrabble was probably legal, but all triple word bonus scores had to be distributed equally among the collective players for the greater glory of the state.

●●●

The Dutch government in the New World thought Peter Minuit had made a bad mistake when he bought the entire island of Manhattan for twenty-four dollars worth of trinkets.

The governors liked the island well enough. They just thought Minuit had been overcharged. Now you couldn't even buy a trinket in New York City for twenty-four dollars.

●●●

Why was there no bodyguard protecting Abraham Lincoln at Ford's Theater the night he was shot?

We know his bodyguard went to the theater with the president, but after that there are two contradictory reports, neither of them a shining example of intelligent diligence.

Some witnesses claim that the bodyguard took a seat outside the presidential box and was watching the show when Lincoln was shot. The other theory is even worse—that the bodyguard went to a saloon for a drink and missed the whole thing.

Watch out if you enter into negotiations with the North Korean government.

American officials who've had that pleasure reported that North Korean envoys would sneak into the conference room each night and saw a quarter-inch off each leg of the American chairs. Why? So American negotiators would feel smaller and smaller as the talks proceeded.

●●●

Assistant Secretary of State under Reagan, Elliott Abrams gave lessons for a new generation of politicians on how to testify before Congress when he declared in 1987: "I never said I had no idea about most of the things you said I said I had no idea about."

Set that to music and we've got a hit.

●●●

Giving lessons to political campaigners everywhere was Virginia Senator John Warren, who proved you could make everyone happy during his race for reelection in 1990. Addressing the abortion issue, Warren declared that he was "pro-choice with limitations," but also "pro-life with exceptions."

●●●

Go down about a mile and make a left turn at the dead cat.

In 1987 when a dead cat was left in the middle of a road, the South Carolina Highway Department simply painted the yellow stripe over the cat. The road painters reasoned that dead cat removal was not part of their job description.

Why there will always be an LA: In 1990 Los Angeles Police Chief Daryl Gates suggested to the Senate Judicial Committee that people who used marijuana or cocaine for recreation "ought to be taken out and shot."

So we're pretty sure he was against decriminalization.

●●●

Having a hard time deciding who gets your vote for president? Think about the advantages of electing a total failure for a change. How about a candidate who:

1. failed in business twice.
2. failed to get elected to Congress twice.
3. was twice beaten in Senate races.
4. then suffered a nervous breakdown. Then ran for vice president—and lost that race too.

Would you vote for a man like that? Thank God enough people did to elect Abraham Lincoln president.

●●●

Adlai Stevenson, who ran for president twice and lost, said, "In America anyone can become president. That's one of the risks you take."

But who took the greater risk—the candidates or the electorate?

Thinking about running for office? Here's a winning strategy from political pundit Frank Dane: "Get all the fools on your side and you can be elected to anything."

•••

The brilliant English politician Benjamin Disraeli advised a new member of Parliament not to engage in debate during his first months in office. The new representative protested that his colleagues wouldn't understand why he refrained from speaking out on the issues.

"Better they should wonder why you do not speak, than why you do," Disraeli advised.

•••

When France conducted nuclear tests in the South Pacific in 1995, the French ambassador to New Zealand tried to calm everyone's concerns by explaining, "They aren't bombs. They're exploding artifacts."

•••

Does the following incident explain why we get the politicians we get? Or is it the reason politicians are able to hold so much power over our lives?

In 2003, President Bush gave a televised news conference that was topped in the ratings by a repeat of *America's Funniest Home Videos*.

Religion used to be the opiate of the people. Then opium was the opiate of the people. But nothing in history has melted more minds than bad TV, which is why television is so popular with advertisers and politicians.

"The secret of the demagogue is to make himself as stupid as his audience so that they believe they are as clever as he," Austrian writer Karl Kraus explained.

●●●

What should a president's duties include? Writer and occasional politician Gore Vidal had a suggestion: "The presidential ninnies should stick to throwing out baseballs and leave the important matters to serious people."

●●●

In England, the Speaker of the House is not allowed to speak. Well, maybe that's not so dumb after all.

●●●

A year before Bill Clinton was reelected president, the *Wall Street Journal* predicted that he would lose to "any Republican nominee who doesn't drool onstage."

That gives me great latitude to predict the winner of the next presidential race. After all, I can only do as bad as the *Wall Street Journal*.

So I predict that George W. Bush will lose to any Democratic nominee who is richer than the Bush family, is more popular with big business, has better connections in the Supreme Court, and doesn't drool onstage too often.

Speaking of candidates, here's radio commentator Rush Limbaugh on former Vice President Al Gore: "Idiot . . . liar . . . IQ of a pencil eraser."

●●●

In a 2002 election in the Czech Republic, Christian Democrats handed out free shots of brandy to voters. The Communist Party countered by hiring topless women to hand out their campaign literature.

●●●

Bookmakers around the country were so sure that Tom Dewey was going to beat Harry Truman in 1948 that they refused to take any bets on the presidential election.

Too bad gamblers couldn't get money down on Truman. The odds would have been so great against his winning the race that the payoff would have been enormous when he did win.

●●●

The Texas legislature is as rowdy as the state itself. In 1971, a representative named Tom Moore found a nasty way to show that the reps often had no idea of what they were voting on.

Moore proposed a resolution commending Albert de Salvo for "unconventional techniques involving population control."

The Texas House passed the resolution. De Salvo was the Boston Strangler.

Speaking of Texas, newspaper columnist Molly Ivins reported that a state senator bragged, "If you took all the fools out of the legislature, it wouldn't be a representative body any more."

•••

Finally, we find an honest politician. In Senate hearings in 1989, Chic Hecht listed his qualification for becoming ambassador to the Bahamas: "I love golf and they have a lot of nice golf courses."

CHAPTER FORTY-ONE

Stupid Science:
Catapulting to the Moon and Beyond

"Inventors and men of genius have almost always been regarded as fools at the beginning (and very often at the end) of their careers," observed the Russian writer Fyodor Dostoevsky.

Of course, fools are also often regarded as fools, which makes it difficult to distinguish the ninnies from the geniuses.

But if these scientists studied the problem, I'm sure they'd come up with some interesting solutions.

The U.S. space program spent $18 million on the *Mariner I* to get a close look at the planet Venus. Never made it. A few minutes into its flight, the unmanned *Mariner I* crashed into the Atlantic Ocean.

What malfunctioned? Nothing. The computer controlling the ship's takeoff did exactly what it was programmed to do.

But the programmer had left a minus sign off one of the directions, and that made all the difference.

•••

Taking a different approach to space flight, the African nation of Zambia decided to send its own astronauts to the moon by using a catapult.

Zambian research scientists trained volunteers for the rigors of space flight by sealing them in an oil drum and rolling them down a hill.

•••

Build it stupidly and they will come. The dumb architect who designed the tower of Pisa in the twelfth century built it wrong, laying a foundation too small to support the tower.

Year by year, century by century, the tower has been leaning toward falling over, despite the millions spent to correct the initial bad design.

But stupidity can have unexpected payoffs. Aside from that one dumb mistake, the Leaning Tower of Pisa is rather ordinary as medieval towers go. If it hadn't been built so badly in the first place, they would have torn it down long ago and the tower would never have become a famous historical landmark.

Women in ancient Egypt used an early form of birth control, a contraceptive potion that Egyptian chemists made from honey and crocodile droppings.

•••

American pesticide manufacturers wanted the EPA to relax standards on how much chemical residue could be left on food. So in 2003 they paid test subjects up to $1,500 to drink two pesticides (dichlorvos and aldicarb) each morning for eighteen days to find out if the poisons would ruin their health.

Both pesticides were listed as hazardous and considered possible carcinogens. Who would risk their health and lives for money that would provide no long-term solutions to their money problems? People desperately in need of quick cash, of course. Who would pay them? Scientists in need of ethics.

•••

Rock composer Frank Zappa had unconventional views on most things, including the universe.

"Some scientists claim that hydrogen, because it is so plentiful, is the basic building block of the universe," he said. "I dispute that. I say that there is more stupidity than hydrogen, and that is the basic building block of the universe."

•••

Nikola Tesla was another example of how genius and stupidity can work comfortably together. Tesla invented the alternating current motor, and his studies in electricity rivaled Edison's. Then he withdrew from human contact and became convinced that touching any round surface would lead to illness.

Not all presidents need scientific advisors. Ronald Reagan, for example, found it more efficient to invent his own science.

Here's Reagan on the campaign trail dismissing the dangers of atomic energy: "All the waste in a year from a nuclear power plant can be stored under a desk."

That would have been one amazing desk, big enough to cover up the twenty-five tons of nuclear waste produced each year by an atomic power plant.

●●●

Air pollution isn't a modern invention. The air in London was already so bad in the year 1306 that burning coal within city limits was punishable by death.

●●●

Some things look moronic but aren't. For example, if you happened to be in London in 1898 you might have seen H. Cecil Booth sucking the dust from restaurant chairs with his mouth.

Booth wasn't a lunatic. He was an inventor, experimenting with the concept of suction. After his early oral experiments, Booth went on to invent the dust-sucking vacuum cleaner.

●●●

An epidemiologist wrote a scholarly article in the *Journal of the American Medical Association* about infections you could catch from the sport of mud wrestling. She recommended wrestling in Jell-O instead, doctor's orders.

University of California researchers developed a health food drink that rejuvenated aging rats. Why anyone would want to improve the health of rats was not explained.

•••

In 2000 two computer drives turned up missing at Los Alamos National Laboratories. Call security—the drives contained vital secrets about our nuclear weapons program.

Never mind, call off security. Just found the drives. Someone dropped them behind a copy machine. Oops.

•••

The English scientist Sir Isaac Newton showed his genius early as a boy in the 1600s when he designed and built a windmill, sun-dials, paper kites with lanterns for flying at night, and a water clock with a revolutionary circular dial.

Despite all his early achievements, his mother declared that the boy should become a farmer. Fortunately for the world, he ignored his mother's wisdom.

•••

Medical researcher Oliver Sacks reached this conclusion from his scientific studies: "Nature gropes and blunders and performs the cruelest acts. There is no steady advance upward. There is no design."

When the seventeenth-century scientist Galileo supported Copernicus's theory that the sun was the center of our solar system, he ran up against church authorities, who insisted incorrectly that the earth was at the center of everything since they were on it.

When the Church denied Galileo permission to teach his theories, the scientist argued that it would be foolish if the "same God who has endowed us with senses, reason, and understanding does not permit us to use them."

Papal authorities banned astronomy and persecuted Galileo for years. He was convicted of heresy and imprisoned for maintaining what is now commonly taught in all schools.

●●●

Interesting attempt at scientific reasoning by St. Thomas Aquinas in the thirteenth century: that the earth could not possibly rotate on its axis because a circular motion would be "violent and contrary to nature" and that "nothing violent is eternal."

●●●

In the 1800s, technicians made dentures from the teeth of dead people. The battlefield was a favored place to gather raw material. Often, the robbers didn't wait for dying soldiers to finish with this life before collecting their teeth.

In Europe, these plates became known as Waterloo dentures, while in America they were called Civil War teeth.

John Dee was a sixteenth-century English scientist with a bent for mysticism, astrology, and wife swapping. His eccentric behavior didn't stop him from fooling most of England.

Before Dee died in 1608, he predicted that the world would end by flood on St. Patrick's Day, 1842.

On that day, two hundred years after Dee's death, English authorities were surprised to find thousands of people sitting in boats, loaded with supplies so they could outlast Dee's flood.

The next day, they all climbed out of their boats and went on with their lives.

•••

During the French Revolution, looters broke into the crypt of Louis XIV, the Sun King, and stole the dead monarch's heart.

Mysteriously, the royal heart came into the possession of an English mystic, the Reverend William Buckland, who had been experimenting with ways to achieve immortality.

Buckland reasoned that since kings were the select of God, he might assume some of that deistic favor by consuming the king. So he had Louis's embalmed heart sautéed and roasted, then served to him at Christmas dinner.

As far as we know, the reverend's experiment didn't work. Or if it did, William Buckland has been keeping quiet about it for several hundred years.

Where racism and stupidity collide: Mississippi Senator Ted Bilbo came up with this pseudoscientific justification for discrimination in 1945: that the skull of a black person "ossifies by the time a Negro reaches maturity and they become unable to take in information."

Apparently, ossification of Bilbo's skull didn't prevent him from expounding baloney.

●●●

Scientist and writer Arthur C. Clarke gets the last word here: "It has yet to be proven that intelligence has any survival value."

CHAPTER FORTY-TWO

Dumb Predictions:
The End of Poverty, War, and Chickens,
as Predicted by People Who Got It All Wrong

Never underestimate the ability of the experts to miss it entirely.

But clever experts can get it wrong and still maintain their status. Their secret? Never apologize. Move on. Say something else authoritative. Maybe you'll be right this time. After all, you can't be wrong about everything.

• • •

Before he saved Britain in World War II, Prime Minister Winston Churchill took time out from his political career to make this far-sighted prediction in *Popular Mechanics* magazine.

Before the year 2000, Churchill claimed, farmers would stop raising complete chickens. Churchill saw this old-fashioned approach to poultry farming as a waste of time. Instead, he predicted, farmers would grow chicken breasts and chicken wings without the rest of the bird.

•••

Check out this slick turnaround on a dumb prediction. Charles Russell, who founded the Jehovah's Witnesses, predicted that the faithful would find deliverance before 1914.

When 1914 came and went without deliverance, Russell simply came up with a new prediction: that the faithful would be delivered *after* 1914.

Smartest move an end-of-the-world predictor ever made was not to put an outside cap on the date.

•••

An optimist? Just a guy who doesn't have the facts.

But you'd have to be a raving optimist to keep up with auto maker Henry Ford.

In 1931 during the depths of the Great Depression, when widespread hunger and homelessness swept the country, Ford insisted, "These really are good times, but only a few know it."

Presumably, Ford meant the few, like himself, who had the sense to stash away millions.

•••

Some thirty-five years after Henry Ford cured the Great Depression (well, at least his own), President Lyndon Johnson caught Ford fever and predicted: "It's going to be soon when nobody in this country is poor."

Maybe he meant soon in the big picture sense—you know, any millennium now we'll eliminate poverty.

●●●

Here's psychologist Kenneth Clark warning the country of a new evil in 1936: that people addicted to marijuana "lose all restraints, all inhibitions. They become bestial demoniacs, filled with the mad lust to kill."

Makes you wonder what he was smoking, doesn't it?

●●●

In 1914 Nicholas Butler, the president of Columbia University, made this call: "No civilized people will ever again permit its government to enter into a competitive armament race."

Oh, if he could see us now when nation after nation has built up their armaments to the point where the world could be destroyed a dozen times over on a bad Tuesday.

Or perhaps Butler was being sarcastic, in the Ghandian sense that no "civilized people" have engaged in an arms race because there are no civilized people.

●●●

Variety is an entertainment industry trade paper that reviews movies and plays not so much for quality as to evaluate the chances of box office success. That's why it's so much fun to see how wrong the pros can be. Let's look twice:

1. *Variety* attended the out-of-town opening of a new musical in 1964 and declared, "It seems clear that this is no smash hit, no blockbuster."

The musical? *Fiddler on the Roof*, clearly one of the biggest Broadway blockbusters of all time.

2. "It will be gone by June," *Variety* predicted in 1955, referring to rock 'n' roll. Ah, but they didn't say which June.

●●●

Here's a Universal Studios exec turning down the chance to sign a young actor in 1959: "You have a chip in your tooth, your Adam's apple sticks out too far, and you talk too slow." Guess who? Clint Eastwood.

●●●

Hollywood rejected another actor for a role in a 1954 movie about politics, *The Best Man*, because he didn't have "the presidential look." The actor? Ronald Reagan.

●●●

President Rutherford B. Hayes wasn't the only smart person who thought Alexander Graham Bell's new invention was useless. "That's an amazing invention, but who would ever want to use one of them?" the president asked of Bell's new telephone. Can't imagine, Mr. President.

Who else missed the significance of the invention that went on to connect the world and pester everyone with endlessly bad TV commercials? Western Union.

Bell offered to sell the telephone to the nation's telegraph company. But what was then our only communications giant turned him down. Western Union executives didn't think the phone would ever replace the telegraph.

Guess they needed a wake-up call. Unfortunately, there was no one to give them a wake-up call since they didn't have a phone.

•••

Ouch. David Lloyd George, former prime minister of England, dismissed the world's worries about Adolph Hitler in the days before the Nazis started World War II by predicting that "Germany is unable to wage war."

And even if the Germans managed to scrape together a few blitzkrieg units, we still had nothing to worry about, George assured the world, because "Germany has no desire to attack any country in Europe."

Oh, George, ever hear of Poland, France, Holland, England . . . ? Perhaps it would be simpler to list the countries Hitler *didn't* intend to attack, namely Germany.

•••

The strangest people can miss the strangest things. Here's the great Indian leader of passive resistance, Mohandas Gandhi, evaluating another political leader in 1940:

"He is showing an ability that is amazing, and he seems to be gaining his victories without much bloodshed," Gandhi said. "I do not consider Hitler to be as bad as he is depicted."

•••

Major George Eliot was an American military expert with a talent for shooting himself in the foot with predictions, the exact opposite of which tended to come true.

In 1938 Eliot predicted that "war between Japan and the United States is not within the realm of reasonable possibility."

Because Eliot was a recognized military expert, it must have reassured the nation when he declared that "a Japanese attack on Pearl Harbor is a strategic impossibility."

But Eliot was equally inept on two continents.

In 1939 he assured the Allies that "the chances of Germany making a quick job of overwhelming Poland are not good."

It took Germany only a month to crush all of Poland.

●●●

As a producer of TV shows, Twentieth Century Fox has made millions. But the studio almost made nothing.

In 1946 Fox boss Darryl Zanuck dismissed the idea that television would ever become popular. He predicted that "people will soon get tired of staring at a plywood box every night."

What Zanuck missed was that when people get tired of staring at the boring box, they simply fall asleep in front of the set. TV is the adult babysitter.

●●●

Samuel Pepys was one of the arbiters of British society in the early 1600s. As such, he declared a new play "the most insipid, ridiculous play I ever saw in my life." What so upset him? Shakespeare's *A Midsummer Night's Dream*.

●●●

In 1956 comedian Jackie Gleason reassured a nation of worried parents that America would survive Elvis. "He can't last," Gleason said. "I tell you flatly, he can't last." And away you go, Jackie.

Critic Howard Thompson of the *New York Times* got it 'wrong twice in one sentence in 1968: "Of Robert De Niro and Jonathan Warden, the latter gives at least some evidence of a little talent."

Poor De Niro went on to become one of the great movie actors of his era, and did it all without talent. Jonathan who?

•••

The producers who wanted to put *West Side Story* onstage for the first time needed financing. But they were turned down by every backer on Broadway.

The famed Broadway composing team of Richard Rodgers and Oscar Hammerstein advised the producers to give up the project because they'd never find enough young actors who could handle the difficult songs.

CHAPTER FORTY-THREE

Dumb Sports:
Flying Pitchers and Concrete Linebackers

When you go looking for stupidity in sports, you don't have to start with the athletes.

Notre Dame football coach Norm Van Brocklin points us in the right direction by explaining, "If I ever needed a brain transplant, I'd choose a sportswriter because I'd want a brain that had never been used."

Now let's watch the players try to catch up.

During an Ohio State game, a football fan was unhappy with the plays sent in by coach Woody Hayes. So the fan yelled at Hayes's wife, "Your husband is a fathead."

Anne Hayes shrugged and nailed the fan with the perfect comeback: "What husband isn't?"

•••

One of baseball's greatest pitchers, Rube Waddell, was also one of the game's heaviest drinkers. During a booze bout on a road trip, Waddell announced to teammates that he could fly.

When they hooted him down, Rube yanked open a hotel window and jumped out.

He survived the fall. When he sobered up the next day, Waddell yelled at his roommate Ossie Schreck for not stopping him from pulling such a foolish stunt.

"Stop you?" Schreck countered. "Hell, I bet a hundred bucks you could do it."

•••

Philadelphia Phillies manager Danny Ozark said this about baseball, but it applies to all sports and most everything else too: "Half this game is 90 percent mental."

•••

To that endless list of dumb sports injuries, you'll want to add this one: Milwaukee Brewers first baseman Richie Sexson sprained his neck in 2003 spring training trying to put on a baseball hat that was too small for him.

Obviously, Sexson should have worked on his cap-adjustment technique with the team's cap coach before trying a maneuver that tricky.

• • •

And now back to the press box for this beaut: At a Super Bowl news conference in 2000, a reporter actually asked one of the St. Louis Ram players: "Is Ram a noun or a verb?" Noun on two.

• • •

Here's what can happen when an athlete and a writer get together to collaborate on a book. When he found out he was misquoted in his own autobiography, basketball great Charles Barkley said, "I should have read it."

• • •

Ever wonder why football coaches don't recruit at Mensa meetings? You don't want your linebackers thinking twice about going up against players like Jim Taylor of the Green Bay Packers, who explained his approach to running the ball: "I love to hear the sounds of breaking bones."

• • •

Croquet is not a contact sport. Plenty of people would say it's not a sport at all, but something to do in the backyard while the chicken's grilling.

Then there was the croquet fanatic George Bernard Shaw, the English playwright. In 1950 at the age of ninety-four, Shaw was playing croquet with friends when he threw a tantrum after muffing a shot. He kicked furiously at the ball, slipped, broke his hip, and died from the effects.

When baseball's greatest zany, Bill Veeck, ran the Milwaukee Brewers, he didn't give away caps and bats like other teams. Veeck gave his fans pigeons, horses, and huge blocks of ice.

"No, Charlie, just put the ice in your pocket. You can play with it when you get home."

When the city threw a banquet in his honor, Veeck showed up in a sports shirt because he hated formal attire. All the other men at the event wore tuxedos.

As Veeck accepted his trophy, he told the crowd, "This is the first time I ever saw 1,200 waiters for one customer."

•••

Bronko Nagurski, the great fullback of the Chicago Bears in the 1930s, ran head down, plowing over defenders, often dragging them into the end zone—if they didn't have enough sense to let go.

He explained his unorthodox running style as an act of mercy. With his head down, he couldn't see the fear in the defense's eyes and be tempted to "melt with sympathy."

•••

Jacob Ruppert Jr. was a rich New York brewery owner who bought the New York Yankees in the early 1900s even though he didn't know much about baseball.

Early one season with his team struggling to score runs, Ruppert misinterpreted the old baseball adage that in the spring the pitchers are ahead of the hitters.

"My players are all right," Ruppert expounded to a reporter. "You must understand that the pitchers are now ahead of the catchers."

Back to the great Bronko Nagurski and the time he ran so hard for a score at Wrigley Field that he crashed through the end zone into a brick wall. Nagurski knocked out a dozen bricks and rammed a hole in the wall. He kept playing while they sent in bricklayers to tend to the wall.

On another play, Bronko ran through the Redskin defense, bounced off the goal post, and slammed into a concrete wall.

When he got back to the Bears' bench, Nagurski said, "Gosh, that last guy sure hit me hard."

●●●

Baseball slugger Babe Ruth once got hungry during a game and gobbled down nine hot dogs, a couple sandwiches, and six bottles of pop, finishing off with an apple before taking the field for the next inning.

He got so sick that he had to be taken out of the game and rushed to the hospital, where Ruth lamented, "I knew I shouldn't have eaten that apple."

Maybe his teammate Waite Hoyt was right about the amazing Babe. "He came out of a tree," Hoyt theorized. "He wasn't human."

●●●

Plenty of baseball players are superstitious, but Babe Ruth carried his to an odd extreme. He felt that anyone he met on the street with a physical deformity would bring him good luck for the day's game. During the 1928 season, he hired a man with a humpback to cross his path before every game.

Here's pro golfer Mark Calcavecchia explaining why he keeps an eye on the leader board while playing a tourney: "I like to know whether I don't need to do anything stupid, or whether I need to try to do something stupid."

Most golfers can relate to that sentiment.

●●●

English racehorses in the seventeenth and eighteenth centuries were given odd names that would now sound loopy even to a horse.

Here are some of the favorites: Kiss in a Corner, Why Do You Slight Me, Turn About Tommy, Sweeter When Clothed, Watch Them and Catch Them, Jenny Come Bye Me, Jack Come Tickle Me, and the odds-on favorite, I Am Little Pity My Condition.

●●●

Casey Stengel coached third for the Dodgers when they played in Brooklyn, but he couldn't get that group of misfits to play the game right.

One game Tony Cuccinello tried to stretch a double into a triple, but was called out at third when he ignored Stengel's signal to slide.

"I couldn't do it, Casey," Cuccinello explained as he trotted off the field. "I would have busted all the cigars in my pocket."

●●●

While warming up before a game, Brooklyn Dodger pitcher Frenchy Bordagaray beaned his own manager, Casey Stengel, then went on to pitch a great game.

Bordagaray then came up with an unusual piece of baseball strategy. "I think I can keep on winning," he told Casey, "if I can hit you on the head every day for luck."

Let's have a show of hands for people who would like to put that plan into effect with your own boss?

●●●

In Southern California, the 24-Hour Fitness Gym installed escalators from the parking lot to the gym so that you don't have to climb the fifteen steps to the front door.

Gym buffs can take the escalator, then go inside and climb on the Stair-Stepper so they can burn calories.

Here's a thought, gym rats: If you ran up and down those steps outside for an hour, you could get in a great workout and save the cost of a gym membership.

Three All-world Dumb Sports

1. Marathon slapping:

    In Kiev in 1931, two Russians went for the world endurance record in the obscure Soviet sport of slapping each other across the face. They hung on for thirty hours straight, and they weren't even mad at each other. At least not when they started.

2. Purring:

    In this Welsh game, a man grabs his opponent's shoulders and the two of them kick each other in the shins until one yells uncle. So why is it that the Welsh never conquered the world?

3. Long-distance crawling:

    A Texan named Hans Mullikin crawled two thousand miles from his home state to Washington, D.C. Why? Well, it has to beat purring.

Tris Speaker was one of baseball's greats, but he also managed the Cleveland Indians.

Speaker knew talent when he saw it. Except once, when he declared that Boston Red Sox pitcher Babe Ruth had "made a great mistake when he gave up pitching. Working once a week, he might have lasted a long time and become a great star."

Ruth, working every day, became a pretty fair hitter.

●●●

Back to the press box, where a writer will risk almost anything for a good line. Hornell (New York) *Evening Tribune* sportswriter Rob Roberts came up with a clever bit in 1990 when he ranted, "I'll push a peanut down Main Street with my nose if the Buffalo Bills make it to the Super Bowl."

That was Roberts you saw with the pavement nose later in the season when the Bills ruined his rant by getting all the way to the Super Bowl (before they lost). Roberts hung in there and paid off on his brag.

●●●

Athletes often experiment with strange training routines. But few of them are as strange as the way baseball player Walter Brodie got himself in shape for the 1896 season.

Each day during the off-season, Brodie rode a horse thirty miles, then wrestled with a trained bear. That season, his batting average dropped seventy points.

Our hero worship of great athletes has some flaky spinoffs. For one, a guy who looks like a star may try to pass himself off as the star, for free drinks or more nefarious cons.

One such impersonator had a tricky problem. Facially, he looked a lot like the great center for the Boston Celtics, Bill Russell. Only problem, Russell was nearly seven feet tall, and the look-alike was nine inches shorter.

The fake Russell explained to people he was trying to fool that he'd had shortening surgery so he could fit into his Mercedes.

•••

You don't need to be dumb to be made a fool of, if you're green enough. When rookie Jim Wynn singled in a 1963 game, Mets first baseman Frank Thomas asked him if he'd mind stepping off the bag for a minute so he could "kick out the dust."

Being new to the bigs, Wynn did as he was asked by a veteran. He was promptly tagged out by Thomas, who had hidden the ball in his glove.

•••

After the St. Louis Cards won the pennant in 1964, fans lined up early to get tickets to the World Series. The Cardinals fanatic first in line got his picture in the paper.

When his boss saw the picture, he fired the guy for cutting work with a phony excuse. Even worse, police saw the picture and arrested him on an outstanding warrant.

Three Smart Teams, Three Dumb Teams

1. **Football**
   Smart: San Francisco 49ers
   Dumb: Arizona Cardinals

2. **Basketball**
   Smart: LA Lakers
   Dumb: LA Clippers

3. **Baseball**
   Smart: New York Yankees despite George
       Steinbrenner
   Dumb: George Steinbrenner despite New York
       Yankees

President Gerald Ford was a big sports fan, in his own way. "I love sports," he said. "Whenever I can, I always watch the Detroit Tigers on radio."

●●●

Perhaps the president knew this New Hampshire woman, who built a home on the edge of a golf course, then sued the country club for harassment because so many golf balls kept landing on her lawn.

Baseball umpires don't like smart-mouth players. So when Chicago Cub outfielder Dom Dallessandro gave George Magerkurth a hard time about his calls behind the plate, the ump told him to shut up or "I'll bite your head off."

The outfielder got the best of the umpire when he retorted, "You do and there'll be more brains in your guts than your skull."

● ● ●

The World Bridge Federation tried to convince the International Olympic Committee to add bridge to the Winter Games in 2002. Why the Winter Olympics? Because the Summer Olympics already had too many sports.

But the rule says Winter Olympics sports must be played on snow or ice. That would make bridge far more interesting, to watch it played on a luge run.

● ● ●

During a baseball game in 1880, catcher Miah Murray reached into the stands to made a terrific catch of a foul ball. The fans applauded, and Murray bowed. While he was bowing, the runner on first tagged up and went to second. The cheering continued, and so did Murray's grandstanding—as the base runner made it all the way home from first base, tagging up on a foul ball.

● ● ●

Not just anyone can run a baseball team. You need vision. Philadelphia Phillies manager Danny Ozark had that vision when he evaluated one of his players by saying, "Mike Andrews' limits are limitless."

More dumb sports injuries: A basketball player from Mississippi State slam-dunked a ball, only to have the ball bounce back and knock him unconscious.

•••

Why boxer Mike Tyson could give lessons to the big boys of the WWF: In a challenge to the champ Lennox Lewis before their match, Tyson declared, "I want your heart. I want to eat your children."

Memo to Mike: Work on your right cross. In boxing there is no TKO by child consumption.

•••

Owner of the Cincinnati Reds Marge Schott tried to bring her team good luck before a game by stuffing a lock of her dog's hair down the manager's pants.

•••

Some fans go too far, and then there's comedian Roseanne Barr. In 1989 during game two of the World Series, she mooned everyone in the Oakland Coliseum. Showing true sports grit, the teams managed to finish the game.

•••

When CBS broadcast golf tourneys in 2000, the network dubbed in the prerecorded sounds of birds chirping to achieve that outdoors special effect.

Is fishing a sport? As comic Stephen Wright pointed out, "There is a fine line between fishing and standing on the shore like an idiot."

•••

Slowing down the competition in a sport based on speed? Hmm, odd idea. Yet, it happened to bike racing in 1934.

That's when the sport's ruling body, the Union Cycliste International, permanently banned recumbent bicycles from the sport. Why? Because riders in the chairlike recumbent bikes could go much faster than traditional bike racers.

•••

In 1791 Daniel Mendoza of London became the heavyweight boxing champion of England. But many people in the fight game disputed his title because he wouldn't brawl like all the other tough-guy fighters of the time.

Instead, Mendoza used a jab, footwork, and boxing strategy to win his fights. Many people in boxing considered those tactics cheating.

•••

In 2002 Yankee outfielder Ruben Rivera stole teammate Derek Jeter's glove and bat out of his locker and sold them for $2,500 to a sports memorabilia store. At the time, Rivera was being paid a million dollars to play baseball.

Finally, consider that sometimes you can do something really dumb and it pays off in odd ways.

When baseball slugger Mike Schmidt was five, he climbed a tree and grabbed a power line. The shock knocked him out and stopped his heart. But when he fell to the ground, the impact restarted his heart.

Years later, as a Phillies star, Schmidt said, "I've looked back and wondered why that stupid little kid didn't die. Maybe that's the reason I've always worked so hard, because I don't want to think that I wasted that chance."

CHAPTER FORTY-FOUR

The Power of Stupidity:
You Only Break the Leg of the One You Love

What do people do when they're given too much power? Create human zoos, T.P. shortages, and the unanimous election.

•••

During the Franco-Prussian War in 1871, soldiers stole a thousand paintings by the great artist Camille Pissaro. The soldiers then destroyed the paintings by ripping the canvasses from their frames to create a dry path through a muddy field.

In the sixteenth century, Russia's Ivan the Terrible killed an average of one thousand people a day. Statistically, think about how difficult that was for the czar to manage since he had no modern weapons of mass destruction.

And what if Ivan decided to take a Sunday off or a week at the seashore? A czar could fall behind and there would be hell to pay trying to catch up.

● ● ●

The world's first parking tickets were given out in Nineveh (now Iraq) over two thousand years ago to people who parked their chariots on the king's road.

The fine? Death by impalement. Tough meter maids back then.

● ● ●

The first zoo outside of China was kept by Aztec rulers in the 1500s. The zoo was made accessible to people with disabilities in a fashion that was different than the accommodations we maintain today.

People with deformities were kept caged in the zoo, treated as curiosities by the Aztec elite, just as they treated animals.

● ● ●

In the 1930s Hitler banned Mickey Mouse from Germany. So did Mussolini from Italy, and Stalin from the Soviet Union.

● ● ●

When J. Edgar Hoover was head of the FBI, no agents were allowed to walk on his shadow.

In a 2002 election, some 11 million Iraqis voted to keep Saddam Hussein as their leader for another seven years. Votes against Saddam? Zero.

In America ice cream couldn't win a unanimous vote.

"This is a unique manifestation of democracy which is superior to all other forms of democracies," one of Hussein's election officials explained.

•••

The condemnation of art by the ruling class is not a rabble-rousing tactic created by our own power-loopy politicians. People who think they know it all have been telling artists what to do for centuries.

In 1573 Italian painter Paolo Veronese was dragged before the Inquisition and accused of the crime of irreverence because his painting *The Last Supper* included characters that offended the Church: clowns, drunks and Protestants.

The artist's defense 'was amazingly modern. "I paint pictures as I see fit," he declared.

Surprisingly, he wasn't drawn and quartered for that remark. But the Church did order him to remove the offensive parts of the paintings.

Veronese sidestepped the authorities and lived to tell about it. He simply changed the title of the painting to *Feast in the House of Levi*. The Church couldn't object to drunks and Protestants in a painting about Jews because that's where they thought such outcasts belonged.

Three Megalomaniacal Rulers Competing for the Title of Your Royal Numskull

1. The Chinese Emperor Li Hsui assigned a personal bodyguard to each of his Pekinese. The emperor wasn't worried about dog assassins. He was afraid that bigger dogs would attack his precious little pets.

2. When Holy Roman Emperor Wenceslaus was fixed a bad meal, he had the cook roasted alive. Obviously, this is not the good King Wenceslaus everyone likes to sing about at Christmas time. Or is it?

3. If Queen Ranavalona of Madagascar saw people she knew in a dream, she summoned them to the palace the next morning and had them executed.

Some of the richest men in Europe in the early 1900s were the doubles employed to pretend to be munitions tycoon Sir Basil Zaharoff. While his doubles entertained at society gatherings in Monte Carlo or London, Zaharoff made millions by supplying arms to both sides in wars between Turkey and Greece, then Russia and Japan.

In World War I, he became a billionaire by selling guns and ammunition to all the countries involved.

The Zaharoff doubles did face one threat to their job security: Many of them were assassinated in Zaharoff's place.

●●●

Vlad III Dracula, Prince of Wallachia, was one of the inspirations for Brad Stoker's creation of Dracula the vampire.

The real Dracula (a Romanian word meaning "son of the devil") came up with a unique plan to eliminate poverty from his kingdom.

He invited all the poor people in his realm to a great feast. Then his soldiers nailed the doors and windows shut and set the feast hall on fire. All the poor people burned to death. No more poverty.

●●●

Frederick William I, King of Prussia in the 1700s, spent a fortune to maintain a regiment of giants, the Potsdam Giant Guards, recruited or shanghaied from around the world.

The giants, many of them over seven feet tall, were taught to march alongside the king's carriage and hold hands across the top.

Despite his fancy for giants, the king treated them so brutally that many mutinied or deserted. If they were captured, they were mutilated and thrown in prison.

At the same time that Shakespeare was enlightening the world, the powers that ruled England punished people for swearing by having their tongues torn out, branding them with irons, or executing them.

•••

Europe in the fifteenth century was a blood-soaked place, where the power-hungry were slaughtered by the power-mad. The three charismatic liberators of that warring century—France's Joan of Arc, Italy's Savonarola, and Bohemia's John Huss—were all burned to death by the establishment.

•••

From 1481 and for the next four hundred years, the Catholic Church promoted the auto-da-fé, a public mass burning of people accused of heresy (mostly people of other faiths).

Church leaders somehow missed the great irony that they were torturing and slaughtering thousands of people in the name of Christ, who was tortured and killed for preaching love, peace, and nonviolence.

•••

For centuries Catholics and Protestants tortured and slaughtered each other (and everyone else) in the name of the Prince of Peace. Much of this abuse stems from men of no understanding who lust for power and use religion as an excuse to destroy everyone in their way.

But what of women, kept powerless in so many societies? Take the role-switching case of Blanche Gamond, a French Huguenot of the seventeenth century, who was punished for her religious beliefs by other women.

Six devout Catholic women stripped Blanche, hung her from roof beams by her arms, then beat her senseless, taunting, "Now pray to your God."

Gamond was a mystic, who deemed it an honor to be whipped for Christ, so she was able to transmute her suffering into religious ecstasy.

This irked the women torturing her. "Double our blows," one woman cried, "she does not feel them."

Isn't that the same approach Roman authorities took when they crucified Jesus?

•••

One of Virginia's first congressmen, John Randolph, set a high standard for the behavior of politicians in the 1800s. If his congressional pages displeased Randolph, he struck them with his riding crop.

What nerve! Who did the Congressman think he was, a senator?

•••

William Randolph Hearst used his newspaper empire to attack Orson Welles's great film, Citizen Kane, which satirized Hearst as a power-mad tycoon.

Oddly enough, Hearst's influence was so strong in the 1940s that when *Citizen Kane* was nominated for eight Oscars, the film and the director were booed every time they were mentioned during the Academy Award ceremony.

The people shouting down what is now considered a masterpiece were not Hearst employees. They were Hollywood celebrities and studio tycoons, turning against one of their own to support the man who attacked their industry.

Johnny Carson, the country's most popular talk show host in the 1970s, once started a panic with a bad joke. On his late-night TV show, Carson claimed that toilet paper was "disappearing from the supermarket shelves."

It wasn't. There was no T.P. shortage. But viewers believed Carson instead of their own eyes.

The next day, there was a run on toilet paper in stores all over the country, as Carson's fans bought enough paper to last them for months.

By noon the shelves were emptied. It took three weeks for the overburdened T.P. manufacturers to replace everything that had been bought in the artificial panic.

CHAPTER FORTY-FIVE

Military Stupidity:
Why Generals Aren't in Jail

Why is it that people who miss it entirely are so often promoted to officers?

Haven't you heard of military tradition, soldier? Now shape up and go charge that hill. We're pretty sure the enemy is out of ammunition. And if you do make it back, we'll share some tales of really stupid military maneuvers.

• • •

General Douglas MacArthur overstepped his authority during the Korean War and crossed President Harry Truman, who demanded his resignation.

"I didn't fire him because he was a dumb SOB," Truman explained, "although he was. But that's not against the law for generals. If it was, half to three-quarters of them would be in jail."

•••

When you look at the vast array of deadly weapons available to our military, you may think there is no need to invent more killing machines.

One of Europe's greatest military engineers agreed with that sentiment. He declared, "I will ignore all ideas for new works and engines of war, the invention of which has reached its limits and for whose improvement I see no further hope."

Who was that farsighted military genius? Julius Frontinius, a weapons designer who helped make Rome the leading military power in the first century A.D.

•••

Field Marshall Leberecht von Blücher of Prussia helped defeat Napoleon at Waterloo. But off the battlefield he presented a problem to his allies. He was convinced that French spies were heating floors to burn his feet. So he walked on tiptoe anytime he went indoors.

•••

While visiting Japan in 2002, President George W. Bush said in a speech, "For a century and a half now, America and Japan have formed one of the great and enduring alliances of modern times."

Kind of missed that whole World War II incident, didn't he?

Here's a lesson we can all learn from the U.S. Army: If at first you don't succeed, simply pretend that you have.

During the Normandy invasion in World War II, American generals planned to have the troops land on Omaha Beach, then advance behind bulldozers and tanks that would break through the German defensive fortifications.

But the tanks and bulldozers never made it to the beach. So the troops, taking heavy casualties from German fire, had to devise their own plan under fire. They eventually took the beach by outflanking the German defenders.

After the battle, the generals stood by their flawed strategy, even though it hadn't worked. They simply claimed that everything had gone according to plan.

•••

British scientist Geoffrey Pyke tried to sell the English high command on a bizarre plan to defeat the Nazis in World War II. He wanted to attack German-held oil fields by sending in a wave of St. Bernard dogs toting brandy kegs. The enemy would get drunk, then the English troops would attack.

•••

Not to be outdone by wacky British schemes, American military theoretician Louis Feiser devised a plan to defeat the Japanese in World War II by outfitting bats with tiny napalm bombs. The bats would then be dropped out of planes over Japan, where they would set fire to buildings.

Although the bat bombers never went into battle, the U.S. Army actually tested Feiser's theory. What happened? They burned down one of their own buildings.

In battle when you're not watching out for the enemy, you'd better watch out for your friends.

In World War II the first German soldier wasn't killed by the British, the French, or the Americans. He was killed by his allies, the Japanese, in China.

And the first American soldier wasn't killed by the enemy but by America's allies, the Russians, in Finland.

●●●

When they're looking for someone to help name a new military campaign, do they always recruit a guy whose parents named him Bozo?

In the Vietnam War, there was Rolling Thunder, the air campaign to bomb North Vietnam into submission. As that campaign failed, American soldiers started calling it Rolling Blunder.

Then there was Infinite Justice, George W. Bush's name for his campaign against Muslim terrorists. Problem was the name insulted all Muslims (including those Bush wanted as allies) because they saw it as a sign of religious bigotry.

The campaign was quickly changed to Enduring Freedom, which can also be read in a negative way—as in how much more of this American freedom must we endure, as they liberate us from our bodies by dropping bombs on our heads?

●●●

We may not be the world's policeman, but we're definitely the world's bankroll. Nobody can spend tax money on weird things like the U.S. Army. Except maybe the U.S. Air Force.

The Air Force got to wondering in 1990: Did the noise from its jets bother pregnant horses? They spent $100,000 of our tax money to fund a study to find out. The answer: a definite maybe.

●●●

You should have been in the toilet-seat business in 1989, back before the business went down the tubes. That's when the Pentagon bought toilet seat covers for its cargo planes for two thousand dollars. Apiece.

They could have gotten them cheaper by flying a cargo plane down to the local Kmart.

●●●

Just a bizarre coincidence, but when the Japanese attacked Pearl Harbor in 1941, the U.S. Navy command was known as CINCUS, pronounced just the way no Navy program should ever be pronounced.

●●●

In 1990 the U.S. Army accommodated its powerful political friends by letting select civilians take target practice on Army ranges. Only cost us $5 million.

So maybe when the next war starts, the generals could send some of their country club pals over to fight it.

●●●

The Civil War began when the Confederates attacked Fort Sumter in South Carolina. Although the rebels poured in cannon fire for over a day, no one inside the fort was killed.

Then after the Union soldiers surrendered the fort, they fired a rifle volley in self-salute as they prepared to march out. That tribute killed one of their own men, the first man to die in the Civil War.

●●●

The first book in this stupid series documented the moronic atrocities of the French Revolution, where revolutionaries in their bloodlust to kill everyone else often managed to kill themselves.

But I left out the plight of Antoine Lavoisier, France's top scientist, who was executed by the revolutionaries as a common criminal.

His crime? Being a scientist.

Lavoisier took the guillotine philosophically, commenting that it "saves me from the inconvenience of old age."

●●●

During the Vietnam War, American GIs were equipped with the AR-15 rifle. The weapon performed so poorly that many American soldiers switched to using Soviet rifles captured from enemy troops.

●●●

When General Curtis LeMay was head of the Strategic Air Command during the Cold War, he described circumstances under which he would launch a preemptive atomic strike on the Soviet Union.

When reminded that preemptive strikes violated United States policy, LeMay dismissed the concern, saying, "It's not national policy, but it's my policy."

The biggest blunder of World War II? How about the Japanese attack on Pearl Harbor on December 7, 1941?

Yes, the surprise attack decimated America's Pacific fleet. But it also led the United States to declare war on Japan.

If the Japanese had contented themselves with enslaving the smaller countries along the Pacific rim, the United States might have concentrated its efforts against the Germans and ignored the Japanese.

But Japanese military planners figured the United States was not strong enough to fight two major wars at the same time—in Europe and the Pacific. Oops, slight miscalculation there.

●●●

Remember the Battle of Kiska during World War II? Probably not. Hollywood doesn't make movies about battles like this.

The Kiska offensive was an attempt by a combined U.S. and Canadian force to take the Aleutian Island from the Japanese.

Things went pretty well at first, as Navy ships shelled the island, then 35,000 Allied troops went ashore and took Kiska, only losing twenty-one men in the firefight.

Of course, casualties might have been higher except for one thing: There weren't any Japanese soldiers on the island. All the dead were brought down by friendly fire.

●●●

During World War II, when the Americans and British launched their counterattack with the Normandy invasion, German leaders gave the Allies time to advance off their beachheads because they didn't want to wake Hitler with bad news, knowing the führer's nasty temper.

Every school kid (and lover of bad jokes) remembers that Hannibal crossed the Alps with elephants. But people forget that nearly all the elephants died on the arduous journey.

From this we learn that history rewards the survivors and the riders. Yet, Hannibal would be just another one of history's temporarily successful invaders if he hadn't chosen a unique, though equally temporary means of transportation. History also glorifies spectacular failures.

●●●

In 2002 twenty British Royal Marines stormed a Spanish beach with assault rifles and mortars. When the practice invasion was over, the town policeman approached and explained to the Marines that the beach they meant to practice on was British-held Gibraltar, a few miles to the south.

A British Defense Ministry spokesman apologized for the mistake. "We were not trying to take Spain and have no plans to do so," he said.

●●●

The Roman Emperor Claudius II banned marriage in the year 270 because he believed that married men were too weak to be good warriors. They were always thinking of their wives and children, instead of marching out to die for the greater glory of Rome and Claudius.

The earl of Essex positioned his ships off the Azores in 1597 to trap a Spanish treasure fleet in a blockade. But at the last moment, the earl moved all his ships into new positions. The Spanish ships simply sailed right through the positions that the earl had abandoned and escaped the blockade.

•••

The General Accounting Office found that Navy officers were using government credit cards for nonmilitary purposes in 2003. The officers purchased tickets to sporting events and financed trips to strip clubs, using money they charged to the cards at ATMs located inside the clubs. And these guys are planning our strategy to outwit the enemy?

•••

During World War II, American fighter planes used tracer rounds to help the pilots aim at targets.

But it turned out that if the tracers hit the target, the deadly rounds that followed would actually miss because of differences in the ballistics.

Once pilots got rid of the tracers, they got rid of the enemy's advantage.

CHAPTER FORTY-SIX

The Beached Whale at the Dumb-Off and Other Random Acts of Idiocy

If stupidity defies intelligence, it can certainly defy classification. There is great creativity in stupidity because there are no limits, as we'll see in the tales below:

●●●

After a woman moved to a small town, she called the mayor to complain about a DEER X-ING sign near her house. She explained that deer were being hit by trucks, and she wanted the deer to cross the road somewhere else where it was safer.

How much irony can you stand? A New York man sued the city for injuries when he tripped on a hole in the street.

Why was that ironic? The man worked for the city. It was his job to inspect the streets for holes.

●●●

Even Woodstock never had a rock festival like this one. In India every year the residents of two villages line up on either side of a river for the Stone Throwing Festival, which consists of people throwing stones at each other.

Here's a surprise: hundreds of rock throwers are injured each year.

●●●

In most large cities, out of every ten square miles, cars use four of them. The United States has more than 60,000 acres devoted to shopping malls.

●●●

For every real flamingo in the United States there are seven hundred plastic ones.

●●●

In 2003 an airline attendant alerted authorities to a possible terrorist plot when she opened a bottle of champagne and found no bubbles.

When the plane landed, the suspicious champagne was investigated by experts, who found: flat champagne.

Eleven Slang Terms for "Idiot"

Everyone sees everyone else as stupid—but not me, of course. That us/them view is manifest in the slang terms used by various professions when they talk about customers, civilians, and other people outside their inner circle.

1. TSTL is what nurses and doctors call a patient who is Too Stupid to Live. They call an obese patient who needs help getting out of bed a beached whale.

2. Tabloid editors call any movie star with an unusual personality a Hollyweirdo. What's a trained seal? An expert the tabs keep on file who will offer validation for any ridiculous claim going into the paper.

3. Stockbrokers call certain customers barefoot pilgrims. They're the ones who can be convinced to make investments that will pay off more in commission for the broker than profit for the investor. What do they call small investors? The little people.

4. Fashion designers refer to people who wear ugly clothes as butt soup.

5. Car dealers don't like people who shop for deals, so they call them fleas. What they like worse is a buyer with bad credit. Him, they call a roach.

6. When a funeral director has a customer who orders a simple cremation, without any of the profit-generating frills, that deal is referred to as a shake 'n' bake.

7. In restaurants, customers who act like they don't go out to eat regularly are referred to by waiters as Clampetts, a derogatory term referring to the rubes from The Beverly Hillbillies.

8. Carnies call people who play carnival games they can't win marks. Townspeople are called rubes.

9. In Hollywood a badly written, unprofessional script is called an Iowa.

10. On TV game shows, the staff refers to the situation where all contestants get the answer wrong as a dumb-off. If they think a woman auditioning for the show is overdressed, they call her a hooker. Anyone with a personality that will look dull on the screen is called a Pasadena.

11. Radio talk-show hosts refer to boring callers as maggots.

In 1961 an obscure Canadian fad caught the fancy of college students in the United States: long-distance bed pushing. As a sport, it was like a combo of jogging and napping.

•••

Cambridge scholar Charles Ogden believed that the world would never live in peace until everyone spoke a common language. Toward that end he revised the English language until it contained only 850 words.

Nice try, but I'll bet we all know people (and not the same people) who get by with a vocabulary half that size.

•••

At a business conference, writer Clarence Kelland was asked to introduce a long list of speakers. "The obvious duty of a toastmaster is to be so infernally dull that the succeeding speakers will appear brilliant by contrast," he told the audience. "I've looked over this list, however, and I don't believe I can do it."

•••

In 1982 a New York dog named Lump Lump was given a "bark mitzvah" when he turned thirteen. Four hundred other dogs were invited to the Jewish ceremony.

•••

The small town of Gaston, South Carolina, finally gave in and set up its first stoplight in 1985. Two hours later, a car ran the town's only red light, causing a four-car pileup.

In 1801 an orchestra conductor tried to save the composer embarrassment by skipping much of the last movement of Beethoven's First Symphony. Why? Because the conductor was afraid "people would laugh."

●●●

Everyone knew the *Titanic* sank in the frozen waters of the North Atlantic. But no one knew where the ship came to rest on the bottom of the ocean.

After several expeditions failed to find the *Titanic*, a search team in 1981 asked twenty-eight psychics to predict where the ship would turn up.

They were all wrong. So was the expedition. The *Titanic* was finally found without the help of psychics in 1985.

●●●

Marysville, California, used to hold a town gambling event in which two 150-pound blocks of ice were set out in the sun, and gamblers bet on which one would melt first.

Hard to say whether this proves that gamblers will bet on anything, or that Marysville isn't likely to pass San Francisco as hot spot of the left coast.

●●●

Radio newsman Robert St. John: "If there is a god, he must be looking down, shaking his head, and saying, 'What a mistake I made.'"

Four Dumb Epithets for Cities

Philadelphia got called the City of Brotherly Love because they named it before they knew better. But these cities got stuck with really lame names:

1. The City of Notions: Boston

2. The City of Spindles: Lowell, Massachusetts (because of its textile industry)

3. The City of the Violated Treaty: Limerick, Ireland

4. The Cream City: Milwaukee (because of its cream-colored brick houses)

When cars first came to Tennessee, the city of Memphis passed a statute that a woman could only drive if a man walked in front of the car and waved a red flag to warn pedestrians of approaching danger.

•••

When asked if whiskey made people able to perform tasks more effectively, Dr. William Osler explained, "No, it just makes them less ashamed of doing them badly."

When the treasures of King Tut went on an American tour, a New York City policeman who was assigned to guard the exhibit had a stroke. He sued, claiming he was another victim of the curse of King Tut.

●●●

Lithuania started a new kind of pageant in 2002, a beauty contest to find Miss Captivity among the country's female inmates.

●●●

Absentmindedness can happen to the best of minds.

When Oliver Wendell Holmes searched his pockets, he couldn't find his train ticket. The conductor assured the Supreme Court justice that he could mail in the ticket when he found it.

"The question is not, where is my ticket?" Holmes said, "but where am I supposed to be going?"

CHAPTER FORTY-SEVEN

Smart Thoughts About Stupidity

When you start thinking about stupidity, you may agree with comedian Bill Cosby, who said, "A word to the wise ain't necessary. It's the stupid ones that need the advice."

Or choose your poison:

•••

Cartoonist Bill Watterson (creator of *Calvin and Hobbes*): "The surest sign that intelligent life exists elsewhere in the universe is that it has never tried to contact us."

Irish playwright Sean O'Casey: "All the world's a stage, and most of us are desperately unrehearsed."

•••

Writer Anatole France: "If fifty million people say a foolish thing, it is still a foolish thing."

•••

Anthropologist Desmond Morris: "We may prefer to think of ourselves as fallen angels, but in reality we are risen apes."

•••

Roman philosopher Epicurus in the third century B.C.: "Most men are in a coma when they are at rest and mad when they act."

•••

Philosopher Michel de Montaigne in 1580: "Man is certainly crazy. He could not make a mite, yet he makes gods by the dozens."

•••

Writer Rita Mae Brown: "If the world were a logical place, men would ride sidesaddle."

•••

Educator Laurence J. Peters: "Most hierarchies were established by men who now monopolize the upper levels, thus depriving women of their rightful share of opportunities to achieve incompetence."

Playwright George Bernard Shaw: "It is dangerous to be sincere unless you are also stupid."

● ● ●

Writer Gustave Flaubert: "To be stupid, selfish and have good health are three requirements for happiness, though if stupidity is lacking, all is lost."

● ● ●

Writer Harlan Ellison: "The two most abundant things in the universe are hydrogen and stupidity."

● ● ●

Philosopher Friedrich von Schiller: "With stupidity the gods themselves struggle in vain."

● ● ●

Philosopher Jean de LaBruyere: "There are only two ways by which to rise in this world—either by one's own industry or by the stupidity of others."

● ● ●

Attorney Barry LePatner: "Good judgment comes from experience, and experience comes from bad judgment."

Four Words of Wisdumb
for the Alternatively Brained

1. Look *as* you leap. Since you're not likely to make it anyway, at least you'll enjoy the view on the way down.

2. Every dog will have his day. Hopefully, they won't all be the same day.

3. You will catch more flies with honey than with vinegar. But what are you going to do with all those flies?

4. In these days when stupidity is a growth industry, you see fools all around you. Of course, everybody all around you sees fools all around them too.

Politician Georges Clemenceau: "America is the only nation in history which miraculously has gone directly from barbarism to degeneration without the usual interval of civilization."

●●●

Playwright George Bernard Shaw: "I have defined the 100 percent American as 99 percent an idiot. And they just adore me."

Writer Jonathan Swift: "When a true genius appears in the world, you may know him by this sign: that all the dunces are in confederacy against him."

●●●

Philosopher Georg Hegel: "We learn from history that we do not learn from history."

●●●

Scientist J. Robert Oppenheimer: "The optimist thinks that this is the best of all possible worlds. The pessimist knows it."

●●●

Writer James Thurber: "You can fool too many of the people too much of the time."

●●●

Writer H. L. Mencken: "There's no underestimating the intelligence of the American public."

●●●

Writer George Santayana: "The young man who has not wept is a savage, and the old man who will not laugh is a fool."

●●●

Seventeenth-century scientist John Ray: "Learning makes the wise wiser and the fool more foolish."

Benjamin Franklin: "Wise men don't need advice. Fools won't take it."

●●●

Inventor Charles P. Steinmetz: "No man really becomes a fool until he stops asking questions."

●●●

Industrialist Henry Ford: "Thinking is the hardest work there is, which is probably the reason why so few engage in it."

●●●

Psychologist R. D. Laing: "Insanity is a perfectly rational adjustment to an insane world."

●●●

Hollywood mogul Samuel Goldwyn: "Anybody who goes to see a psychiatrist ought to have his head examined."

●●●

Finally, two thoughts from that great thinker, Unknown:

1. "Artificial intelligence is no match for natural stupidity."
2. "The difference between genius and stupidity is that genius has its limits."

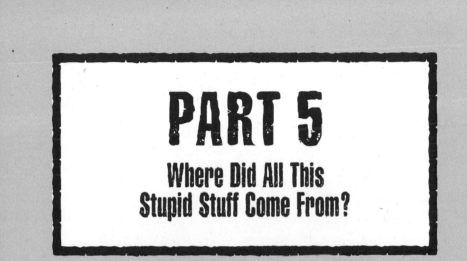

PART 5

Where Did All This Stupid Stuff Come From?

CHAPTER FORTY-EIGHT

Ask Forty-five Stupid Questions, Get Forty-four Stupid Answers

1. Is life just one stupid, nasty, pointless thing after another?

No, of course not. Often, several stupid, nasty, pointless things can happen to you at the same time.

•••

2. What are the odds that we humans are the dumbest race in the universe?

With a universe as big as ours, the good news is that it's unlikely we're the single dumbest race in the whole joint.

Sure, it's possible. But the odds are on our side that when God scraped the bottom he didn't come up with us.

That honor probably belongs to an insignificant race in a backwater solar system that goes around praying to God on Sundays and killing each other Monday through Friday—and sometimes Saturday, depending if they didn't get the job done right during the week.

What is that prayer heard all over this not-the-dimmest fuzzy object in space? Thank you, Lord, for this incredible thing you gave us, life, and the brain to realize we're alive and that we owe it all to you.

Now just sit quietly for a few minutes because we have to go over there and kill all those people who must have gotten their lives and brains from someone else.

●●●

3. Do you think more people would be able to follow the ten commandments if they weren't so complicated? Like maybe God could simplify them next time around; condense them into one or two really important commandments.

Most people don't realize that the ten commandments *are* the *Reader's Digest* version of God's rules. Here's what actually happened when Moses tried to come down from the Mount with the ten commandments:

GOD: Oh, Moses.

MOSES: You talking to me?

GOD: You're the only one up here besides me, and I don't talk to myself.

MOSES: What now, God?

GOD: You forgot eleven through twenty.

MOSES: These stone tablets are pretty heavy, Lord. I could take down forty, fifty commandments if You'd put them all on paper.

GOD: Like to, but you haven't invented paper yet.

MOSES: You're all-powerful, couldn't You move a few inventions up on the schedule? Paper would be nice. Some of those lightweight sandals with the cushion tread. I wouldn't object to ice cubes. This desert water doesn't taste so hot coming out hot all the time.

GOD: Moses, already you're forgetting the eleventh commandment: Thou shalt not whine.

MOSES : Right, right.

GOD: And number twelve: If you've got any questions about why life is the way it is, keep it to yourself.

MOSES: Right, because if You wanted to explain things You would have. It's not like this stuff slipped Your mind.

GOD: So Moses, take the next ten with you.

MOSES: Look, I'll come back for them. I promise. As soon as I can get people to follow the first ten.

GOD: Don't forget.

Moses forgot. Don't you make the same mistake. Write us today for a copy of the Forgotten Commandments, numbers eleven through twenty. Be sure to include a self-addressed return stone tablet.

●●●

4. With the spread of nuclear weapons and other life-destroying technologies, is there any upside to the direction we're headed?

With our advance warning system, about thirty to forty minutes before the end of all life as we know it, you'll have a chance for the sale of a lifetime.

90 percent off everything in stock. Everything. Everywhere.

Hardware, software, underwear. Salt and pepper shakers, popcorn makers, bread bakers, cruise missiles.

We mean everything. Buy one, get a thousand free, if you act now.

How can we make an offer this crazy? Because we're crazy. You know that.

•••

5. Can you judge a person's IQ by how much he recycles, so that the smarter you are the less garbage you produce?

Recycling demonstrates a psychological need to think we're solving another problem that can't be solved.

People have been producing garbage ever since they bought the odd notion that civilization was a goal instead of a collective personality defect.

Much of that ancient garbage is now treasured by museums as valuable artifacts of cultures past.

So don't feel guilty about tossing garbage. Think of it as helping some future Yale anthropologist get a cheap Ph.D.

Garbage: So what if it piles up? We have more important things to do. Waste is a terrible thing to mind.

•••

6. Have you ever met a dumb rocket scientist?

People are always saying, "You don't need to be a rocket scientist to figure *that* out."

Actually, there's only *one* job where you *do* have to be as smart as a rocket scientist—being a rocket scientist.

One more thought it doesn't take a rocket scientist to think: Whom do rocket scientists refer to when they want to be modest and imply that they're not as smart as someone else?

You don't have to be a supervisor of rocket scientists to figure that out.

7. What's the world's biggest problem?

Overpopulation. And I could name names.

The solution is simple: Everyone in the world picks a number from a hat. All number fives have to go. That would free up a lot of apartments in New York City.

Where would they all go? Hey, I just solved overpopulation. Get someone else to work out the details.

●●●

8. Can you ever win an argument with an idiot?

Let's say you maintain the radical opinion that "it's cold outside."

A philosopher might argue: "How do you define cold?"

A mystic would counter: "What do you mean by outside?"

A Democrat could contend: "If it was cold outside, the government would have alerted us to the danger."

But an idiot will argue: "You can't stay warm in the closet."

You might be tempted to say, "I wasn't talking about the closet."

Or: "Let's go outside and see if it's cold or not."

Or: "Even a moron can tell when it's cold."

None of these arguments will do you any good. The idiot will simply refute your logic with: "No, it's my closet and you can't play."

The only way to win an argument with an idiot is to think like an idiot, which isn't as hard as you might expect.

So the next time you want to prove to an idiot that it's cold outside, say: "Since no one knows for certain if the inside is part of the outside, all cold is relative to my uncle, and the government hasn't voted on the issue yet, let me in that closet now."

Then grab the idiot, throw him out, lock the door behind you, and consider yourself lucky to have won once in your life.

•••

9. Are stupid people part of the problem or part of the solution?

Stupid people are our only hope. Consider pollution, which is getting worse day by day. But it's just not bad enough.

If our poisoned air and six or seven polluted oceans were really a problem, some genius would solve it.

No one's come up with a solution, so how bad can it be?

If you really want to do something about pollution, pitch in and make it worse. Let's not deprive some bright young scientist of the chance to win the Nobel prize for Really Great Science That Actually Does Something by solving pollution and saving what's left of the world.

Pollute as if your life depended on it because no pollution = no solution.

•••

10. Free will or fate? Is it stupid to try to resolve that debate?

"You are who you are and there's nothing you can do about it," Phillip said. "You can't be who you're not."

"No, you are who you think you are," Megan said. "Until one day your thinking changes and you realize you only thought you were who you were."

"No, you are who you can get away with being," Rachel said. "Who you can convince other people you are. You can say you're a guru, but if no one follows you, then you're not."

"No, you are who we allow you to pretend to be," Chris said.

"Not true," Gabriel said. "You are only the illusion of who you are."

"Excuse me, folks. I hate to ruin the fun, but none of you are who you think you are. You are all who I thought you were."

"Hey, pal, who do you think you are?"

"The guy who thought you up in the first place."

"Maybe you only think you thought us up."

"I can prove it."

"How?"

"The same way God does. By stopping."

●●●

11. Can we cure stupidity?

Sure, join the Society for the Unspecifically Unhappy or the National Organization to Make Sure We Haven't Forgotten Anything by sending two thousand dollars to Post Office Box 2000, Needmoney, New Jersey.

These groups are devoted to curing stupidity by becoming rich enough not to care any more.

●●●

12. If you are an idiot, what line of work should you go into?

Politics is always an attractive option. Our elected officials have already proven that any idiot can do the job. The trick is getting the job.

There's a lot of competition because of the graft and corruption. Also, there's no actual work to be done once you've mastered the handshake.

But for people just starting out in the idiot business, I recommend crime. It's America's largest growth industry. You don't have to be union to get work, and your competition tends to be even dumber than you are.

Best of all, there's job security. If you choose a career in bank robbing, for example, you don't have to worry that the bank will be sent overseas to be robbed for less by cheap foreign labor.

●●●

13. If idiotology is a new field of study, how can you tell in which direction we're moving? Were people dumber before, and now are smartening up? Or were we smarter then, and now growing dumber day by day?

If people were dumber and are now getting smarter, then idiotology wouldn't be a new field of study. Scientists would have stumbled upon it a long time ago because their primary observations concern the obvious.

●●●

14. Are there any advantages to being stupid?

Four, making it an attractive lifestyle choice.

1. You won't have to worry about losing your mind when you grow old if you lose it when you're young.

Good riddance to overrated straw anyway. The Scarecrow's brain never would have hurt if Dorothy had left him alone.

2. The progressive dumbing-down of America can be taken as a compliment. Everyone else is trying to become more like you.

And with the help of advertising and our government's policy of investing in smart bombs and dumb kids, they're going to make it. Meanwhile, you can sit around waiting for everyone to catch up.

3. Sarcasm relief. We are all bombarded by the cruel, thought-less comments of miserable people.

You? Blithe. The snide comments and sarcastic barbs shot in your direction will fly right over your head. While other people have their feelings crushed, you'll go blithely on your way. Or would if you had any idea what "blithely" meant.

4. Greater range of food options. Butter-dipped pork rinds? You bet. Cereal made from sugarcoated sugar? Mmm, I'll have seconds. Extra cheese baked into the pizza box so you can eat the whole thing without having to figure out which is the pizza and which is the cardboard? Sounds good.

You'll never feel guilty for eating garbage once you go brain-less. After all, if it were really bad for you, why would they be selling it?

● ● ●

15. I read somewhere that April is the cruelest month. But I've never had any special problem with April. Is this a tax protest thing, or am I missing something?

April used to be the cruelest month back when they put a poet in charge of cruel accounting.

T. S. Eliot noticed that in April you not only have taxes, but also war, famine, illness, nasty accidents, and, on top of all that, the blues.

What Eliot failed to note, perhaps because his poetic license expired, was that right after April you get May, which also has war, famine, illness, accidents, and a deeper shade of blue. Plus, pile on top of that the remembrance of the cruelties of April, and you have a new leader in the cruelest month race.

Until June, when ditto occurs.

July? The same. August? See July.

The cruelty mounts month by month because none of these problems ever go away. Then you get to February, which not only has its fair share of misery and memories, but also takes on the whole problem of that extra *r*.

We all want to spell it as we call it: Febuary. But the English teacher who crawled inside our heads in fifth grade won't let go, and there's nothing crueler than that.

Then comes March, which luckily is the uncruelest month because we know that no matter what terrible things happen to us in March, it's not going to be as bad as what's coming next: another April, which is the cruelest month, as the poet instructs us.

●●●

16. Are the French and Japanese smarter than Americans because they teach their children to speak foreign languages at a young age and we don't?

They're supposed to be able to speak a foreign language. They're foreigners.

●●●

17. Everyone knows by now that it's stupid to take drugs, unless you really love fried eggs. So why do so many people continue to do something so dumb?

We could have won the war on drugs by now if we had saved those Keystone Kops' billions we wasted chasing drug dealers from one side of the street to the other, and spent it on research to invent a better drug with fewer nasty side effects.

Those fried-egg drugs? Take out the drug reference and it makes just as much sense to say: These are your brains on TV. Here are your brains behind the wheel of an SUV. These are your brains after a really bad junior high school teacher got hold of them.

There's a world of fried brains out there, and they weren't all fried by drugs.

But you'll never wipe out a substance that makes people think they're having a good time even if they're not.

• • •

18. Is failure a sign of a subpar intelligence?

For too long people have been telling you that you're a failure just because you fail. Don't let all that negativity get you down.

Each year the Chicago Cubs fail to win the World Series. Do you think that gets them down? No, they bank their millions just like the champs, then go out the next year and fail all over again.

Failure is a humanitarian response. If you don't fail, someone else has to. Each time you fail, you give them a chance to succeed. You're a nice guy.

Remember, if at first you don't succeed, you may have found a lifestyle you can live with.

• • •

19. Who's dumber, crooks or lawyers?

Victims are. Because we allow these two groups to run our society when we could get rid of them both in one easy step.

We *can* eliminate crime in our lifetime. How? Make it all legal. Everything.

The way it is now, crime attracts the worst kind of people: criminals. No more crime, no more crooks.

Once we legalize crime, then everyone can do it. Crime will become as American as speeding or cheating on your taxes.

•••

20. Do smart people throw away money more intelligently than stupid people?

Absolutely, as a recent study proved when researchers examined the spending habits of people with and without IQs. They found that:

Stupid people buy: mood elevators, security systems, guns, subscriptions to *National Enquirer*.

Smart people buy: higher priced mood elevators, better security systems, larger guns, subscriptions to *Vanity Fair*.

•••

21. Why do magazines assume we're idiots?

It's a profitable assumption. Take *Vanity Fair*, a magazine for rich idiots, which ran an ad from what used to be Citibank but now is repositioning itself as Citi—a lifestyle choice instead of a place to open a checking account.

The ad advises us to "amass a fortune . . . in friends" because "they're the only ones who can tell you what you're worth."

Apparently, now that it's no longer a crass commercial bank, Citi is not bothering to keep track of your money. They're relying on your friends to do that.

In the photo, a woman is dressing as five pairs of hands tug at her white dress. Being rich in friends means never having to adjust your own clothes.

Or perhaps, the ten hands belong to Citi's nonbanking staff. Freed from having to waste their time keeping track of your money, the ex-bankers can help you with more important things, like looking good.

●●●

22. If we go into a war with God on our side, and they're fighting against us in the name of God, what's God to do?

Play defense. Can't you see that battle where God actually protects every mother's son and daughter by knocking aside all the bullets like some Super-Arnie?

They shoot at us, but they all miss. Then we shoot at them, but we all miss too.

It would get so frustrating to drill instructors everywhere, that right there it'd be worth it.

But then some general would order an old-fashioned bayonet charge. Now God really has to get to work. We stab at them and they sidestep, sidestep, sidestep. Then they try to club us with their blunderbuss butts, but we duck and weave like a pre-rope-a-dope Ali.

Finally, everyone gets so wiped out from all that missing they collapse in a big, nonlethal heap, and someone says, "Anyone got a beer?"

And the battle can't be won so the war has to end, and God goes, "Damn, why didn't I think of that before?"

●●●

23. Is it smarter to light a single candle or curse the darkness?

More people have been killed by candles than cursing.

You'd think people would remember to put the candles out before they catch the drapes on fire. But people are so busy patting themselves on the back for being so candle-lightingly optimistic that they forget to practice proper wax safety.

Meanwhile, people who curse the darkness are doing their part to protect the environment, while developing command of a full variety of curses that will come in handy when things go really bad.

Take a close look at the universe. It's filled with more darkness than light. If God wanted the world to be heavy on light and light on cursing, He wouldn't have put so much space between so few stars.

●●●

24. Why do the idiots always rise to the top?

They're handpicked by the top brass, who don't want someone smart coming in and making them look bad by comparison.

●●●

25. Does watching TV make you stupid? Or do you have to be stupid first?

Studies show the average American watches seven hours of TV a day. That's not nearly enough. If you put your mind to it, you could double that.

If everyone watched TV fourteen hours a day, we'd cut our traffic jams in half. We'd also reduce the spread of sexually transmitted diseases because TV sex is the only safe sex. Tele-living is just like ordinary living, only safer.

26. Why are smart people moaning and groaning all the time?

The more you whine about how stupid everything is, the longer God lets you live because He sees that you get it.

●●●

27. If you've already done the stupidest thing you'll ever do, isn't it all looking up from there?

Not quite. Nothing you can do is ever as stupid as it will become once your neighbor finds out about it.

●●●

28. Where have all the smart people gone?

Gone to flowers everyone.

Right off the top, we know they haven't gone to D.C. The last smart person in Washington was seen running from the Capitol screaming a warning: "They're not pod people."

If our government officials had come from outer space, that would explain a lot. But no, they come from America, and that's a scary thought. Apparently, this *is* the best we can do.

NYC, LA, Akron? No, no, no. If you were smart, would you live there?

You'll find most of the smart people in universities, where they hide out from the world because they've figured out what the rest of the world is like.

You'll also find wise guys in monasteries, where they seek enlightenment through reflection and meditation. And as soon as they find it, they make sure not to pass it on to the rest of us.

They realize if they showed other people how to become enlightened, the marketing boys would sell us Nirvana perfume so we can smell like heaven, and everyone would get caught up in the enlightenment rat race. There they may find a better breed of rat, but it's still a race.

•••

29. Are artists geniuses? Or do they just get away with telling us they're geniuses because nobody knows anything about art?

All great art is motivated by one desire: not to have to work for a living.

Art does not require intelligence. If brains were any advantage to an artist, then Harvard MBAs would have painted the Sistine Chapel.

•••

30. Is it smarter to look before you leap or jump right in?

It's smart to look before you leap, but only if you look an hour and a half before you leap.

That way you will have plenty of time to come up with a good excuse for why you leaped after you looked and saw what you were leaping into.

•••

31. Are doctors as smart as they claim to be?

Experts estimate that one in fifty doctors is a fake, with no medical degree—and that doesn't count actors who play doctors on TV.

These impostors practice medicine anyway, some of them as effectively as real doctors.

Either we have some very smart impostors, or it's not as hard to be a doctor as the medical schools want us to believe.

●●●

32. Why are movie stars so fabulous until you actually meet them, when total jerkism seems to set in?

You'd be a jerk too if you were paid millions to romance a movie camera. Take Brad Hunk, your typical movie star.

Somehow he inspires millions of thirteen-year-old girls and suburban housewives to dream of the moment they stumble onto Brad at the mall, and he says, "You're the one I've been looking for all my life. All those Hollywood stars, the models, they mean nothing to me."

Yet Brad knows how inadequate he really is because a year ago he was folding shirts at the Gap. He doesn't know what he did right to deserve his incredible break or he would have done it after one day of working at the Gap.

Now Brad's a god walking the earth, worshipped by fans and managers. Every dumb thought he used to have is now a telling insight, written down by journalists who keep wondering why they didn't become movie producers instead of copying down the pronouncements of handsome idiots.

Brad now strides through the indefinite world with the confidence of a young prince surveying his father's harem. But even with the full resources of the beauty industry working on their behind, movie stars can never be good lovers because lovers merge with the other, and a movie star merges only with his box office.

33. What is the dumbest holiday?

In the spirit of Christmas, we go to overcrowded stores whose merchandising would have appalled Christ. We waste precious resources wrapping presents so the wrapping can be torn off and thrown away. We spend too much money for things we don't need and wonder why the holiday leaves us feeling empty.

On Easter and Halloween, we overdose our children with candy, knowing that within the hour we'll be yelling at them to stop tossing baby brother up against the wall to see if he sticks.

On Groundhog Day, we celebrate the ability of a rodent to predict the weather.

But clearly the favorite holiday of idiotologists everywhere is April Fools' Day, when we celebrate the fact that we are stupid enough to hold a celebration of how dumb we are.

●●●

34. Aren't phobias a sign of intelligence? There are things we should be afraid of, right?

You bet. People in power who have sharp implements in their hands. A politician is the last person in the world you'd want running with scissors, especially nuclear scissors.

But that's not what we're afraid of. We're afraid of spiders, our most common phobia, even though we're a thousand times bigger and a million times meaner than they are. When's the last time a spider swatted at you with a rolled-up newspaper?

More people are afraid of spiders than cancer, sociopaths, or being bored to death at pool parties by people in Speedos who have enough stomachs to outfit the whole neighborhood.

You're more likely to have a zonked-out rock 'n' roll singer fall on your head than to die of a spider bite.

35. They give out Nobel prizes for physics, chemistry, medicine, literature, economics, and peace. Doesn't that prove that we've got at least six smart people around here?

Prize winners are a small circle of friends, who take turns giving out prizes to each other, not to the rest of us.

They don't give out Nobel prizes for handicapping the football pool, channel surfing, whining, petty crimes, or living in a messy house—the things most of us are good at.

●●●

36. Humans have invented hundreds of languages, all of them incredibly complex. Surely that proves intelligence?

No, but it makes talking a lot more fun. Language ability is more of a paradox than a sign of intelligence.

For example, when we want to tell someone that words fail us, we have to use words to get the idea across.

●●●

37. Where do most idiots go, to heaven or hell?

Most everybody, smart or stupid, goes to hell.

For starters, every religion condemns the foolish followers of every other religion. They can't all be right, although they could all be wrong.

Then there are the nonbelievers who are going to hell for not believing there's a hell to condemn other people to.

This leaves a couple of saints and a buddha or two with a shot at heaven.

But not to worry. Have fun. If you have fun and get sent to hell for it, then you'll be with all the other people who got sent to hell for having fun—the party crowd.

The few people a century who stand a chance of getting into heaven will be honing their harp skills while perfecting pure thoughts. So guess who's going to throw the best party?

•••

38. Are ignorant people smarter than the highly educated?

We'll let you know as soon as the professors turn in their research.

Meanwhile, consider this: An ignorant farmer, walking through the woods at the edge of his farm, came upon a coiled rattler. Without thinking twice, the farmer raised his shotgun and killed the snake before it could strike.

Loss of the snake subtly shifted the area's ecological makeup. Without the rattlesnake, the population of wood rats increased rapidly.

Searching for food, the rats invaded the farm, bringing with them a disease that killed the farmer's chickens.

He treated the survivors with a chemical that saved some chickens but seeped into the soil, where it destroyed his corn harvest. Without a cash crop, the farmer couldn't pay his mortgage and lost the farm.

Fed up with his ineptitude, the farmer's wife ran off with an Indian snake charmer.

Despondent and completely clueless as to why life was so unfair, the ex-farmer wandered into the big city, where he became a street-corner drunk. He was killed in a knife fight over a bottle of cheap whiskey outside a skid row bar called the Snake Bite.

A few hundred miles away, an educated farmer with a Ph.D. in organic interdependency was walking through the woods at the edge of his farm when he came across a coiled rattlesnake.

As he raised his shotgun, the educated farmer thought about the consequences of killing the snake: how it might upset the delicate ecological balance he'd carefully nurtured. Further, his presumptive shooting would be unfair to snakes and other living creatures. Plus, it might come back to bite him at harvest time with increased vermin population and other problems that a snakeless ecology could introduce to the art of sensitive cultivation.

While the educated farmer was projecting these consequences in a nonlinear fashion, the snake struck and killed him.

There, I hope that answers your question.

•••

39. Since the experts so often turn out to be wrong, shouldn't we be getting smarter experts?

Planes crash. Ships sink. Rockets explode. The power goes out. The toast burns.

We train the best soldiers in the world, give them the finest equipment, then send them out on impossible missions and they fail. That's why the mission was impossible, as the generals conclude in their follow-up report.

It takes a wise man to admit that he's wrong. Therefore, a wise man could never be an expert.

•••

40. If primitive people were so smart, why did they create us?

They had a sense of humor before they knew that there was anything to laugh at.

If civilization manages to self-destruct, we will have achieved an irony none of us will be around to appreciate—thereby creating no irony at all, how ironic—by turning civilized people back into primitive people once again.

●●●

41. Isn't marriage just another form of marketing?

Genuine marriage: Doesn't taste as good as passion, but it's less filling.

There's always money to be made from any product that can be improved by words like *genuine* (beer) or *true* (love). But the money will be made by the people who service the product, not by the people who consume it.

●●●

42. Is there a new dumb trend coming into fashion?

Tough question, since all fashion trends are dumb. But watch out for extend marketing. For example, women will soon be buying giant tubes of bodystick because lipstick is not just for lips any more.

Why should your mouth get all the attention? Isn't your neck kissable? How dare they ignore the inside of your wrist?

Now through the magic of bodystick you can send out signals of where you'd like to be kissed next.

●●●

43. Is mankind too dumb to live?

No, we survive because of our ferocious stupidity. Only idiots would live in endless warfare that kills millions of people.

Yet, without all our wars, the planet would be jammed with millions of more people and where would we put them? Underground was a stupid solution, but effective.

●●●

44. In the first stupid book you said the future was looking pretty dumb. Now it is that future. So were you right or what?

You make the call—although if you're smart enough to do that you're probably too smart to do it.

First, count the wars, the oppression, random cruelty, the way wealth taunts poverty, the continuing destruction of the only world we've got.

Everybody knows we're screwing up big time. Nobody stops. But hey, the president's happy we're still shopping.

●●●

45. Any hope for the future?

Has to be. You can't have hope for the past.

The future was invented so we'd have someplace to put all the hope that keeps springing eternal.

You ever notice how hope always springs? It doesn't slip or sashay or walk calmly to the nearest exit.

Hope has to spring because if it doesn't take a flying leap, it's not going anywhere.

CHAPTER FORTY-NINE

Twenty-one Stupid Solutions to Problems You Didn't Even Know We Had

1. Bad money

I have nothing against old presidents who are no longer with us, but if they're no longer with us and we didn't know them personally, why do we keep their pictures in our pockets?

Wouldn't it make more cents to sell that space off to corporations? They've got most of our money anyway. So why shouldn't they pay for the naming rights?

- Disney would sponsor the one-dollar bill because that's a Mickey Mouse denomination anyway.

- The twenty-dollar bill, built Ford tough.

- The MasterCard fifty-dollar bill: You'll never get one of these with American Express.

- The quarter? Mickey D's. Just get rid of the eagle and imprint the coin with the Macdonald's quarter pounder with cheese.

- The dime? Sponsored by Wal-Mart, only now it's marked down to six and a half cents.

●●●

2. Car cheats

Most people feel dumb when they buy a car. You could switch to riding a bicycle. Okay, but seriously, there is a way to get over feeling cheated.

Just follow this advice from the National Association of Concerned Car Salesmen: If we sell you a lemon, shut up and make lemonade, you pathetic loser.

Sure, our cars are lousy. You think you can make them any better, you're welcome to come down and try.

Maybe they do break down at the most inconvenient moment. So what? That's life, in case you haven't noticed.

You can whine about it, or you can look at that leaky radiator as half full, an opportunity to better yourself.

Do you realize you'll burn off 890 calories just by pushing one of our lemons into the repair shop? And the more time your car spends in the shop, the less air pollution your kids have to breathe. We're doing our part to clean up American air with American-built cars.

Making something that works most of the time is job one. Advertising is job two, three, four, five. All right, and one, too.

3. Unwanted senility

Social security will shortchange you in your old age. And you don't want to end an occasionally dignified life eating cat food and sitting at bus stops pretending you have someplace to go.

But now we can make lingering illness and debilitating diseases a thing of the past.

How? By stopping the senseless slaughter of our young soldiers—and subbing in the senseless slaughter of very old soldiers.

Let's not send our sons and daughters around the world to kill other people. Let's send our grandparents.

War: the lasting solution to the problems of old age, coming soon to a disputed territory near you.

●●●

4. Unhappy fat

Fat people are looked down upon as dumb by skinny people. But really, they're just differently weighted.

Skinny people are from Pluto. Fat people are from Jupiter.

Skinny people get all the good press because photo editors pull the strings.

If supersized people launched their own PR campaign, it would go something like this:

We're fat. The way people were meant to be. Can't see your toes? We've seen them, and believe us you don't want to.

So have seconds. Do your part to fight the international diet conspiracy of skinny losers who are afraid to live large, or extralarge.

We're not twice as big as they are. We're twice as good.

So eat up. The more of you there is, the less room there is for them.

5. Ugly no more

People who buy *People* tend to associate intelligence with good looks. Is there any real connection?

Sure, if you're beautiful—smart move. And call, we'll do after-lunch.

But if you're ugly and dumb, at last there's a solution, and it comes from an unexpected source. Listen in:

"Say Marge, I couldn't help but notice . . ."

"What, Sally?"

"You're really ugly, Marge."

"I know, Sally, but what can I do about it?"

"Haven't you heard? Avis has a wonderful new program that can help ugly people like you."

"Sounds too good to be true. How does it work?"

"Simple. All the really ugly people . . ."

"You mean like me?"

"That's right, Marge. All the real clock stoppers move to New Jersey."

"Hmmm. Why New Jersey?"

"Remember when we had all the gun nuts move to Montana? Same principle."

"Makes sense to me, Sally. Ugly people go to Jersey."

"You'll feel more at home with your own kind, and the rest of us won't get nauseous."

So remember, beauty (like intelligence) may only be skin deep. But that's as far as anyone looks.

6. Beating the market

Every system for picking winners on the stock market turns out to be a loser. But now there is an investment plan that won't make you feel like an idiot.

It's manic depression: the investment strategy for the post-Enron years.

How does it work? Simple: Buy when you're low. Sell when you're high.

Any psychiatrist can cure manic depression. We'll show you how to turn your up-and-down cycle into a moneymaker, because nothing reflects your own violent mood swings like the stock market.

Our system will make you rich, then poor, then rich again. If you're manic-depressive, or would like to be, you may never find mental stability. But you can achieve financial security. And who needs sanity when you're rich?

●●●

7. Guaranteed love

They say any fool can fall in love. What about a complete idiot? Is there really someone out there for every dunderhead?

Yes, it no longer matters how dumb you are because every day your chances of finding true love get better and better.

Odds used to be a million to one you'd never find the perfect mate. But as the world population grows, those odds keep improving in your favor.

The secret to true love is that you've been looking in all the wrong places. Stop searching for romance in Beverly Hills and Palm Beach. Those beautiful people are all taken.

Look for your perfect mate where the love professionals look: China, India, the Bronx. There's a reason these are the most over-populated countries in the world. They're full of young lovers, looking for someone just like you.

As an idiot, you'll understand that overpopulation isn't a problem threatening to destroy the world's resources and bankrupt the planet. It's all about romance.

How can there ever be too many lovers in the world?

•••

8. Republican air

Every time we elect Republicans, our environment goes to hell. Is this a coincidence?

Studies show that only 67 percent of the air is actually poisoned by pollution. Simple Republican math will tell you that means 32 percent of the air is good, old-fashioned American oxygen.

And because the Republicans are in charge, all that good air remains absolutely free to everyone, regardless of race, religion, or lung power.

Ask yourself: What have the Democrats done for your cardio-vascular system lately?

The challenge for right-thinking Americans is how to get hold of that good 32 percent and send the bad air to developing countries, where it doesn't matter what they breathe because they don't have any Republicans over there.

The answer is the Republican Sniff. You probably thought we had our noses in the air because we were snobs. Nothing could be further from the truth.

The Republican Sniff is the only way to search out that 32 percent of the air that's still breathable.

So you can sit there and breathe the old, tired Democratic way. Or you can join us and breathe free again.

Air: brought to you by the Republican Party. And they say we never gave you anything.

●●●

9. Don't just say no

If all the people who just say no to drugs have been just saying no for so many years, how come we still have so many drugs?

Because just saying no to drugs is a stupid answer, when you could say so much more.

With our home-study program, you'll learn to say nay, nix, nope, nowise, noways, by no means, by no manner of means, on no account, in no respect, not in the least, not by a long shot, and not by a long chalk to drugs.

Now that'll get dealers to sit up and listen.

Let's face it—half the people who just say no to drugs are high when they say it. Why not put that time to better use?

With our vocabulary enrichment course, you won't just be lying around in a drug-induced stupor. You'll be lying around in a drug-induced stupor *and* improving your word power at the same time.

Our thesaurus is designed specifically for people who are too stoned to look anything up. We don't arrange words alphabetically or by subject, like those straight word finders. Our book has no order whatsoever. So you'll feel right at home wandering aimlessly through the absurd pages and improving your mind at the same time.

When your parents complain, "Why are you wasting your life getting high?" you can reply, "I'm not wasting my life. I'm dissipating my existence."

We've turned thousands of drunks into inebriates and fifty-seven junkies into alternative consciousness facilitators. We can do the same for you. Word power to the people!

●●●

10. That fifth doctor

You know those TV commercials where four out of five doctors agree? Ever wonder: What if the fifth doctor is the smart one, and the other four are like the idiots you go to?

The American Mediocre Medical Association offers this advice: four out of five doctors agree—stop whining.

Headache? Muscle ache? Where have you been, pal? That's nothing compared to the alternatives.

You could have phlebitis, phlebutus, or even phlebootius.

Your hair could be falling out in clumps. So could your toes.

Spinal chord leakage. Brain seepage. Intestinal gnats.

And that's just off the top of our heads.

So when you have minor headache or backache pain, or hear "Achy Breaky Heart" on golden oldies radio, doctors recommend you keep it to yourself. No one wants to hear your petty problems all day long.

Take two aspirin. Take four. Who cares? Just don't call us in the morning.

The Only Doctors You'll Ever Be Able to Go to Association: From now on, nothing but the truth.

●●●

11. Driven gay

In every car commercial on TV, sexy women are always turning to ogle any guy in a new car. Think about how many awkwardly dumb problems this creates for gay guys.

Homosexual men in good cars who are besieged by the unwanted advances of gorgeous women need a car of their own—the Gay Car.

You're not like other men. Why should you drive their cars? When you slip behind the wheel of a Gay Car, women will move back to Tulsa, Oklahoma.

What else can they do when you're driving the Gay Car, the only car ever made that will never drive women crazy?

•••

12. Leftover idiots

At last there's help for the idiots left out of all those other idiot guidebooks. Here are two excerpts from *The Stupid Idiot's Dumb Guide to Moronic Career Success*.

1. So you want to be a bank robber?

They'll give you the money, no problem. Don't even need a gun. Just tell them you have one. We guarantee they won't say, "Can you pull it out and shoot someone, please, to prove you mean it?"

Crowd control inside the bank—that's your problem. Most people who use banks will experience unnecessary anxiety when looking down the barrel of a gun. It's your job to calm them down.

Instead of threatening to shoot everyone, pass out peanuts and diet sodas. Then they'll do anything you tell them. Hey, it works for the airlines.

2. Thinking about a career in drugs?

You don't want to waste all your time getting deadbeat clients to pay their bills. Most dealers simply sell to the wrong demographic. Drug users make lousy customers because they're so stoned they can't keep their business straight.

Who should you sell to? Members of the Rotary and Kiwanis clubs, upstanding citizens who always pay their bills on time.

•••

13. Happy money
You've probably heard that money can't buy happiness. Rich people have been telling that one to poor people for generations.

The truth is money can't buy *you* happiness, but it's done pretty well by us.

Of course, the life of the wealthy isn't all fun and games.

All right, it is all fun and games. But we're used to it. You wouldn't like it. Being rich isn't for everyone.

Do you have any idea how dreary those banquets can be? Resort, resort, resort—please.

The yacht? A constant headache. If it's not the helicopter pad that needs polishing, it's the crew jumping ship in the Bahamas. And you can never keep sand out of the carpets. Jet lag? You don't want to know.

Rich people. We're not better than you are. . . . All right, we are.

•••

14. Phones for boneheads
Every night we get phone calls from phone companies offering us new phone services. You may ask them, "You got a phone service that prevents phone companies from calling me up?" They don't.

But at last there's a company that's less stupid than all the rest. The phone service from Ma Tell-and-Tell.

Other outfits offer cheaper rates and better service. But only Ma Tell-and-Tell gives you what the other phone companies can't: something to talk about.

When you sign up, they'll let you in on some of the hottest gossip in show business, sports, politics, and other celebrity rackets.

Like which eighty-eight-pound starlet is sleeping with what hot, young president? And who else is she sleeping with that he doesn't know about? Ma even knows whom she's going to sleep with next, which only her agent knows about.

How do they get such great gossip? Hey, they're the phone company. If they can't listen in, who can?

To sign up, just dial 1-800-Say-What.

●●●

15. Inner football

Football: It's not just a game. It's spending the kids' inheritance for a bad seat to watch guys you hate get beaten up by other guys you would hate if you knew them better.

But don't think of season tickets as a stupid investment in idle worship. Think of it as a stupid investment in therapy.

You could spend $150 an hour to have some scruffy chin who couldn't crush a beer can on his forehead tell you you're all screwed up. Wasted money. You already know that.

Your team knows it too. That's why they soak you for the rights to be double-soaked for season tickets, even though they haven't won a Super Bowl in twenty-five years and aren't planning to.

Why should they go to all that effort to win when they can get rich by losing?

That's why they cram you into seats too small for your butt, then stuff you with Polish sausages and beer so that the seats get tighter as your butt swells each exciting week of the season.

That's why every player on the team has been convicted of aggravated assault. And guess what? Not one of them has ever served a day in prison. Why? Because they're football players, you dope. Society needs them. But it doesn't need you.

That's why they always seat a fat slob right behind you who spills beer down your back and busts your ear drums with a stupid horn that scientific studies have proven has absolutely no effect on the outcome of the game.

All this and less for only eighty-five dollars for a three-hour session. Plus $17.50 luxury tax, $8.50 to park in a muddy field, and a seventeen-cent charity surcharge.

No matter how much they soak you, it's still cheaper than psychoanalysis. And the results are the same: You get to vent. Plus, if you sign up now, they'll let you throw things at the players. That's why they wear helmets. If you hurt one, don't worry. There's always more where they came from.

Football: America's game. The Gestalt-Lombardian Interpersonal Therapy is free.

● ● ●

16. Sweet-smelling knuckleheads

Plenty of products try to express a smart lifestyle. But is there anything besides Slurpees and Gap clothes designed for the dumb lifestyle?

Yes, they're just starting to market dumb products now.

For example, there's Ennui, the fragrance that reflects your lifestyle. Sort of.

At last you can smell the way you really feel. With Ennui, the fragrance that's hard to describe. Or put on. Or care about.

Ennui. Perfume for a man. Or a woman. Or whatever.

Every half-full, half-empty bottle of Ennui comes with a self-squirting applicator. Because the way you feel, who can be bothered?

With each purchase of fifty dollars' worth or more, you get absolutely nothing, absolutely free. Because that's the way life really is.

●●●

17. Industrial boo-boos

You've seen signs like this at manufacturing plants: "Another forty-seven minutes without a serious industrial accident." But are industrial accidents a sign of worker stupidity or the result of management planning?

Neither. They're arranged by an outfit little known outside executive circles called Industrial Magic. Here's what their brochure offers:

> Industrial Magic: Because accidents happen. Don't they?
>
> Corporate layoffs? Downsizing? Firing the bums? Who are you kidding? Let's face it: The old way to get rid of workers you don't want anymore is cruel, humiliating, and dangerous.
>
> We have a new way: industrial accidents. Because the worker who dies on the job won't be coming back the next day with an Uzi looking for a manager.

Put Industrial Magic to work for you. Whether it's a supervisor who's too highly paid. Or a plant full of beer-guzzlers who don't know how to shut up and work overtime for free like the Chinese. Our industrial experts will arrange the perfect accident that will downsize your corporation without the fuss, the guilt, or the severance package.

One phone call will get us started. Ring twice, ask for Pete. Industrial accidents: the new way to say goodbye to old problems.

Be sure to ask your Industrial Magic agent about our new retirement fund. We're planning the future. You're not in it.

•••

18. The final diet

If you just want to tell people you're on a diet, then any diet plan will work. But if you actually want to lose weight and keep it off, then there's only one plan for you: the Ethiopian Diet.

In just four easy steps you will accomplish 25 percent more than you can in three easy steps.

Step 1: We take all your money and leave you in total poverty.

Step 2: You live on surplus food charity just like those svelte Ethiopians.

Step 3: We hire armed thugs to steal your surplus food scrap and resell it to us.

Step 4: Right before you die, you'll never have looked thinner.

19. Out-dancing depression

America seemed to be moving forward. Then it didn't. Then it kind of did. Now, who can tell? So youth wants to know: Is there a dumb way to get America moving forward again?

No, but we can get America moving from side to side.

Let's make every other Thursday National Dance Day. You'll feel a whole lot better and we'll get America back on its feet.

Here's an upbeat dance song to get the party started, number forty-five with a bullet from Shady Lady and the Pitz, "Everything Is Like a Prozac Delirium Except When I Got My Da-Da-Dancing Shoes On."

> Life stinks. War kills.
> No one thinks. Nothing thrills . . .
> So let's dance. Boogy-da-boogy. Let's dance.
> God's dead. Hope's gone.
> Stale bread. Elton John.
> So let's dance. Boogy-da-boogy. Let's really dance.

●●●

20. Better death

If life is so dumb, what's our alternative?

Death. It's the only time that the idiot and the genius have the exact same chance of success.

Life? Been there. Done that. So maybe it's time to cast off your old tired life and get ready for something new and exciting.

Well, new anyway. Death, the only game in town where everyone can play. No experience necessary. No rules. No dress code. Come as you are.

In the game of death, everyone's a winner. But you can't play if you don't die.

Death: the ultimate thrill ride.

•••

21. The tax lottery

We've seen plenty of dumb attempts to fix our tax system, even though no government system can be fixed. It can only be broken in a different way.

But the IRS could make paying taxes popular by taking a tip from the lottery.

To pay your taxes, you'd file an IRS scratch card, Form 1040SC-RA-TCH. Then on April 15, the weatherman with the slickest hair would draw the winning numbers from the IRS drum. One tax player in ten million wins the IRS lottery and goes tax free for life.

Of course, that wouldn't help the IRS get rich people to pay their taxes. But free drinks handed out by IRS agents in rhinestone-studded G-strings should take care of that problem. Hey, it works for Vegas.

CHAPTER FIFTY

Stupidity by the Numbers

Eight Stupid Signs from Around the Globe

1. On a Burmese river road: "When this sign is under water, this road is impassable."
2. In a Nairobi restaurant: "Customers who find our waitresses rude should see the manager."
3. In an Indian maternity ward: "No children allowed."
4. At the Budapest Zoo: "Please do not feed the animals. Give all food to the guard on duty."
5. On a restroom hand dryer along an American turnpike: "Do not turn on machine with wet hands."

6. In a German cemetery: "Do not pick flowers from any but your own grave."
7. In a Parisian hotel elevator: "Please leave your values at the front desk."
8. At a dry cleaners in Rome: "Leave your clothes here and spend the afternoon having a good time."

•••

Two Spectator Sports That
Could Easily Be Made Less Dumb

1. Hockey wouldn't be such a dumb sport if they just got rid of the puck.

   Then we wouldn't be distracted from watching big lugs hit each other with sticks. They could get rid of the ice skates too while they're at it.
2. *The Nutcracker* wouldn't seem like such a dumb ballet if the rats won every now and then.

•••

Three Dumb Questions We Have No Answers To

1. If doctors and lawyers work in professional buildings, who works in amateur buildings?
2. Why do they always run us around in circles? Couldn't they run us in ovals or rectangles or figure 8s for a change?
3. Why are those ants always bragging they can lift thirty-two times their own weight? Big deal. I can lift thirty-two times their weight too. With one hand.

Three Dumb Theories of Creation

1. Human beings were one of God's early models. Now that God's off creating other races, He's worked out most of the bugs.
2. A superior race from another galaxy dumped us here, then ran away and has been hiding from us ever since.
3. It took more than one god to create this big a mess. Picture two gods hanging out at the Cosmic Café knocking back a few.

   BIG JOE GOD: People, they'll believe anything.

   FRANK "GOODIE" GOD: You think yours are gullible. I told mine that I created them because I loved them.

   BIG JOE: And they believed you?

   GOODIE: They've got no sense of humor. I mean, after all the earthquakes, fires, hurricanes, accidents in the shower, plus the itching, they still think I'm setting up some kind of Club Med for them after they're through down there.

   BIG JOE: Pathetic, isn't it? They'll swallow any story that makes them feel like they've got a shot. Why don't we create something a little smarter next time?

   GOODIE: Yeah, but let's have another round first.

●●●

Three Ideas So Dumb They're Brilliant

1. Mood rings for cars.

   Every time you squeeze the steering wheel, lights indicate your mood to other drivers.

   Watch out for that road-rage Volvo with the red light coming up on your left.

You see that T-Bird cruising the drag? Look at her amber light; she's just teasing.

2. All-loaner used car lot.

    Have you ever put your own heap into a shop and had any problems with the loaner? Mechanics keep loaners in top shape because they're advertising their mechanical skills.

    Plus, people don't trash loaners as they do rental cars. Everyone sends karmic signals back to the mechanics: If I take care of your car, give me a break and take care of mine.

3. Height-sensitive movie theaters.

    Before you get in to see the movie, everyone lines up in order of height, short to tall, so you'll always be sitting behind someone you can see over.

    Hey, it works in grade school. It'll work at the movies.

●●●

Three Goofy Ideas That Used to Be Smart but Boy, Do They Sound Dumb Now

1. Go West, young man.

    Two letters: LA.

    If Horatio Alger had only said, "Go Midwest, young man," you'd still be able to park in Hollywood and get from the Valley to Malibu in under five hours.

2. A fool and his money are soon parted.

    If he's such a fool, how did he get the money in the first place?

    And if he and his money are soon parted, how come they weren't parted sooner than when they are parted? Why were they waiting for you to come along?

    More accurately: A fool and his money are soon partied.

3. This country is going to hell in a handbasket.

    Who carries a handbasket these days? What the hell is a handbasket anyway? As opposed to a footbasket or a fannybasket?

    Why would you carry your stuff around in a basket when you can choose from a wide range of handbags, purses, fanny packs, backpacks, and multitasking omnipacks?

    So relax, this country isn't going to hell in a handbasket. Clearly, we're going to hell in an SUV. It's so much faster that way.

●●●

Three Things You Should Never Say to an Idiot

1. What makes you think so?
2. Would you like to hold my collection of crystal antiques?
3. Welcome, come on in.

●●●

Three Things You Hope You
Never *Have* to Say to an Idiot

1. Sure thing, boss.
2. Yes, dear.
3. Can you clarify that, Mr. President?

●●●

Three Things That Mean Big Trouble
If You Have to Say Them to an Idiot

1. But Your Honor . . .
2. Are you sure you have to operate, Doc?
3. You want us to charge which hill, General?

Three Businesses Only an Idiot Would Run

1. Day Two, a restaurant that serves only leftovers.
2. The Double Bill, a theater that shows two movies at the same time, so if you get bored with one you can watch the other.

   Here's the schedule for the split screen:

   Gone with the Wind and the Lion
   A Few Good Men Don't Leave
   The Man Who Would Be King Kong
   My Favorite Year of Living Dangerously
   Dead Man Walking Tall
   Bob and Carol and Ted and Alice in Wonderland
   The Good, the Bad and the Ugly American
   The Princess Bride of Frankenstein
   The Thin Man on the Flying Trapeze
   Working Girl, Interrupted
   The Russians Are Coming, the Russians Are Coming Home
   Blue Steel Magnolias
   Odd Man Out of Africa
   Nine to Five Easy Pieces
   Bob and Carol and Ted and Alice's Restaurant
   Shakespeare in Love with the Proper Stranger
   A Man and a Woman for All Seasons
   The Maltese Falcon and the Snowman

3. Rent-a-Lemon Car Rental: Doesn't matter how much you beat up these junkers. Even we don't want them back.

Three Rejections of Greatness
by Fools Who Couldn't See It

1. Ignace Paderewski was told his hands were too small to play the piano. He became one of the greatest pianists of all time.
2. When engineer Guglielmo Marconi developed his theory of radio transmission, the scientific authorities of his day dismissed the notion, explaining that his ideas ran contrary to the laws of physics.
3. Enrico Caruso was told to abandon opera because his voice sounded like "wind whistling through a window." He kept whistling in the wind and became the greatest operatic tenor of his time.

•••

Two Dumb Blonde Jokes Versus Two Dumb Men Jokes:

1. The dumb millionaire is driving the wrong way down a one-way street. A cop pulls him over and asks, "Where do you think you're going?"

    "I don't know," the millionaire replies. "But I must be late because everyone else is coming back."
2. What do you call a man with half a brain?
    Gifted.
3. Why do psychiatrists charge blondes half price?
    They only have half a brain to analyze.
4. Why do blondes get only half an hour for lunch?
    So their bosses won't have to retrain them.

Actually, I reversed them. The first two jokes were originally dumb blonde jokes. Numbers 3 and 4 were originally dumb men jokes. But they work just as well the other way around, don't they?

• • •

Four Dumb Jobs

1. Actor

    Movie director Alfred Hitchcock disliked actors because they were hard to manage. Here's the great manipulator dreaming of the perfect actors: "Disney, of course, has the best casting. If he doesn't like an actor, he just tears him up."

2. Newspaper editor

    "An editor should have a pimp for a brother," writer Gene Fowler suggested, "so he'd have someone to look up to."

3. Lawyer

    "Lawyers are the only persons in whom ignorance of the law is not punished." Which attorney basher said that? The attorney Jeremy Bentham.

4. Politician

    "Being in politics is like being a football coach," Senator Eugene McCarthy said. "You have to be smart enough to understand the game, and dumb enough to think it's important."

Six of the Dumbest Things
the Human Race Has Ever Done

1. Create cities.

    Monstrously overcrowded cities are not even a modern invention. Constantinople, capital of the Byzantine Empire, was home to over a million people as early as the ninth century.

    But not happily. Hundreds of thousands of poor people were drawn to the city, thinking it had to be better than life in their miserable villages.

    They lived in the city's slums in such abject misery and squalor that their major hobby became rioting. Persecution of the poor became a prime city function, like sweeping the streets.

    Is this any way to live? Apparently so, since it's still done that way in mammoth cities all over the world.

    What if there were no huge cities? Then no sieges, no traffic jams, no plagues, thin walls, or dumb neighbors.

    You wouldn't have panhandlers on every corner if there weren't so many corners.

    No cities, no organized crime. No streets, no street gangs.

    Madness due to the stresses of overpopulation? Gone. Man goes mad on a mountaintop, who knows? Man goes mad downtown, he upsets the office staff on their way to lunch, requires police intervention, inspires other madmen to let loose.

    No cities, no ennui. Out in survival land, people are too busy to be bored.

    So what do cities give us in exchange for all that numskull misery? A few good museums, some great restaurants, more hills to be king of.

Plus, better chances for plain guys to find good-looking girlfriends. It's a numbers game, and cities give you numbers.

2. The ten commandments.

Not complaining about the value system. All good. But too many of them.

Who are the top ten home-run kings of all time? The ten biggest box office hits? People can't remember ten of anything.

"Was that 'don't covet my neighbor's ox'? Or my neighbor's ass?"

God would have gotten a much better return on his moral investment if he had condensed. One good commandment would have done the job, and we'd all remember it: Thou shalt not be such a jerk.

3. The power behind the throne.

The king's not that big a problem. Everyone knows how to fool tough guys. Make them ruler of all they survey. That tends to keep them mollified. Your biggest challenge is making sure they don't survey too much.

But the powers behind the throne never stop meddling. They want more because they know that over the hill in the next tough guy's land, the powers behind that throne are just like them: They want more.

These guys are always buzzing in the king's ear: See those other guys over there? We'd better wipe them out before they wipe us out.

If there were no powers behind the throne, there would be no throne.

4. Short skirts. Long skirts. Makeup. Fashion.

How many centuries of women-hours have been wasted trying to look a little better for a little while?

If women took all that time they spend putting on and taking off makeup and shopping and studying what fashion is going to do to them next, and devoted that energy to fixing all the dumb things men have done to screw up the world, we wouldn't be in such a mess today.

5. Synonyms.

The English language means too many things. If we had fewer words, we'd lead smarter, happier lives with less stress.

Right now, we not only have stress. We have tension, pressure, anxiety, apprehension, trepidation, misgivings, and disquietude.

Life would be easier if we only had stress.

But English is designed to drive us all mad, in case the rest of the world isn't up to the job.

Your boss says, "Jones, you idiot," and you don't know where you stand. Sounds bad, but is it?

"Jones, you idiot" could still be a rung up from "That moron Smith in accounting." Or not.

Synonyms make people who know a lot of words feel superior, and that makes people who don't know as many words feel like punching them in the nose. Which leads to a lot more stress for everyone.

6. To-do lists.

Before to-do lists, we did the minimum we could get away with. If some task was really important, it didn't have to be remembered. It had to be *done*.

The operational rule: If whoever was in charge of nagging forgot about it, then you didn't have to do it.

Until the to-do list came along. To-do lists gave us obligations and guilt. Made it much less convenient to forget.

Now we preplan our planning meetings. But only after we prioritize the agenda for our preplanning session.

We keep lists that track our other lists.

We buy special pads of paper just for lists. When we run out, we write down on another list: "Buy new list pads."

Is there a way to break the terrible list habit? Sure, everything beyond number seven on any list—throw it away. It's not that important or it would work its way into the top five.

You ever wonder what the to-do lists of famous people were like?

Moses' To-Do List

1. Meet with Pharaoh.
2. Buy locust insurance first. *Then* meet with Pharaoh.
3. Figure out a good route to the promised land *before* leading that bunch of whiners into the desert.
4. When you go up the mountain to get God's commandments, take wheelbarrow. Stone tablets are heavy and there's no telling how many rules God will come up with once He gets started.
5. While up there, see if God has any ideas for something new to eat. People getting tired of matzo, matzo, matzo.

Theodore Roosevelt's To-Do List

1. Go hunting tomorrow.
2. If press hangs around, remember to find an animal and set it free. Maybe they'll name it after me. Teddy rabbit sounds good. Maybe Teddy deer.
3. Avoid bears at all costs.
4. Consider whether motto should be "Walk swiftly and carry a small stick" or "Walk safely and carry a medium-size stick." Can't decide.

Four Areas Where Foolish Spell Checkers Are Taking Over

Since only a few third graders can still spell, we let our computer's spell-checker make decisions for us, thereby correcting things we didn't even know needed correcting.

1. Rock bands
   If it were up to our spell-checker, Mötley Crüe would be changed to Motley Crude.
   The Doobie Brothers: The Doughboy Brothers
   Simon and Garfunkel: Simian and Garfunkel
   Lovin' Spoonful: Loin Spoonful
   The Byrds: The Birdies
   The Allman Brothers Band: The Alumna Brothers Band
   Kool and the Gang: Koala and the Gang
   Manfred Mann: Mannered Man
   The Isley Brothers: The Islet Brothers
   Emerson, Lake and Palmer: Emerson, Lake and Paler

2. Movies
   Butch Cassidy and the Sundance Kid: Butt Cased and the Sundance Kid
   Shrek: Shrike
   Forrest Gump: Forrest Ump
   Ben-Hur: Ben-Hurry
   Unforgiven: Unforgotten
   Rambo: Mambo
   Stalag 17: Stag 17
   Superfly: Superbly
   Tora! Tora! Tora!: Torn! Toro! Torero!
   The Guns of Navarone: The Guns of Nazarene
   Mr. Blandings Builds His Dream House: Mr. Blandness Builds His Dream House

3. Books
   The Hunchback of Notre Dame: The Hunchback of North Dame
   Anna Karenina: Anna Keratin
   Jane Eyre: Jane Eye
   Barry Lyndon: Barry London
   Les Misérables: Lease Miserable
   The Picture of Dorian Gray: The Picture of Doorman Gray
   Wuthering Heights: Withering Heights

4. Pop culture favorites
   Betty Boop: Betty Oop
   Tinkerbell: Thinkable
   Godzilla: Good Will

●●●

Two Dumb Future Trends

1. Combo books.
   To increase our lagging productivity in reading, publishers will combine books. We can double our reading through-put with combo books like these:

   Lake Wobegon Days of the Locust
   The Old Man in the Gray Flannel Suit and the Sea
   Romeo and Juliet and Franny and Zooey
   101 Dalmatians Flew Over the Cuckoo's Nest
   The Petrified Forrest Gump
   Tender Is the Night of the Iguana
   The Wings of the Lonesome Dove
   The Maltese Falcon and the Snowman

2. Movie marketing, phase II: Beyond product placement.

    Hollywood will realize vast new fortunes (which they can stack on top of their vast old fortunes) when they take product placement off the screen and into the stores. Movies will go retail with products like:

    Gone with the Windex: Tomorrow will be another dirty day. That's why down in the South we keep our vision clear with a window cleaner that frankly doesn't give a damn about dirt.

    A Bug's Life Spray: The only bug spray that makes insects so darn cute, you'll treat them as guests, not pests.

    Tootsie Rolls: The candy bar for people who are questioning their sexual orientation. Open at either end.

    It's a Wonderful Life Insurance Company: You're in safe hands with Jimmy Stewart.

    Malcolm X-ray Labs: We see into your body . . . and through their lies.

    Who Framed Roger Rabbit Picture Frames: Your pictures aren't bad. They're just framed that way.

    Thelma and Louise Dating Service: If you can catch them, you can date them.

    The Dirty Dozen: Eggs the way nature intended them.

Five Signs That Our Legal System
Wouldn't Be Much Wackier If It Had
Been Created by Goo-goo Heads

When you think about our laws, they don't have to make sense. What's legal and illegal in our society is often just prejudice.

1. Using a sexy woman to sell everything from beer to autos: legal.
   Using a sexy woman to sell sex: illegal.
2. Having sex with someone you just met in a bar and probably will never see again, then giving her fifty dollars for tickets to a church raffle: legal.
   Having sex with someone you just met in a bar and probably will never see again, then giving her fifty dollars without the raffle tickets: illegal.
3. Taking drugs that make you want to hit the guy next to you with a barstool: legal.
   Taking drugs that make you want to hug the guy next to you in a drum circle: illegal.
4. Killing hundreds of people if the president says it's okay: legal.
   Killing one person without the president's okay: illegal.
5. Strong guy beats up weaker guy: illegal.
   Strong guy puts on gloves and beats up weaker guy: not only legal, but you can sell tickets to it.

●●●

Three Dumb Rules for Pilots

1. It's better to be down here wishing you were up there than up there wishing you were down here.

2. The propeller is a big fan in the front of the plane that keeps the pilot cool. Every time it stops, the pilot breaks out in a sweat.

3. Don't drop the aircraft in order to fly the microphone.

•••

Three More Dumb Rules for Pilots

1. Flying is the second greatest thrill. Landing is the first.

2. Learn from others' mistakes. You won't live long enough to make them all yourself.

3. Don't forget the difference between God and a pilot. God doesn't think He's a pilot.

•••

Four Examples of Our Dumb Language

No matter how highly educated we are, most of us end up uttering silly phrases like these:

1. "Without further ado . . ."

   That's so unfair. It means you've already had your ado, but I don't get mine. The time to undo ados is before you get to the further part.

   But no one ever offers: "With ado, I'd like to introduce a guy who needs no introduction . . . the guy who popularized use of the salad fork and is well liked by many of his cousins. . . ."

   Hey, the only guy who needs no introduction is Jesus. Everyone else can use as much ado as they can get. Otherwise, why would there be someone figuring out where the ado cut-off line should be?

2. Premature ejaculation.

   Has any woman ever said, "Oh, Harold, that was such a mature ejaculation"?

   What if she says, "Sorry, too late." Does that make it postmature?

3. "That's like comparing apples and oranges."

   Why can't apples and oranges ever get along? They have so much in common: We eat both of them. They're fruit. You can juice either one. They're more or less round. They're good for you. They appear in the same sentence more than any other fruits.

   Not so hard to compare them after all, is it?

4. "Don't count your chickens before they hatch."

   Really? Have you ever tried to count them after they hatch? They're all over the place. You're chasing one, missing four.

   Then you think: All right, I'll hire a few chicken counters to help out. But how can you know how many chicken counters you'll need unless you count them before they hatch?

   In fact, eggs turn out to cause endless problems. We say, "Don't put all your eggs in one basket."

   What are you, like, made of baskets?

   Let's say you've got a dozen eggs. If you put one in one basket, then the other eleven in another basket—you're still putting all your eggs (all eleven of them) in one basket.

   Eventually, you'll need an infinite number of baskets for an infinite number of eggs, one in each. Then where are you going to put all those baskets? In a bigger basket!

   "You can't make an omelet without breaking a few eggs."

Seemingly so incontrovertible, leaving aside the U.S. Army. But that egg-breaking crack completely misses the point of modern life: So few of us can make an omelet even *after* breaking eggs.

What can we do about it except switch to oatmeal? Nobody counts oats, and they don't hatch. You don't have to put them in baskets, and you couldn't break them if you wanted to.

●●●

Five Everyday Things We Couldn't Get Right

1. If your house has two bathrooms, odds are one of them does not contain a bath.
2. In the kitchen we put cups in the cupboard. But we don't put plates in the plateboard.
3. We call them glove compartments, although no one keeps gloves in them.
4. Parkways don't lead to parks.
5. We eat eggplants without eggs, hamburgers without ham, and pineapples that have neither pines nor apples. We also pick at sweetmeats, which are meatless candies; and sweetbreads, which are unsweetened, breadless meat.

●●●

Six Signs That the Inhabitants of Our Daily Comic Strips Are Dumber Than the Inhabitants of Anywhere Else

A quick look at idiots who have been gainfully employed in comic strips gives us:

1. The lead character in *Hagar the Horrible*, *The Born Loser*, and *Andy Capp* (and Andy's wife is not too bright either).

2. Lieutenant Fuzz in *Beetle Bailey*, Jon in *Garfield*, Jonathan the brokerage-house boss in *Bulls 'n' Bears*, Artie in *Geech* (and maybe Merle), a tie between Brad and Tiffany in *Luann*, Moondog in *Monty*, Sluggo in *Nancy*, the pig in *Pearls Before Swine*, Royboy in *Soup to Nutz*, and the king in *Wizard of Id*.

3. In a few strips, just about everybody is an idiot; for example, *Li'l Abner*, *Charlie*, and *Dilbert*.

4. You'll find dumb dads starring in *The Buckets*, *Big Nate*, *Betty*, and *Rose Is Rose*.

   The dad in *Drabble* is saved from the list because his son, Norman, dumb-trumps everyone else.

5. Two of the most popular strips of all time present interesting challenges on the Stupid-O-Meter.

   Peanuts is too kid-kind to have a real idiot. But Marcie and Sally are mostly clueless. The free-spirited Snoopy is often out of touch with the world, but that may be a sign of his intelligence, not his stupidity.

   Doonesbury is populated with a variety of conditional idiots.

   Duke is sporadically stupid, depending upon the pharmaceuticals involved.

   Roland the reporter says stupid things all the time, but he is occupationally stupid because he works for TV news.

   Boopsie is one of the few dumb women working in comics, but her feeblemindedness never slows her down.

   Zipper is an interesting second-generation airhead, as blissed out as Uncle Zonker but with a diluted injection of Zonker's magic.

6. One of the best strips of all time had no idiots at all: *Calvin and Hobbes*.

    The ingeniously diabolical little boy and his stuffed tiger are something rarely seen in comic strips: two best friends who together take on the world.

    Bill Watterson, the genius behind the strip, chose not to take the obvious route and make the parents idiots. Calvin may sometimes get the best of them, but you can see where the boy inherited his stubborn deviousness.

    It's interesting to see whom Watterson often casts in the role of the strip's idiot.

    Take the panel where Calvin mourns the death (there's something you rarely see in comic strips) of a baby raccoon he found in the woods and (with the help of those non-idiot parents) tried to save.

    "I didn't even know he existed a few days ago and now he's gone forever," Calvin laments. "It's like I found him for no reason."

    A true friend, Hobbes has little consolation except his steady presence at Calvin's side.

    "Still in a sad, awful, terrible way, I'm happy I met him," Calvin realizes, then hits the kicker: "What a stupid world."

    Watterson knows that the world will take care of the idiocy for you.

●●●

One Warning Sign That America's Getting Dumber

There are students who enroll at the Dunkin' Donuts Training School and then don't pass. Yes, America now has people too stupid to work in a doughnut shop.

CHAPTER FIFTY-ONE

What's the Dumbest Thing You've Ever Done? Eighteen True Stupid Stories from Real People Just Like You, Except They're in the Book and You're Not

1. From winery owner June Smith

After enrolling my husband Jim in the national Jim Smith Society, we went to the convention in Washington, D.C., and left the name of the hotel with our business partner.

But when he needed to reach us, he had a terrible time, because everyone in the hotel was named Jim Smith!

2. From writer Ann Parker

When I was a kid I thought it might be interesting to see what happened when you lit a whole pack of matches at once. Wow, it was impressive.

The fire startled me so much that I dropped the matchbook into the trash can in my parents' bedroom. The tissues in the can immediately ignited.

Panicked, I grabbed the nearest thing to douse the fire—and sprayed my mom's perfume on the flames, which promptly shot up three feet.

I escaped from this mini-inferno amazingly well: no burns, the house didn't burn down, and my folks never found out. Thank goodness for metal trash cans and quick-burning tissues.

●●●

3. From bookstore owner Aillee DeArmond

I have never done anything stupid. But when I was eighteen, my parents went to Europe, leaving their car in my care.

Three of us went to town to get cigarettes. As I turned off Pacific Avenue, the guy sitting next to me lit a cigarette. Then he tried to light one for me off his, but kept the lit cigarette in his mouth and the unlit one in his hand.

This guy is a real idiot, I thought. While I was marveling at his stupidity, I ran into a parked car, which smashed into another parked car, which then bumped the car parked behind it.

A four-car accident and I was the only driver. The message here is that it is better to be well lit when driving.

4. From food columnist Donna Maurillo

I hosted some official visitors from Italy, who were in our city on a cultural exchange. Despite my Italian heritage, my language skills are a bit spotty. But that didn't keep me from showing off.

When one of the visitors couldn't find his glasses, I told him in Italian that he was "a little forgetful."

His reaction was dead silence. Only later did I realize that I'd called him "a little testicle."

●●●

5. From grief counselor Gabriel Constans

As a teenager I agreed to photograph some friends streaking naked (remember when that was a big thing?) through our local mall.

I didn't realize it was the same day the Boy Scout and Girl Scout troops were showing their projects in the mall. Some of the parents were *rather* upset.

●●●

6. From professional volunteer Anne Butterfly

When I was a seat filler one year at the Academy Awards, I stepped into my gown moments before we were to take our places for the show.

But I was wearing four-inch heels and cut a twelve-inch slit up my leg and fell flat on my face. Then I found out we could wear any old comfortable shoes under our formal gowns because we wouldn't be seen on camera. Some of the seat fillers even wore athletic shoes.

7. From writer Jane Parks-McKay

"When I was a teenager, I fell for a guy who worked at the gas station near our home. My dad lent me his hot Ford Cougar, which I later commandeered permanently.

I felt the *only* way I could see this guy was to burn up a tank full of gas fast, then go visit him at the station.

Not once did it occur to me—even when my Dad asked about the high gas bills—to get a *little* gas and go in to the station more frequently!

I did go out with the guy, but ended up liking his brother instead.

•••

8. From librarian Chris Watson

After working at a school fundraiser, my son and I had our picture taken together. When the photo was dropped on my desk at work, I was shocked to discover how much my son, at seventeen, looked like me at forty-eight. I pointed out the likeness to everyone I met.

That night when I showed the photo to my son, he looked at me and frowned. "You're kidding, right?" he asked. "You know they pasted a copy of my head onto your face, right?"

Sure enough, when I looked closer, I saw my son's baseball hat, distinctive jaw and smiling eyes peeking at me from under my own mane of hair. How could I be so blind?

The answer is that mothers of teenage boys will take any opportunity to get closer to their sons.

The other answer is that there are none so blind as those who will not see. I guess my bifocals weren't working that day.

9. From newspaper reporter Brenda Moore

Many other people have done this too—only usually they're male. I asked a woman when her baby was due; and, of course, she wasn't pregnant.

The moment was made worse by the circumstance. I was having my annual OB-GYN checkup, flat on my back, feet in stirrups, the whole humiliating bit. Luckily she was the nurse, not the doc, so I was spared any physical harm.

•••

10. From TV reporter Benjamin Dover

When I was three years old, the world seemed like a simple place to figure out. For instance, anytime you saw a cord protruding from an appliance, you simply plugged it in the wall and the item would go. Blenders would blend and fans blow cool air.

One day I noticed an old electric extension cord in the trash that my parents had thrown away, and saw an opportunity to upgrade my tricycle to an electrically powered vehicle. It was so obvious! According to this three-year-old's logic, anything with a cord plugged into the wall became motorized.

I wrapped the two exposed ends of the extension cord around the metal frame of the tricycle and secured the cord with electrician's tape. Then with great anticipation, I plugged the end of the extension cord into the electrical outlet in the garage.

But instead of zipping around on my motorized trike, I was rudely educated about the perils of electricity. But the breakers kicked in and did their job, turning the juice off while I lay wincing on the cement floor of the garage.

11. From minister Becky Irelan

I couldn't drive a car when I became a pastor. I would ride my bike in town, but had to have folks in the church drive me around to visit the outlying farms.

One day I visited a farmhouse where the woman's husband was dying of a brain tumor. My driver that day was old Ann, accompanied as always by her dog, a Yorkshire terrier named Trinket.

I went in to pray with the man. Then the dog and I headed for the back door. Several steps ahead of my elderly driver, I turned into the kitchen and saw the *pile*. Without a second's hesitation, I grabbed a handful of Kleenex and scooped up the poop.

Then I stopped. What was I going to do with it?

I couldn't put it in the kitchen garbage; it would smell. I couldn't turn around and head for the bathroom; the ladies were right behind me.

So, hoping for a trash can in the yard, I stuffed it into my purse—just in time for my parishioners to catch me in the act. I had a very red face. We all had a very good laugh.

What did I learn from the poop-in-the-purse episode? I had only been trying to save my driver from a little embarrassment. While that may have been a noble intention, my efforts didn't succeed in making the dog poop disappear.

It was just one of those inconvenient reminders that we can't always fix everything for everybody. When we try, we end up looking pretty foolish.

For those who make a habit of taking on everyone else's piles of problems, listen up: The job opening for Savior has long since been sewed up.

12. From medical sonographer Robin Cunningham

It was Easter break and we didn't have a hotel reservation in Zihuatanejo. But my husband Bill is an optimist. "We'll find a place," he said, "no worries."

Playa del Sol, the only hotel with a vacancy in that Mexican town, was worthy of a spread in *Architectural Digest*. But we were the kind of travelers who pored over *Latin America on $3 a Day*, so I knew the price would be way out of our league. But Bill said, "Let's go for it!"

They gave us a kitchenette, a sumptuous bedroom, and a bathroom nicer than my own home. A view of the ocean and right on the beach. I wanted to live there. This was the nicest hotel room I'd ever been in.

I was tired of carrying around all our papers, my camera, and traveler's checks. So I looked for a place to stash them before we took off for town. Under the mattress seemed so cliché and the freezer too obvious. So I alighted upon the brilliant idea of putting our papers, passports, tickets, and money in the bathroom trash can. I put some paper towels on top to hide them, and we took off.

Going to town turned out to be a wild night in a tequila bar with ex-pats and lunatics. We danced on the tables and ran around in the moonlight on the sand. The rest is lost for eternity, but when we got back I was clearheaded enough to check for my stash.

The wastebasket in the bathroom was empty. I shrieked. Bill ran in and started laughing. All our stuff had been carefully laid out on the countertop like little children put to bed.

We had never been in a hotel where they emptied your garbage mere hours after you arrived, so I did not anticipate that possibility. I was thrilled that I had not lost my valuables, but I felt like we had exposed our inexperience in a uniquely idiotic way.

When I opened my eyes the next morning, it was very bright in the room. Not only had we fallen asleep with the curtain wide open, but our room faced the *palapa* restaurant so the other guests dined in full view of our crumpled bodies for God knows how long that morning.

My first vision was of Bill's face, which appeared to be covered in dried blood. "Are you bleeding?" I asked.

He got a funny look on his face, and said, "Are you?" Bill ran his finger over my cheek and popped it in his mouth. "Chocolate!"

On the pillows were the mints we had fallen asleep on. "Jesus, they should have asked us for references before they let us in here!" Bill said. I couldn't believe the level of lameness we'd managed. And we had not even been there one whole day.

In the *palapa* the young bartender came over to our table and, in the most gentle way, said, "My wife cleans your room, and she is worried that you will lose your things if you put them in the garbage. *Por favor, no en la basura.* She wanted me to ask you not to do that anymore."

The sweet part of this story is that Arturo and Rosa looked out for us for the rest of the week. They showed us the safe in the office, where we left our valuables. We managed to eat mints every night instead of sleeping on them.

●●●

13. From psychologist Offra Gerstein

A couple I was counseling discussed the wife's affair and used the man's name repeatedly. Later in the session, I referred to the husband by the lover's name. Blush time.

14. From travel writer Karen Kefauver

In the days before 9/11, airport security was more lax, giving dumb travelers a greater opportunity to exercise stupid errors in judgment.

Traveling from San Francisco to my parents' home in Washington, D.C., at Thanksgiving was a stupid decision in the first place. Then we landed in Pittsburgh, where I had to transfer for a flight to Virginia's Dulles Airport, which was close to D.C.

When I boarded the second plane, I was irritated that some idiot was sitting in my assigned seat. I found another one. Then I found out that this plane was flying, not to Dulles, but to Washington's National Airport.

I begged to use a cell phone, contacted my stepmom, and told her I had gotten on the wrong plane. Meanwhile, my dad had miraculously recognized my luggage at Dulles, picked it up, and gone home. My stepmom dashed to National to collect her very embarrassed stepdaughter.

It was one of the dumbest mistakes I ever made. But since my parents so kindly remind me of it frequently, I have never repeated it.

●●●

15. From actor Daniel Hughes

When I was seven, everyone thought Jason and I were best friends because our families were together so often. But I hated him.

Jason was a bully who outweighed me by fifty pounds and would break my toys, steal things from me, and take every opportunity to humiliate me in front of people.

On the Fourth of July, our families had a barbecue at my house. Jason "accidentally" broke the legs off one of my action figures and poured juice over my head.

I decided to play a trick on him. I climbed onto the roof of the garage toting a watermelon the size of my torso. I held the watermelon over my head and called to Jason.

When I saw the top of his head, I threw the melon as hard as I could. It hit him square on the head. The watermelon burst and I ducked out of sight, laughing my head off.

The next thing I heard was Jason's mother screaming in horror. "Call an ambulance!" someone howled. I peeked over the edge of the roof and saw Jason laying face down in an awkward position, his arm twitching and watermelon everywhere.

I was certain I had killed him. I think everyone else was too. The ambulance took him away. Jason's father tried to have me arrested. I was not. Our families have never spoken since.

Jason did not die, although he was knocked out cold. He wore a neck brace for a few days and recovered quickly. I was grounded for the remainder of my life.

When I went back to school in the fall, everyone said I had tried to kill my best friend, and no one would play with me. My friends eventually warmed up to me, but the story that I tried to kill Jason followed me all through high school. Jason never looked me in the face again.

●●●

16. From book editor Marilyn Green

Faux Pas was the pet gerbil in my sorority house at Michigan State. I took Faux Pas home for the Christmas holidays and my dog ate him . . . all but the tail.

Thinking that all gerbils look alike, we went to the pet store and bought another one. Turns out all gerbils may look alike, but not all gerbils know how to swim.

Faux Pas's caretaker came to me, hands on hips. "Marilyn, what happened to Faux Pas?"

"What do you mean?" I replied. I never let on.

•••

17. From actor Bruce Burns

I was doing *Oliver!* and choreographed one of the dances. The actress and I doing the dance had an Astaire–Rodgers kind of move where we moved past each other, then grabbed and came back.

But one night, I couldn't remember if I was supposed to be upstage or downstage when I passed her. So my brilliant decision was to go for the middle.

Naturally, I knocked her down. I was mortified that I had forgotten my own dance. But in a dance number you can't stop. So I helped her up and we went on.

•••

18. From movie publicist Buff McKinley

The most ridiculous thing I've ever done was offer the following smug reply to a snotty flight attendant who said I couldn't sit with my friends on a crowded flight: "That's okay, we just won't tell you where we hid the bomb."

This was in the late 1970s and I was a smart-ass kid, with no idea that I was committing a federal offense. That fact was politely explained to me by the nice federal agent who met me at the gate in LA.

PART 6
Looks Like We're De-stupifying Again

CHAPTER FIFTY-TWO

How to Get Smarter by Cribbing from Actual Smart People

When you put this book down and go back out into the world, you can be mostly smart or mostly stupid. I recommend mostly smart. Less competition.

To help you make the leap, here are some sharp tips from people who found a home in the world of the mentally unchallenged.

1. Get started.

- Preacher Richard Evans: "Don't let life discourage you. Everyone who got where he is had to begin where he was."
- Thomas Edison: "Opportunity is missed by most people because it is dressed in overalls and looks like work."
- Henry David Thoreau: "If you have built castles in the air, your work need not be lost. That is where they should be. Now put foundations under them."

•••

2. Keep moving.

- Poet Henry Wadsworth Longfellow: "The lowest ebb is the turn of the tide."
- Writer John Hershey: "I have great contempt for intelligence all by itself. Coupled with energy and willingness, it'll go. Alone, it winds up riding the rails."
- Playwright George Bernard Shaw: "When I was a young man, I observed that nine out of ten things I did were failures. I didn't want to be a failure, so I did ten times more work."
- Car manufacturer Henry Ford: "Nothing is particularly hard if you divide it into small jobs."
- President Calvin Coolidge: "We cannot do everything at once. But we can do something at once."

•••

3. And when you're ready to quit, start moving again.

- Writer André Gide: "One doesn't discover new lands without consenting to lose sight of the shore for a very long time."

• Philosopher Ralph Waldo Emerson: "The hero is no braver than an ordinary man, but he is brave for five minutes longer."

• Violinist Fritz Kreisler (responding to a woman who had exclaimed, "I'd give my life to play as you do"): "Madame, I did."

• Minister Ralph Sockman: "Give the best that you have to the highest you know, and do it now."

●●●

4. **When they tell you it can't be done, you may be on to something.**

• Inventor Charles Kettering: "The Wright Brothers flew right through the smoke screen of impossibility."

• Poet Struthers Burt: "Men are failures, not because they are stupid, but because they are not sufficiently impassioned."

• Greek historian Plutarch: "Many things which cannot be overcome when they are together, yield themselves up when taken little by little."

• Writer Samuel Butler: "Life is like playing a violin solo in public and learning the instrument as one goes on."

• Politician John Foster Dulles: "The measure of success is not whether you have a tough problem to deal with, but whether it's the same problem you had last year."

5. Follow a real leader, if you can find one.

- Businessman H. Gordon Selfridge: "The boss says, 'Go!' The leader says, 'Let's go!'"

- Therapist Paul Goodman: "Few great men could pass Personnel."

- Business magnate J. Ogden Armour: "Nothing will make more for loyalty and energy in an organization than the knowledge that employees are being promoted continually from the bottom. It gives men ambition, it gives them pride; and pride and ambition . . . will keep a man working at top speed when money is merely a by-product."

- Roman philosopher Lucius Seneca (to Emperor Nero): "However many you put to death, you will never kill your successor."

- Mount Holyoke College founder Mary Lyon: "Trust in God—and do something."

●●●

6. Don't waste your time.

- Inventor Charles Kettering: "You will never stub your toe standing still. But the faster you go, the more chance you have of getting somewhere."

- Songwriter Noël Coward: "I write at high speed because boredom is bad for my health."

- Writer Samuel Johnson: "While you are considering which of two things you should teach your child first, another boy has learnt them both."

- English politician Lord Chesterfield: "Take care of the minutes for the hours will take care of themselves."

- Philosopher Ahad Ha-am: "Wise men weight the advantages of any course of action against its drawbacks, and move not an inch until they can see what the result of their action will be. But while they are deep in thought, the men with self-confidence come and see and conquer."

- General Electric chairman Owen D. Young: "Being slow and sure usually gets around to being just slow."

- History professor C. Northcote Parkinson: "During a period of exciting discovery or progress, there is no time to plan the perfect headquarters."

- Motivational speaker Dale Carnegie: "Ask yourself what is the worst that can happen. Then prepare to accept it. Then proceed to improve on the worst."

- English politician Sir Barnett Cocks: "A committee is a cul-de-sac down which ideas are lured and then quietly strangled."

- Business advisor Charles Brower: "The good ideas are all hammered out in agony by individuals, not spewed out by groups."

- Art historian Bernard Berenson: "Each day as I look, I wonder where my eyes were yesterday."

7. Copy the clever moves.

- English politician Lord Chesterfield: "Be wiser than other people if you can, but do not tell them so."

- Scientist Linus Pauling: "The best way to have a good idea is to have a lot of ideas."

- Writer Samuel Butler: "To do a great work, a man must be very idle as well as very industrious."

- Wanda Landowska (a master of the harpsichord): "I never practice. I always play."

- Businessman Robert Wieder: "Anyone can look for fashion in a boutique or history in a museum. The creative person looks for history in a hardware store and fashion in an airport."

- Writer A. H. Weiler: "Nothing is impossible for the man who doesn't have to do it himself."

- Business advisor Charles Brower: "There is no such thing as soft sell and hard sell. There is only smart sell and stupid sell."

- Newspaper publisher E. W. Scripps: "Never do anything today that you can put off till tomorrow . . . Most things that you do not have to do today are not worth doing at all."

- Historian Arnold Toynbee: "History not used is nothing, for all intellectual life is action, like practical life."

8. **Wisdom, courage, vision.**

- Baseball player Vernon Law: "Experience is a hard teacher because she gives the test first, the lesson afterwards."

- IBM president Thomas Watson Jr.: "I never hesitated to promote someone I didn't like. The comfortable assistant—the nice guy you like to go on fishing trips with—is a great pitfall. Instead, I looked for those sharp, scratchy, harsh, almost unpleasant guys who see and tell you about things as they really are. If you can get enough of them around you, and have patience enough to hear them out, there is no limit to where you can go."

- Minister Doug Larson: "Wisdom is the reward you get for a lifetime of listening when you'd have preferred to talk."

- Newspaper publisher E. W. Scripps: "When you find many people applauding you for what you do, and a few condemning, you can be certain that you are on the wrong course because you're doing the things that fools approve of. When the crowd ridicules and scorns you, you can at least know one thing, that it is at least possible that you are acting wisely."

- Book publisher Elbert Hubbard: "Every man is a damn fool for at least five minutes every day. Wisdom consists in not exceeding the limit."

- Lecturer and writer Helen Keller: "To know the thoughts and deeds that have marked man's progress is to feel the great heartthrobs of humanity through the centuries. And if one does not feel in these pulsations a heavenward striving, one must be deaf to the harmonies of life."

- Merchant J. C. Penney: "Courage is a quality which grows with use. It may take nerve to give up a position where you are doing fairly well and to take a lower one somewhere else. But if you have courage and ambition you can do it. The breaking away is the hardest part."

- Inventor Thomas Edison: "Genius? Nothing! Sticking to it is the genius! Any other bright-minded fellow can accomplish just as much if he will stick like hell . . . I failed my way to success."

- And finally, the John Wayne method of acting, straight from the Duke: "Talk low, talk slow, and don't say too much."

Works for a lot of other things too.